Econometric Methods for Postgraduate-Level Research

Econometric Methods for Postgraduate-Level Research

A Practical Guide with Examples

AFRICA WORLD PRESS
TRENTON | LONDON | CAPE TOWN | NAIROBI | ADDIS ABABA | ASMARA | IBADAN | NEW DELHI

AFRICA WORLD PRESS
541 West Ingham Avenue | Suite B
Trenton, New Jersey 08638

Cover design & Book design: LiteBook Prepress Services

Cataloging-in-Publication Data may be obtained from the
Library of Congress.

ISBNs: 978-156902-954-4 (HB)
978-156902-851-1 (PB)

CONTENTS

INTRODUCTION

This book introduces postgraduate-level students and researchers to commonly used econometric and statistical methods of data analysis. The methods covered in the book are commonly used for performing quantitative and qualitative data analyses in socioeconomic, demographic, public-health and socio-behavioural studies. The book is especially helpful to learners who wish to acquire basic skills in quantitative and qualitative data analysis by using statistical packages such as SPSS and STATA. Theoretical principles are outlined, followed by easy numerical examples, along with steps that need to be followed for performing data analyses and interpreting results obtained from data analyses. The book has two aspects (quantitative and qualitative data analyses). As part of the quantitative aspect, the book stipulates theoretical principles, steps needed for data analysis, and the interpretation of results of data analyses. The book provides easy examples to follow on how to use the American Psychological Association (APA) citation-and-referencing style. Examples are provided for journal articles, books, and Internet-based reports and sources of information. A sample proposal, a questionnaire of study, and a list of interview questions are provided for learners to follow. These documents are custom-made to requirements that apply to postgraduate-level studies at Tshwane University of Technology.

The book also provides steps on how to use appropriate goodness-of-fit tests for all procedures of quantitative and qualitative data analysis. Such tests are required for assessing the theoretical reliability of fitted models. As part of the qualitative aspect, the book provides learners a practical example of thematic analysis, which is a commonly used method of qualitative data analysis. The book enables learners to write research proposals and perform quantitative and qualitative methods of data analysis. Raw data sets are used for illustrating theoretical principles. The book performs the analyses of raw data sets in the statistical packages SPSS and STATA. Easy steps that need to be followed by learners are outlined and provided in all parts of the book.

Requests for raw data sets used in the various chapters of this book may be made to the author by email through the email address: Zeleke.Worku@gmail.com

The author wishes to extend his deepest appreciation to Professor Henrik Halkier of Aalborg University in Aalborg, Denmark, Professor Stephen E. Little of the Manchester University in the United Kingdom, and Professor Alicia L. Carriquiry of Iowa State University in Ames, Iowa, USA. The author appreciates comments and suggestions on the book and intends to keep producing updated versions of the book to learners. Enjoy your reading!

UNIT 1

SAMPLING TECHNIQUES AND SAMPLE SIZE CALCULATIONS

The importance of using Quantitative Research Methods

Quantitative research is empirical research in which the researcher explores relationships using numeric data. Surveys are the primary method of quantitative research. Surveys ensure statistical accuracy. In cases where a representative sample is drawn from the population of study, results obtained from quantitative research can be generalized to the population of study. Quantitative research that is based on a large and good representative sample enables the researcher to estimate the parameter of interest along with the variance of estimation.

Characteristics of a Good sample

- Probability sampling used for selection of units from the population
- Large in size
- Units are selected at random
- Sampling frame used
- Free from bias
- Allows maximum variability
- Units drawn based on proportional allocation with regard to size
- Most suitable sampling technique used for selection of eligible units

Commonly used Types of Surveys

1) Postal surveys (Sending questionnaires by post)

Postal surveys are paper-and-pencil instruments that are mailed to respondents. They are self-administered by the recipient, which means there is little control over the feedback. However, they are the most convenient for respondents, who can complete them in the place and time of their choosing. Mail surveys are best for the collection of sensitive information, because they provide anonymity for the respondent. They provide the best opportunities for both random samples and targeted random samples. They are the least expensive way to collect data from large numbers of people.

2) Telephonic surveys (Conducting interviews by telephone)

Telephonic surveys are conducted over the phone by trained interviewers or by automated systems. Telephonic surveys are good for reaching "low incidence" respondents – populations of people that are very small within the general population. They also allow for relatively quick data collection.

3) Computer-based surveys (Conducting surveys by use of computers and the Internet)

Computer-based surveys are conducted by use of computers, e-mails, and the Internet. They enable the researcher to conduct complicated research by use of modern technology, with online assistance. Computer-based surveys are inexpensive to conduct, and ensure speedy data collection and reporting. Respondents can answer questions at their own pace and at their convenience. Respondents who do not have access to computers and the Internet, however, cannot take part in computer-based surveys.

4) Personal surveys (Conducting surveys by use of personal interviewers or enumerators).

Instant surveys are conducted by using personal interviewers or enumerators. Personal surveys are expensive to do but are highly effective. Example: Estimating the proportion of teenagers at a shopping mall.

5) Hybrid surveys (Surveys in which a combination of various techniques is used in order to improve efficiency).

How to select a Suitable Survey Method

In selecting a survey method, the following factors should be considered:

1) Identify your objectives. What do you want to find out?
2) Determine suitable criteria of inclusion and exclusion for the study.
3) Determine the sample size of study and power of study. How many responses are needed in order to produce reliable results?
4) Determine a suitable timetable of activities for the survey.
5) Determine the cost of the survey.
6) Prioritise your needs appropriately (sample, timeframe, budget, and complexity). In cases where there is no money for large samples, use a telephonic survey. In cases where instant response is needed, use a computer-based survey. In cases where a large number of responses is needed, use postal or telephonic surveys. In cases where the cost of study is small, use postal or computer-based surveys. In cases where the questions in the survey require interaction with respondents, use a telephonic or computer-based survey.

Sampling and Sampling Errors

Survey error consists of causes that undermine the reliability of estimated results. Some of the causes of error could be avoided by ensuring precision during data collection. However, random sampling errors are causes that cannot be avoided.

Types of Errors in Surveys

a) Sampling error

Random variability in sample estimates that arises out of the randomness of the sample selection process. Sampling error cannot be avoided unless the entire population of study is sampled.

Precision can be quantified (estimation of standard errors, confidence intervals)

b) Non-sampling error (bias)

Non-sampling error is estimation error that arises from sources other than random variation.

Example: Non-response, under-coverage of survey, poorly trained interviewers, non-truthful answers, non-probability sampling. This type of error is called bias. Non-sampling error could be avoided by improving the precision of measurement and the resources available for the study.

Comparison between Sampling and Census Surveys

Census surveys are precise but are quite difficult and expensive to conduct. By contrast, sampling surveys are prone to random sampling error even though they are cheaper and easier to conduct.

Procedures for Selecting a sample

- Articulate your research questions precisely, and identify measurable indicators based on which of your research questions could be answered adequately.
- Construct the sampling frame of study. The sampling frame consists of all potential sources of data for your planned survey. The sampling frame must be up-to-date and complete.
- Determine the sample size of study.

Determine the sampling technique to be used for selecting units from the population of study into the sample. In other words, what sampling method should be used? Example: Probability sampling versus non-probability sampling. Examples of probability sampling techniques are simple random sampling, stratified sampling, cluster sampling, and systematic sampling.

Probability sampling ensures the selection of units from the population of study based on objective criteria. Probability sampling ensures random selection as well as the estimation of the variance of estimation. Results obtained from probability sampling could be generalised to the population of study. Probability sampling is used extensively in quantitative studies.

Non-probability sampling is a sampling procedure in which eligible units are selected based on subjective criteria such as convenience and purpose. Non-probability sampling does not adhere to objective criteria of selection. The selection of units and the sample size of study is based on convenience, resources available for the study, or the specific purpose of the study. Non-probability sampling does not guarantee random selection and is prone to selection bias. Non-probability sampling is used extensively in qualitative studies.

Commonly used Probability Sampling Techniques

- Simple random sampling
- Stratified random sampling
- Cluster sampling
- Systematic random sampling

Commonly used non-Probability Sampling Techniques

- Convenience sampling
- Purposive (targeted) sampling
- Quota sampling
- Judgmental sampling
- Expert sampling
- Snowball sampling

Simple Random Sampling

Simple random sampling allocates the same probability of selection to every unit in the population of study. The table of random numbers, pocket calculators, ballot papers, coins, and dice are used for randomly selecting units from the population of study into the sample.

Stratified random sampling

Stratified random sampling is used when the population of study could be split into distinct blocks of similar units. From each stratum, units are selected based on proportional allocation with regard to size. Example: Use gender (male, female), place of residence (rural, urban), level of income (low, moderate, high) as stratification criteria. The strata are internally homogeneous and externally heterogeneous. You must select units from each distinct stratum.

Cluster Sampling

Cluster sampling is used when the population of study could be split into distinct clusters. The strata in stratified sampling are analogous to the clusters in cluster sampling. Data is gathered only from those clusters that are relevant to the study. Within each cluster, data is gathered by using suitable sampling techniques. Example: Use cluster sampling to gather data from a random sample of 1, 000 South Africans affected by flood. To do so, you go to clusters where there has been damage due to flood. The strata are internally homogeneous and externally heterogeneous. It is not essential to select units from each cluster.

Systematic Random Sampling

Systematic random sampling is used in cases where the population of study resembles no visible pattern with regard to the variable of interest. The sampling interval is denoted by k = N/n where N is the population size and n is the sample size. After the required sample size has been calculated, the first eligible unit is selected at random. From then on, every kth record is selected from the list. The process is continued until all n units are selected from the population into the sample.

Sample size of study for studies involving proportions

The initial sample size of study is denoted by n_0, and is determined using the formula shown below in Equation (1):

$$n_0 = \frac{Z^2_{1-\frac{\alpha}{2}} \times P(1-P)}{d^2} \qquad \textbf{Equation (1)}$$

In most cases, the value of α is fixed at the 5% level.

$\alpha = 0.05$ = level of significance

$Z_{1-\frac{\alpha}{2}} = Z_{1-\frac{0.05}{2}} = Z_{1-0.025} = Z_{0.975} = 1.96$ = value of standard normal random variable at the $\alpha = 0.05$ level of significance

d is the margin of error

P is the proportion of people who are affected. If there are no estimates, the value of P is fixed at 50%.

The final sample size of study is given in Equation (2):

$$n = \frac{n_0}{1 + \frac{n_0}{N}} \quad \textbf{Equation (2)}$$

In Equation (2),

n_0 is the initial sample size of study

N denotes the population size

Adjustment for Dropouts

Let f denote the proportion of people who drop out of the study for various reasons. The adjusted sample size of study is given by:

$$n_{adj} = \frac{n}{1-f}$$

Commonly used Statistical Tests in Quantitative Research

Parametric tests are used in studies in which the variables of study are continuous and/or the sample sizes of study are large.

Example: The two-sample t-test used to compare two competing brands of painkillers with regard to time (in minutes) needed to bring about relief from pain; $n_1 = n_2 = 30$.

Non-parametric tests are used in studies in which the variables of study are categorical and/or the sample sizes of study are small.

Example: The Mann-Whitney U-test used to compare two independent groups of patients; $n_1 = n_2 = 9$

Results from parametric tests are reliable.

Results from non-parametric tests are not so reliable.

Examples of Commonly used Parametric Tests

The one-sample t-test (Used to find out if the true average value is equal to a hypothesized value)

Example: To find out if the pollution level in a public source of drinking water exceeds the level recommended by the City Council

The two-sample unpaired t-test (Used to compare averages of 2 unpaired or independent groups)

Example: To compare CD4+ counts of two independent or unpaired groups of patients; $n_1 = n_2 = 30$

The two-sample paired t-test (Used to compare averages of 2 paired or related groups)

Example: To compare CD4+ counts of the same group of HIV-positive patients before and after a treatment; $n = 30$

The one-way Analysis of Variance (ANOVA) test (Used to compare 3 or more groups)

Repeated measures ANOVA (Used to find out if there is a significant difference among varieties, treatment methods, trials, etc

Multiple linear regression analysis (Used to study the relationship between an outcome variable Y and several explanatory variables related to Y (X_1, X_2, ….., X_k)

Logistic regression analysis (Used to study the relationship between a categorical outcome variable of study Y and several explanatory variables that are related to Y (X_1, X_2, ….., X_k)

Factor analysis (Used for data reduction)

Principal component analysis (Used for identifying and quantifying key sources of variation at a single level)

Discriminant analysis (Used for identifying and quantifying differential factors)

Survival analysis (Used for identifying and quantifying key predictors of survival based on hazard ratios); Requires a longitudinal study design.

Multilevel analysis (Used for identifying and quantifying key sources of variation at various hierarchical levels)

Time series analysis (Used for detecting and quantifying factors that vary as a function of time)

Statistical Packages suitable for Quantitative Data Analysis:

STATA

SAS

SPSS

S-PLUS

MLWin

Basic concepts of Statistical Estimation

Statistics is a field of study concerned with (1) the collection, organisation, summarisation, and analysis of data, and (2) the drawing of inferences about a body of data when only a part of data is observed.

A parameter is the true value or characteristic of a population. It cannot be known precisely. It can only be estimated based on a sample estimator or statistic. An example of a parameter is the true average monthly income of all South Africans. This figure cannot be known for sure unless data is gathered from the entire population of South Africa. The true average monthly income of all South Africans is estimated based on a representative sample drawn from the population. The sample mean is used for estimating the population mean.

Quantitative research methods utilise data sets and robust statistical methods of data analysis. Data entry and analysis is performed in statistical packages such as STATA, SPSS, SAS, S-PLUS, etc. Interpretation of results of data analysis is based on the theory and principles of inferential statistics. For this reason, it is vital to know both the theory of statistical principles and their practical application. Statistical data consists of all available information arising from observations, experiments, surveys, public records, registers, empirical evidence, etc. The accuracy of statistical data sets determines the degree of utilisation of statistical results of data analysis.

A variable is a characteristic that takes on different values in different persons, places, or things. Some examples of variables include heart beat rates, heights of people, income, and weight.

A quantitative variable is a variable that can be measured objectively. Examples of quantitative measurements are age in years, weight in kg, body temperature, volume, income in Rand, etc.

A qualitative variable is a variable that cannot be measured objectively. Examples of qualitative variables are gender (male, female), marital status (single, married, divorced, widowed, other), language group (English, Zulu, Xhosa, Sotho, other), health status (healthy, sick), etc.

Types of Variables of Study

Continuous variables are variables that could be measured without gaps. Examples of continuous variables of studies are the age of a person in years, the weight of a person in kilograms, volume in cubic litres, distance travelled in kilometres, temperature in degrees centigrade, CD4 count, red blood cell counts, viral load count, number of hours of study, number of pages of a book read, length of time taken to complete a task, and monthly income in Rand.

Discrete variables are variables that can take only values with interruptions or gaps between them. There are three kinds of discrete variables:

- **Discrete nominal variables** are discrete variables that can only take values which have no particular order. Example: Gender could be male or female. Order does not matter. It only matters that males differ from females.
- **Discrete ordinal variables** are discrete variables in which order matters. For example, the degree of satisfaction in the quality of services provided (1 if excellent, 2 if very good, 3 if good, 5 if poor, 5 if very poor) denotes a discrete ordinal variable in which order matters. As one goes from 1 to 5, the degree of satisfaction decreases.

- **Discrete numeric variables** are discrete variables whose possible values are numbers. For example, family size can only be positive (1, 2, 3, 4, 5, etc). It is possible to quantify or compare two family sizes.

Measurement Scales

Measurement is defined as the assignment of numbers to objects or events according to a set of rules. The various measurement scales result from the fact that measurement may be carried out under different sets of rules.

The nominal scale: The lowest measurement scale is the nominal scale. As the name implies, it consists of 'naming' observations or classifying them into various mutually exclusive and collectively exhaustive categories.

The ordinal scale: Whenever observations not only differ from category to category but can be ranked according to some criteria, they are said to be measured on an ordinal scale.

The interval scale: Unlike nominal and ordinal scales, the interval scale is truly quantitative. The interval scale enables us to order measurements. It also enables us to measure the distance between any two measurements. An example of the interval scale is the measurement of temperature in the Celsius scale. A temperature of zero Celsius does not indicate the absence of heat.

The ratio scale is the highest level of measurement. The ratio scale consists of a truly zero value. For example, measurements such as height, weight, and length are based on the ratio scale, and can actually be equal to zero.

Analysis of Continuous and Categorical Variables

There are two broad categories of variables (continuous and categorical). Statistical methods of data analysis vary depending on whether our variable of study is continuous or categorical. It is difficult to learn much from raw data. Planning and intervention are often made based on class intervals, and not based on individual observations. This explains why we often transform raw data into grouped data before analysis is done. The analysis of continuous variables requires statistical procedures such as averages, standard deviations, and correlation coefficients. For example, the average monthly income of employees of the South African Reserve Bank along with the standard error of estimation. By contrast, the analysis of categorical variables requires procedures such as frequency tables and proportions. Example: The proportion of males and females.

Summarising Discrete Variables

Total frequency = Total number of observations in data set = Sample size of study

Relative frequency = Proportion of the number of times an observation occurs in a data set

Cumulative frequency = The total number of observations that are less than or equal to a specific observation

The first step in summarising data is to construct a frequency distribution.

Example: Suppose that we gather data from 61 female and 39 male respondents by using a questionnaire as part of a study. The distribution of respondents can be summarised as follows by using a simple frequency table in which the two genders are displayed.

Table 1: A simple frequency table for the distribution of gender

Gender	Frequency	Relative frequency
Female	61	0.61 = 61%
Male	39	0.39 = 39%
Total	100	1.00 = 100%

Graphical methods for Discrete Variables

Discrete variables are often presented graphically using bar charts or pie charts. Bar charts and pie charts can be plotted easily in spreadsheets such as Excel. In a bar chart, frequency is measured using the length of the bar. In a pie chart, proportion is measured in areas. A pie chart is suitable for number of categories less than or equal to 5. For several categories, it is better to use bar charts. It is possible to assign titles and legends to bar charts and pie charts.

Figure 1 shows a bar chart for the distribution of gender which is based on the information displayed above in Table 1. The bar chart shows that the number of men is 39, whereas the number of women is 61.

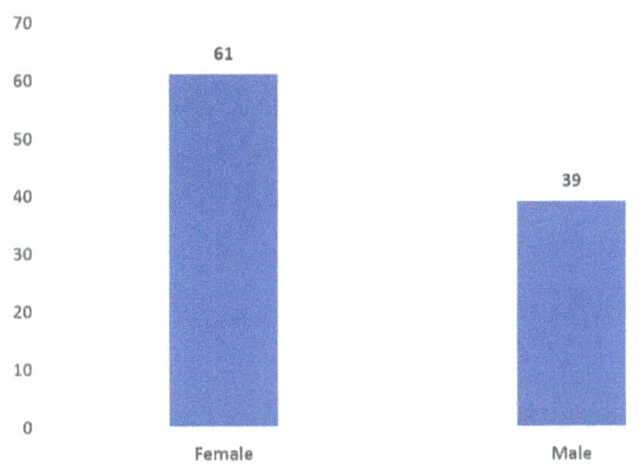

Figure 1: A bar chart for the distribution of gender

Figure 2 shows a pie chart for the frequency distribution displayed in Table 1 above. The pie chart shows that the number of men is 39, whereas the number of women is 61.

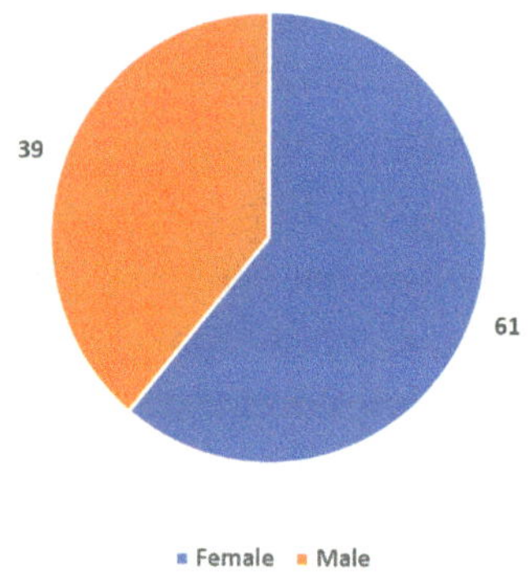

Figure 2: A pie chart for the distribution of gender

How to sketch a stalked bar chart in Excel

A survey is conducted by gathering data from 6,090 women. The number of contraceptive users is 5,012. The number of non-users is 1,078. Table 2 shows the age categories of 5,012 women who use modern contraceptive methods and the age categories of 1,078 women who do not use modern contraceptive methods. It is desired to sketch a stalked bar graph in Excel to provide a graphical summary for the data displayed in Table 2.

Table 2: Distribution of contraceptive use by age category (n = 6,090)

Age category	Number of contraceptive users	Number of non-users
15 to 19 years	843	168
20 to 24 years	770	180
25 to 29 years	600	131
30 to 34 years	2,799	599
Total	5,012	1,078

Enter your data in Excel as follows:

15 to 19 years	843	168
20 to 24 years	770	180
25 to 29 years	600	131
30 to 34 years	2,799	599

Highlight your raw data in Excel
Click on Insert
Click on Recommended charts, Clustered column, OK
Delete chart title
Click on + on right hand side of bar chart
Click on Data labels, Outside end
Highlight and delete Y-axis values and X-axis values

Right click on Excel graph
Click on Select data
Click on Series 1
Click on Edit
Type new name for Series 1 (Users)
Click on OK

Click on Series 2
Click on Edit
Type new name for Series 2 (Non-users)
Click on OK

Save your stalked Excel bar chart (See Figure 3)

To copy bar chart from Excel to MS Word

Open MS Word, and leave an active window
Go back to Excel, and highlight entire graph
Click on Edit
Click on Copy
Go to MS Word
Click on Edit
Click on Paste

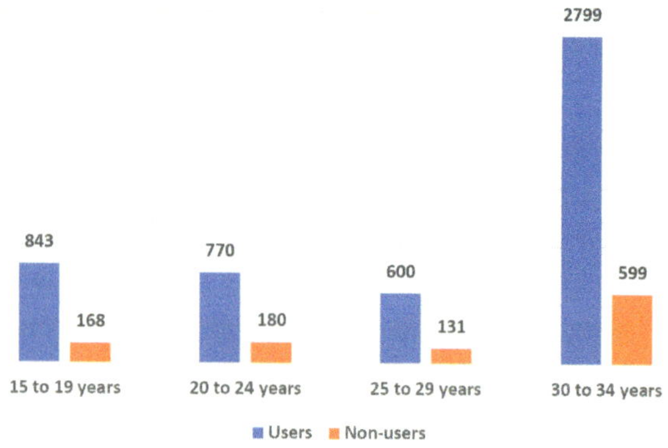

Figure 3: A stalked bar chart for contraceptive use by age category

Two frequency distributions can be compared using a stalked bar chart. Usually it is very useful to represent both frequency distributions by bar charts plotted in the same graph

The Stem-and-Leaf Plot

A stem-and-leaf plot summarizes data by listing. The unit of measurement is used for constructing a stem-and-leaf plot. The plot is useful for identifying the modal observation.

Procedure:

- List all the observations in the data set in an ascending order.
- Decide how large the stem and leaf should be. For example, the stem could be 10, the leaf could be 1.
- List the stems in a column with a vertical line to their right.
- For each value, write the leaf portion in the same row as its corresponding stem.

Example:

The weights in kg of a random sample of n=100 people who took part in a community based nutrition survey are shown below:

82, 64, 44, 85, 52, 48, 47, 33, 47, 49, 60, 59, 52, 49, 49, 62, 91, 88, 71, 48, 62, 61, 76, 44, 67, 75, 82, 91, 88, 78, 72, 74, 40, 59, 52, 78, 59, 60, 67, 69, 60, 51, 45, 58, 47, 58, 47, 58, 79, 56, 49, 68, 61, 54, 58, 54, 67, 66, 77, 79, 56, 72, 60, 41, 52, 49, 49, 62, 91, 88, 71, 67, 82, 61, 76, 44, 67, 75, 82, 91, 88, 81, 82, 74, 40, 59, 52, 78, 59, 60, 67, 79, 80, 57, 65, 58, 79, 56, 49, 73

Use a stem-and-leaf plot for summarising the raw data set.

Solution:

The data set is captured in Excel, SPSS or STATA formats as data1. Note that the unit of measurement for this raw data set is equal to 1. A stem-and-leaf plot could be obtained in STATA as shown below.

```
. use c:\bos\data1.dta, clear
. su weight, detail

                        weight in kgs
-------------------------------------------------------------
      Percentiles      Smallest
 1%         36.5             33
 5%           44             40
10%           47             40       Obs                 100
25%           52             41       Sum of Wgt.         100

50%           61                      Mean              63.98
                        Largest       Std. Dev.      14.14926
75%           76             91
90%           82             91       Variance       200.2016
95%           88             91       Skewness       .1745792
99%           91             91       Kurtosis        2.10218

. stem  weight, digits(1)

Stem-and-leaf plot for weight (weight in kgs)

  3* | 3
  3. |
  4* | 001444
  4. | 57777889999999
  5* | 12222244
  5. | 66678888899999
  6* | 000001112224
  6. | 5677777789
  7* | 1122344
  7. | 556678889999
  8* | 0122222
  8. | 58888
  9* | 1111
```

The stem is 10.

The leaf is 1.

The number 49 appears 7 times in the data set. No other observation in the data set appears 7 times. As such, the mode is 49 (the most frequent observation in the data set). The stem-and-leaf plot makes it easy to identify the mode.

The following stem-and-leaf plot is obtained from SPSS (data1.sav)

```
weight in kgs Stem-and-Leaf Plot

 Frequency    Stem &  Leaf

     1.00        3 .  3
      .00        3 .
     6.00        4 .  001444
    14.00        4 .  57777889999999
     8.00        5 .  12222244
    14.00        5 .  66678888899999
    12.00        6 .  000001112224
    10.00        6 .  5677777789
     7.00        7 .  1122344
    12.00        7 .  556678889999
     7.00        8 .  0122222
     5.00        8 .  58888
     4.00        9 .  1111

 Stem width:   10
 Each leaf:    1 case(s)
```

How to sketch a bar chart in Excel for the variable age category

Age category in years	Percentage
20 years or less	11%
21 to 30 years	24%
31 to 40 years	28%
41 to 50 years	25%
51 years or more	12%

Capture your raw data in Excel as shown above
Click on Insert, recommended charts, clustered bar chart, OK

Delete chart title
Click on + on right hand side of bar chart
Click on Data labels, Outside end
Highlight and delete Y-axis values and X-axis values

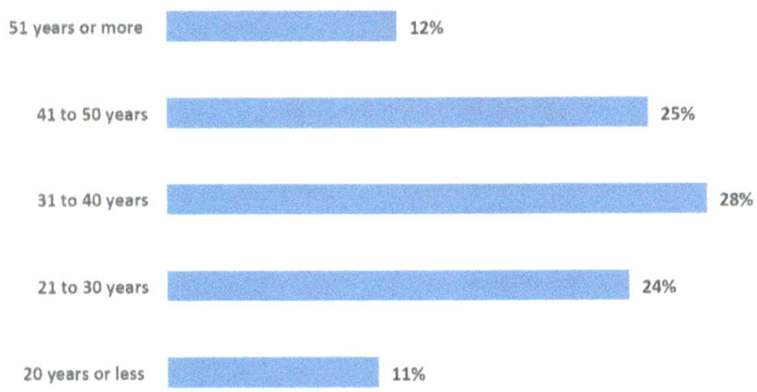

Figure 4: A bar chart for age categories

How to sketch a histogram for a continuous variable in STATA

Open up the STATA data set data1.dta and sketch a histogram for the weights in kilograms of the 100 people in the data set.

Open up the raw data set data1.dta in STATA
Click on Graphics
Click on Histogram
Select the variable as weight
Click on Density plots
Click on Add normal density plot
Click on OK

```
. use c:\bos\data1.dta, clear

. histogram weight, normal
(bin=10, start=33, width=5.8)
```

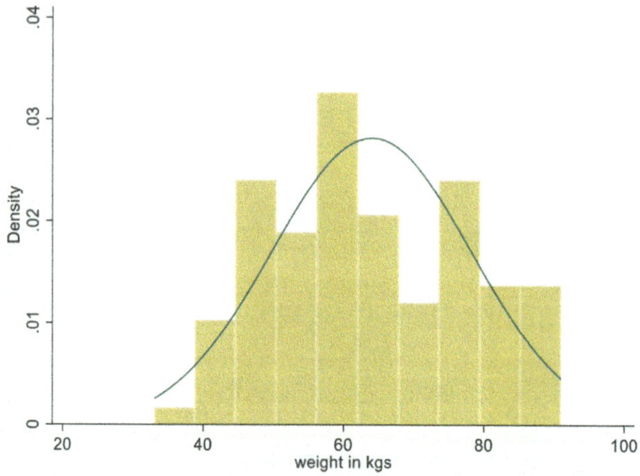

Figure 5: A histogram in STATA for the weights of 100 people in kilograms

How to sketch a box plot for a continuous variable in STATA

Open up the STATA data set c:\bos\data1.dta and sketch a box plot for the weights in kilograms of the 100 people in the data set.

Open up the raw data set c:\bos\data1.dta in STATA
Click on Graphics
Click on Box plot, Vertical
Select the variable as weight
Click on OK

```
. use c:\bos\data1.dta, clear

. graph box weight
```

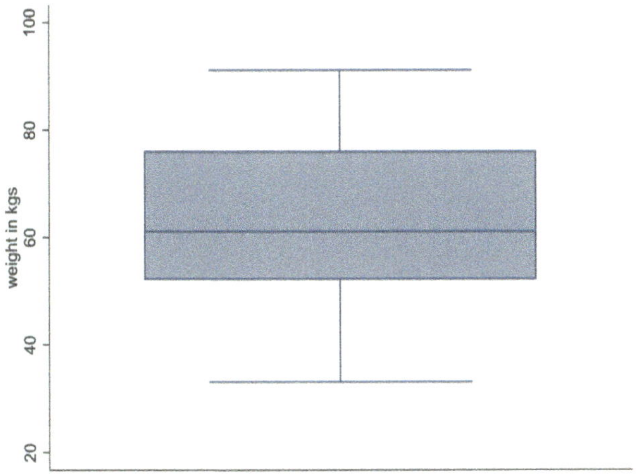

Figure 6: A box plot in STATA for the weights of 100 people in kilograms

In Figure 6,

The bottom part of the rectangular box is the first quartile or 25th percentile (52)

The solid line in the middle of the rectangular box is the 2nd quartile or the median (61)

The upper part of the rectangular box is the third quartile or 75th percentile (76)

The lowest horizontal line closest to the X-axis is the smallest observation in the data set (33)

The highest horizontal line at the top of the plot is the largest observation in the data set (91)

```
. use c:\bos\data1.dta, clear

. su weight, detail

                        weight in kg
-------------------------------------------------------------
      Percentiles      Smallest
 1%         36.5             33
 5%           44             40
10%           47             40       Obs                 100
25%           52             41       Sum of wgt.         100

50%           61                      Mean              63.98
                        Largest       Std. dev.      14.14926
75%           76             91
90%           82             91       Variance       200.2016
95%           88             91       Skewness       .1745792
99%           91             91       Kurtosis        2.10218
```

Differences between Quantitative and Qualitative Methods

Researchers routinely gather information or massive data on several variables of study in order to predict the likelihood of future events. The underlying assumption is that events occur repeatedly under similar circumstances, and knowledge of the past contributes to the accurate prediction of future events. Quantitative and qualitative methods of data gathering and analysis are complimentary to each other, as the shortcomings of one method are compensated for by the strengths of the other method. In cases where a researcher has adequate resources for collecting and analysing data, it is advantageous to use a combination of both quantitative and qualitative methods of data collection and analysis. This is commonly referred to as the use of a mixed, sequential approach to data collection and analysis. For example, consider a study in which results obtained from quantitative data analysis identify 3 influential predictor variables that affect the outcome or dependent variable of study. Subsequent analysis is conducted on the top 3 influential variables by using qualitative methods of data collection and analysis. This approach is sequential in nature in which quantitative methods are used first, and further analysis is carried out by using qualitative methods. In such cases, results obtained from quantitative and qualitative methods should be integrated with each other so that feasible recommendations can be made with a view to manage plans of intervention effectively.

Quantitative methods are research methods dealing with numbers and factors that are measurable. By contrast, qualitative methods are methods based on factors that cannot be measured quantitatively. Qualitative methods of data collection and analysis are used extensively in cases where subjective phenomena and unique perspectives need to be understood, explained, and accounted for satisfactorily. For example, qualitative methods are suitable for assessing and evaluating the extent to which residents and ratepayers of the City of Tshwane are satisfied with the quality and efficiency of routine municipal services that are provided to them by municipal employees. Qualitative data is gathered mostly by conducting in-depth interviews. Such interviews are transcribed, coded, and tallied. Themes are created out of codes and categories. A common method of conducting qualitative data analysis is thematic analysis. The reliability of qualitative data analysis is assessed by using multiple sources of credible information such as personal observation, past and present records and reports, subject matter opinion, and findings obtained from a critical review of the literature. This process is commonly referred to as triangulation.

In some studies, a combination of quantitative and qualitative methods of data collection and analysis are used on a sequential basis. Often, quantitative analysis is conducted to identify influential predictor variables by using univariate, bivariate, and multivariate methods of statistical data analysis. Following that, subsequent qualitative research is carried out on the influential predictor variables identified by using quantitative research.

Results obtained from qualitative data analysis should be integrated with results obtained from quantitative data analysis in order to ease the task of making feasible recommendations. In most cases, qualitative data is gathered by conducting individual or focus-group interviews. Members of a focus group must share similar characteristics in terms of the research questions that need to be answered. In most cases, eligible participants are selected for conducting qualitative studies based on purposive sampling. That is, participants must be highly knowledgeable, well experienced, and firmly grounded in the area of research that needs to be investigated.

In the course of conducting individual in-depth qualitative interviews, the researcher needs to know when to stop interviewing eligible participants of the study. The researcher should stop interviewing eligible participants when a state of saturation is reached. A state of saturation is reached when responses obtained from new participants of study reduce to a repeat of responses obtained from eligible participants who have already been interviewed as part of the same study. When saturation is reached, no new information is obtained from eligible participants. For example, consider a qualitative study in which 12 eligible participants are chosen for the study. It is possible that a state of saturation is reached after individual interviews are conducted with participants 1 to 8. That is, the researcher confirms that responses obtained from participants 9 to 12 are similar to responses obtained from participants 1 to 8. When that happens, there is no need to use interviews conducted with participants 9 to 12 in the study. In practice, it is highly beneficial to conduct interviews with all 12 eligible participants of study. Doing so enables the researcher to collect all available data and discard duplicate views and opinions from the data collected as part of the study.

Individual and focus group interviews are commonly used for gathering data in qualitative studies. For example, 1-hour-long individual in-depth interviews are often used for gathering information from participants of qualitative studies. Focus groups consist of participants who share similar views, background, perspectives and experience with regards to the aims and purposes of study. Participants of focus groups should be homogeneous but not familiar with each other. Familiarity among focus group participants introduces bias into the study.

The ability to measure variables of interest objectively is a common feature of quantitative or statistical methods of research. Statistical methods enable researchers to measure parameters of interest and account for precisions of estimation. For example, it is possible to estimate the true average monthly income of South Africans by drawing a representative sample from the population of study. The true monthly average income is a parameter value. It is not possible to determine the exact value of a parameter precisely unless data is collected from all units in the entire population of study. Doing so is cumbersome and costly. It is more efficient to draw a representative sample from the population of study, and use the sample mean as an estimator of the true or population mean. Whenever a sample is drawn out of a population, the precision of estimation depends upon how well the sample reflects the population of study.

In management, business, socio-economic, and behavioural studies, postgraduate level research is carried out by using purely quantitative, purely qualitative, and mixed methods. Mixed methods use a combination of quantitative and qualitive methods of data collection and analysis. The choice of such methods depends upon the aims and objectives of study as well as the availability of enough of the resources that are required for data collection.

Quantitative research methods heavily rely on statistical inference. Statistical methods involve gathering quantitative and qualitative data in order to estimate population parameters. Statistical inference has two goals: estimating parameters based on samples, and the assessment of the theoretical reliability of estimates. Advocates of quantitative methods argue that only by using such methods can the social sciences become truly scientific. Advocates of qualitative methods argue that quantitative methods tend to obscure the reality of the social phenomena under study because they underestimate or neglect the non-measurable factors, which may be the most important. The modern tendency is to use qualitative and quantitative methods in conjunction with each other, because the two methods are often complementary and support each other.

Ensuring Validity and Reliability

A researcher needs to know that what is being measured as part of the study is what is intended to be measured. This task is accomplished by ensuring validity. Ensuring content validity enables the researcher to be able to measure variables of study accurately and objectively. Content validity is ensured by conducting a pilot study before the actual study is conducted. A pilot study can be conducted by administering the questionnaire of study to a simple random sample of eligible participants of study. Conducting a pilot study enables the researcher to refine the questionnaire of study in the field. Participants in the pilot study can also comment on the suitability of questions that are listed in the questionnaire of study. In a qualitative study, a pilot study can be conducted by conducting individual and/or focus-group in-depth interviews with a random sample of a few eligible participants of study.

In the fields of management, business, socioeconomic, and behavioural studies, reliability and internal consistency are ensured by using the Cronbach Alpha test of reliability and internal consistency. Cronbach Alpha coefficients (Bell, Harley and Bryman, 2022) with magnitudes of 0.75 or above indicate that tools used for the measurement of variables are reliable and internally consistent enough.

Statistical Packages

Statistical packages such as SPSS, STATA, and SAS are often used for quantitative data analysis. These packages are used to perform data entry and analysis. Raw data can be transferred from one system to another easily. In most cases, raw data sets are captured by using an Excel spreadsheet. The choice of a statistical package does not alter results of data analysis. An efficient use of statistical packages requires an understanding of theoretical statistics.

UNIT 2

RESEARCH FOR POSTGRADUATE-LEVEL STUDIES

The main purpose of research

The relationship between the researcher and supervisor

The role of the immediate supervisor

The role of internal examiners or moderators

The role of external examiners or moderators

The role of the research committee

The role of the ethics committee

The role of the statistical advisor

The role of the donor or sponsor of research

Research standards and minimum requirements

The identification of a suitable research problem

Informal presentation of results of study

Formal presentation of results to immediate supervisor

Procedures of review of a study report (accountability for utilized resources, acknowledgement of all sources of research information and tools, accuracy and authenticity of analytical results, contribution to the literature and potential stakeholders, adequacy of research standards)

Formal evaluation of research proposal or thesis (stages 1 and 2)

Valid reasons for the complete rejection of a proposal or thesis (compromised standards, plagiarism, unwarranted discrepancy between approved objectives and end results of study)

Procedures of grievance or complaint by researcher

Essential Elements of a Research Proposal

Research proposals are similar, although there are variations depending on the specific objective of the proposal. Proposals are often written to seek financial and administrative support for a research grant, a training grant, an academic qualification, a conference presentation, or curriculum development. A typical research proposal produced for research and/or academic purposes consists of the following components:

Title of study

Abstract of study

Introduction of study

Background of study

Literature review

Objectives (general and specific) of study

Rationale of study

List of variables of study and their levels (types of variables and their measurement)

Examples of data collection procedures (interviews, questionnaires, and records)

The design of questionnaires

Methods and Materials

- Study design
- Sample size of study and data collection procedures
- Determination of the most suitable sampling technique
- Statistical methods of data entry, editing, manipulation, and analysis
- Brief summary of alternative procedures of data analysis from the literature

Expected outputs of study

Limitations of study

Ethical considerations

The cost of study

Action plan of study

List of references used in the study

Abstract of Study

The abstract is a brief statement of the topic, procedure, and projected outcome of the project. The abstract of the final report is often similar to the abstract in the research proposal. Usually, the size of an abstract is half a page.

Table of Contents

The table of contents lists (with final page numbers) the location of each separately titled section of the report, usually following the sequence above from abstract through appendices. To the professional reader (who as such is faced with lots of reading and appreciates conveniences), the table of contents also indicates at a glance what material is covered.

Introduction to Study

The Introduction will be the first major section the reader encounters, so you want to make it as effective as you can to encourage further interest. The Introduction states the broad problem objectives, helps introduce the project subject, and explains why the problem is worth solving and who will be interested in the solutions. If the proposal is being prepared for an off-campus project sponsor as well as an advisor, make certain the value of solving the problem is clear to the real-world sponsor.

Some questions to cover here are the subject of the proposal, the goals, the sub-goals, the potential benefactor of the proposed research activity, how the research is going to be done, how the results of study are going to be used, and what methods are going to be used to conduct the proposed study.

Background of Study

The background of study explains the reasons that prompted the researcher to embark on the current study. Usually, this is a summary of acute problems faced by the community involved due to lack of concrete findings about what is actually going on with regard to the proposed research problem.

Literature Review

A literature review is a summary of what has been done by other researchers, and what the major findings are. A good research proposal is based on a thorough literature review. The literature review shows how and why the present researcher agrees or disagrees with what has been reported by other researchers in the past. All claims in the literature review section must be backed up by concrete reference. Good questions to answer in this section are:

1) What studies have been done by others so far, and what techniques of study and analysis were used?
2) How is the proposed study different from other studies? What unique contribution to the literature will this study make?

The problem statement is a succinct summary of the literature review.

A robust review of the literature is supported by a theoretical framework of study. That is, evidence of local and international best practice is provided as part of the literature review. It identifies what has been done and known until now, where the gap in the literature is, and how this gap can be filled by using appropriate methods and materials of study.

Methods and Materials of Study

The methods and materials section of the research proposal is the heart of the proposal because it shows how the researcher intends to carry out the proposed study. The section must convince the advisor that the researcher clearly understands the task, has a logical time plan for solving problems, and has identified all the resources needed.

Some of the other questions the reader will expect you to answer in this section are:

1) What are the tasks and sub-tasks identified to achieve your objectives?
2) What specific methods and materials will be needed to carry out the proposed activity (data analysis, interpretation of results, etc)?

3) What data are needed for the project and how will they be collected? If the project requires a survey or interviews, the design of this instrument (especially the selection of participants) must be explained and justified.
4) What statistical methods of data analysis will be used to analyse this data, and where else has this method or process been used?

Action Plan of Study

An action plan provides a time table of major research activities that will be carried out as part of the proposed study.

Cost of Study

The cost of study shows the amount of money needed to conduct the proposed study. This section will have a breakdown and must be supported by suitable evidence, such as quotations from the relevant service providers.

List of References

The list of references provides a list of all cited materials in the various parts of the proposal. All cited materials must be included in the list of references according to the referencing style recommended by the academic or research institution in which the study is carried out. Example: Students who are enrolled at Tshwane University of Technology (TUT) are allowed to use the American Psychological Association (APA) style of citation and referencing in their research proposals and dissertations.

Appendices

Appendices contain materials too lengthy for inclusion in the text, or not directly relevant. Certain kinds of raw data, background materials, geographical maps of the sites of study, letters of ethics approval for the proposed research, proof of financial assistance, letters of institutional support, relevant newspaper articles, government gazettes, etc fall under Appendices.

UNIT 3

DESCRIPTIVE ANALYSES

A parameter is the true characteristic or value of a population of study. For example, the true monthly average income of all South Africans is a parameter. The exact value of a parameter cannot be known unless data is gathered from the entire population of study. However, a parameter can always be estimated using a sample estimator or statistic. For example, the true monthly average income of all South Africans can be estimated using the sample mean by drawing a representative sample from the population of study.

Statistical tests are broadly classified into 2 categories: parametric and non-parametric tests. Parametric tests are based on large sample sizes. Parametric tests are based on the normal distribution and assume that the sample is a true representative of the population of study. To use parametric tests, the variable of study must be continuous or else the sample size of study must be very large. In cases where the sample size of study is less than 30 or in cases where the variable of study is discrete, non-parametric tests are used. Results from parametric tests are theoretically more reliable than results from non-parametric tests.

Descriptive measures consist of measures of central tendency (the mean, mode, and median) and measures of variation (the variance, the standard deviation, the coefficient of variation, the range). The mean, mode, and median are called centres of central tendency or measures of location. The mean is the average value. The mode is the most frequent observation. The median is the centre of balance of the set of data. Measures of location or central tendency are used to determine the centre of distribution of the given set of data. Measures of variation are used to assess the precision of estimation. Descriptive statistics relies basically on measures of location and variation.

There are 2 types of variables: discrete and continuous. Discrete variables are analysed using frequency tables and bar charts. Continuous variables are analysed using the mean, mode, and median, standard deviation, variance, and histogram. There are two broad categories of discrete variables: nominal and ordinal. An example of a nominal variable is the sex of an individual, which can either be male or female. The order between males and females does not matter; it only matters that males are different from females. An example of an ordinal variable is a 5-point level of satisfaction in which 1, 2, 3, 4, and 5 denote various categories arranged in an increasing or decreasing order of satisfaction. Categorical data analysis is used to analyse discrete variables of study.

A test of hypothesis is done to find out whether a hypothesis is true. Statistical tests of hypotheses are done at a level of significance denoted by α, usually fixed at the 5% level. The usual level of α is 5% because most researchers are willing to tolerate an error in judgement of 5%. The null hypothesis is rejected if the probability value (P-value) falls below α. Otherwise, the null hypothesis cannot be rejected at at the same level of significance. In cases where the null hypothesis cannot be rejected, the researcher works under the assumption that the null hypothesis is correct.

Inferential statistics uses sampling distributions of the sample mean, the sample proportion and the sample variance. Point estimates are used to provide rough estimates of parameters. Interval estimates provide confidence intervals (lower and upper bounds) for parameters. For example, a 95% confidence interval for the true average gives a 95% assurance that the true average lies between the lower bound and the upper bound.

Type 1 and Type 2 errors

A Type 1 error is the mistake of rejecting a true null hypothesis. The probability of Type 1 error is denoted by α (the level of significance of the test being made). A Type 2 error is the mistake of accepting a false null hypothesis. The probability of a Type 2 error is denoted by β. It is impossible to minimise both α and β at the same time. Statisticians often fix the value of α, and minimise the value of β. The power of a test is a measure of the ability of the test to reject a statistical null hypothesis when the null hypothesis is not true. The power of a statistical test is equal to $1 - \beta$. In most statistical tests, the value of α is fixed at the 5% level. The power of most statistical tests is 80%.

Examples of Commonly used Parametric Statistical Tests

The following are examples of commonly used parametric statistical tests:

- To test the null hypothesis that the mean is equal to a hypothesised value, the one-sample test on the mean is used.
- To test the null hypothesis that the proportion is equal to a hypothesised value, the one-sample test on proportions is used.
- To compare the averages of 2 groups with each other, the two-sample test on the mean is used. If the samples are independent of each other and the variable of comparison is continuous or if the sample size per group is at least 30, the two-sample unpaired t-test can be used.
- To compare two related or paired samples with each other, the two-sample paired t-test is used.
- To compare two proportions with each other, the two-sample test on proportions is used.

- To compare 3 or more groups with each other with regard to one variable of comparison, the one-way analysis of variance (ANOVA) test is used.
- To investigate the relationship between one continuous outcome variable and one continuous explanatory variable, simple linear regression analysis can be used.
- To investigate the relationship between one continuous outcome variable and several explanatory variables, multiple linear regression analysis can be used.

Statistical Assumptions

Statistical assumptions are general assumptions about statistical populations.

Statistics, like all mathematical disciplines, does not generate valid conclusions from nothing. In order to generate interesting conclusions about real statistical populations, it is usually required to make some background assumptions. These must be made with care, because inappropriate assumptions can generate wildly inaccurate conclusions. The most commonly applied statistical assumptions are the following:

1) Independence of observations from each other
2) Independence of observational error from potential confounding effects
3) Exact or approximate normality of observations
4) Linearity of graded responses to quantitative stimuli

Most parametric tests are based on the maximum likelihood method of estimation that asserts that all of the information in a sample is contained in the likelihood function. The parameter value which maximises the likelihood function is the value which is most strongly supported by the evidence. Statistical inference is inference about a population from a random sample drawn from it or, more generally, about a random process from its observed behaviour during a finite period of time. It includes point estimation, interval estimation, hypothesis testing, and prediction. Diagnostic measures or goodness-of-fit statistics are used in statistical data analysis in order to assess the theoretical reliability of estimated statistical models. A simple diagnostic measure suitable for multiple linear regression analysis is R-squared. It measures the percentage of explained variation. An R-squared value less than 75% indicates that the fitted model is not so good.

Sampling Techniques

Samples are drawn from populations of study. It is too costly and difficult to gather data from each individual unit in the population of study. For this reason, the researcher draws a sample from the population of study using sampling techniques. It is essential to determine the sample size of a study before the study can be conducted. The researcher must make sure that the sample is a good representative of the population of study.

The quality of the study depends on the quality of the sample drawn from the population of study. A good sample is random, large in size, free from bias, and one that allows maximum variability. The most commonly used sampling techniques are simple random sampling, stratified random sampling, cluster sampling, and systematic random sampling.

In simple random sampling, a sampling frame is used. A sampling frame is the list of all units constituting the population of study. Each of the N units in the population has an equal probability of being selected into the sample. The table of random numbers, ballot papers, etc, are used to select n out of N units at random.

Stratified sampling is used when the population of study can be split into k distinct strata (blocks of similar units). The strata are internally homogenous and externally heterogeneous. Often, data is gathered from each stratum by using proportional allocation with regard to size. In stratified sampling, data is gathered from each distinct stratum.

Cluster sampling is used when the population of study can be split into k distinct clusters (blocks of similar units). The clusters are internally homogenous and externally heterogeneous. The researcher gathers data from some of the clusters constituting the population of study. In cluster sampling, data need not be gathered from all clusters. Selection of clusters depends on availability of data needed for study, simplicity in gathering data, relevance to the research problem being investigated, and availability of data. Often, multi-stage cluster sampling is used to gather data.

Systematic sampling is used when the population shows no specific pattern. A sampling interval $k = \frac{N}{n}$ is used for selection of eligible units from the population of study into the sample. The first unit is selected at random. From then on, every k^{th} unit in the list is selected into the sample. The process of selection is continued until a total of n units are selected.

The above techniques are probability sampling techniques because eligible units are selected from the population into the sample based on probabilities of occurrence in the population of study. Probability with regard to size ensures the selection of units in accordance with how abundantly they occur in the population of study. There are sampling techniques that do not require probabilities of occurrence. Such techniques are called non-probability sampling techniques. An example of a non-probability sampling technique is snowballing, in which the researcher selects the first k observations into the sample and disregards the rest. Non-probability sampling techniques are theoretically much weaker than probability sampling techniques.

Sample Size of Study for a Descriptive Cross-Sectional Study

The purpose of a descriptive cross-sectional study is to estimate basic statistical parameters, such as proportions of attributes and averages. To determine the sample size of study, it is necessary to know the proportion of the desired attribute from previous studies or from a pilot study. The researcher determines the level of significance of study and margin of error.

The initial sample size of study is denoted by n_0, and is given by:

$$n_0 = Z^2{}_{1-\frac{\alpha}{2}} \times \frac{\hat{P}(1-\hat{P})}{d^2}$$

In the above expression, d denotes the margin of error, α denotes the level of significance of test, $\hat{P}$ denotes the proportion of attribute from the literature, and Z denotes the standard normal random variable.

The final sample size of study is denoted by n, and is given by:

$$n = \frac{n_0}{1+\frac{n_0}{N}}$$

In the above expression, N denotes the population size of study.

The sample size of study is often adjusted for dropouts as shown below:

$n_{adj} = \frac{n}{1-f}$ where f denotes the expected proportion of dropouts.

The adjusted sample size is larger than the unadjusted sample size of study.

Example:

It is desired to draw a representative random sample of farmers from a community in which a total of 10,000 farmers live in order to estimate the proportion of farmers experiencing food shortage. It is known from a study conducted a year ago that 12% of farmers at the site of study experience food shortage. Determine the adjusted sample size of a cross-sectional, descriptive study, assuming a 5% level of significance, a margin of error of 0.058, and a 20% dropout rate. (Use $Z_{0.975} = 1.96$).

Solution:

$N = 10{,}000,\ \alpha = 0.05,\ \hat{P} = 0.12,\ 1 - \hat{P} = 0.88,\ d = 0.058,\ f = 20\% = 0.20$

$$n_0 = Z^2_{1-\frac{\alpha}{2}} \times \frac{\hat{P}(1-\hat{P})}{d^2} = Z^2_{0.975} \times \frac{0.12(0.88)}{(0.058)^2} = (1.96)^2(31.39) = 120.54 \cong 121$$

$$n = \frac{n_0}{1+\frac{n_0}{N}} = \frac{121}{1+\frac{121}{10000}} = 119.55 \cong 120$$

$$n_{adj} = \frac{n}{1-f} = \frac{120}{1-0.20} = 150$$

Hence, a random sample of 150 farmers must be drawn from the site of study using a suitable sampling technique.

Commonly used Statistical methods of Data Analysis

In what follows next, commonly used statistical methods of data analysis are discussed along with practical examples. Numerical examples are given in the statistical packages STATA and SPSS. The methods illustrate the analysis of raw and grouped data sets, one-sample tests and confidence intervals, two-sample tests and confidence intervals, the Pearson chi-square test of association, simple and multiple linear regression and correlation analysis, and logistic regression analysis.

Measures of Location or Central Tendency for Raw Data

Measures of location or central tendency measure the centre of distribution being analysed. The mean is used to locate the average value of the observation. The mode is used to locate the most frequent observation in the data set. The median provides the centre of balance of the data set.

Raw data is a collection of observations that have not been systematically organized or arranged. Grouped data is statistical data provided in terms of class intervals.

Measures of location or central tendency can be obtained for both raw data and grouped data.

Suppose that a raw data set consists of n observations X_1, X_2, ….., X_n. The mean or the average of the n observations in the data set is given by:

$$\overline{X} = \frac{\sum_{i=1}^{n} X_i}{n}$$

In cases where some of the observations occur repeatedly, the following expression is more convenient to use:

$\overline{X} = \frac{\sum_{i=1}^{k} X_i f_i}{n}$ where f_i denotes the number of times observation X_i occurs.

The mode $\hat{X}$, is the most frequent observation. It is possible to have more than one mode in a single data set.

The median is denoted by X_{med} and gives the centre of balance of the data set.

To find the median, we first need to rearrange the n observations in an increasing order. In n is odd, the observation in the middle becomes the median. If n is even, the average of the middle 2 observations becomes the median.

Example:

Consider the 10 observations 1, 2, 2, 2, 2, 3, 3, 3, 4, 4. Find the mean, mode, and median.

$$\overline{X} = \frac{\sum_{i=1}^{n} X_i}{n} = \frac{26}{10} = 2.6$$

$\hat{X} = 2$ because 2 appears more frequently than the other observations.

$$X_{med} = \frac{2+3}{2} = 2.5$$

Measures of variation for raw data

Let x_i denote the ith observation in a raw data set consisting of a total of n observations. Let k denote the number of distinct observations in the data set. Let f_i denote the number of times the ith observation occurs in the data set. Then,

The variance is given by: $S^2 = \frac{\sum_{i=1}^{k} f_i \left(x_i - \overline{X}\right)^2}{n-1} = \frac{\sum_{i=1}^{k} f_i x_i^2 - n\overline{X}^2}{n-1}$

The standard deviation is given by: $S = \sqrt{Variance}$

The coefficient of variation is given by: CV = $\frac{S}{\overline{X}}$

The range is given by:

R = Largest observation – Smallest observation

Example in STATA

The weights in kg of 100 people selected for a nutrition study from a rural village at Kwa-Zulu Natal are shown below:

82, 64, 44, 85, 52, 48, 47, 33, 47, 49,

60, 59, 52, 49, 49, 62, 91, 88, 71, 48,

62, 61, 76, 44, 67, 75, 82, 91, 88, 78,

72, 74, 40, 59, 52, 78, 59, 60, 67, 69,

60, 51, 45, 58, 47, 58, 79, 56, 49, 68,

61, 54, 58, 54, 67 66, 77, 79, 56, 72,

60, 41, 52, 49, 49, 62, 91, 88, 71, 67,

82, 61, 76, 44, 67, 75, 82, 91, 88, 81,

82, 74, 40, 59, 52, 78, 59, 60, 67, 79,

80, 57, 65, 58, 47, 58, 79, 56, 49, 73

Determine all measures of location and variation for the raw data set shown above.

Solution:

First, capture the 100 observations shown above into STATA, Excel, SPSS, or any other statistical package that is available to you. Suppose that the data set is captured in STATA, and saved using the file name data1.dta. The data set data1.dta is saved on the computer on the C directory in a folder called bos. Thus, the path directory for the data file data1.dta is written as **c:\bos\data1.dta**. The following STATA procedure could be used for obtaining all relevant summary statistics for the raw data set.

```
. use c:\bos\data1.dta, clear

. su  weight, detail

                          weight in kg
-------------------------------------------------------------
      Percentiles      Smallest
 1%         36.5             33
 5%           44             40
10%           47             40       Obs                 100
25%           52             41       Sum of Wgt.         100

50%           61                      Mean              63.98
                        Largest       Std. Dev.      14.14926
75%           76             91
90%           82             91       Variance       200.2016
95%           88             91       Skewness       .1745792
99%           91             91       Kurtosis        2.10218
```

The average weight is 63.98 kg. The 25th percentile is 52 years. The 75th percentile is 76 years. The median age is equal to the 50th percentile or 61 years. The inter-quartile range is the difference between the 3rd quartile (76) and the 1st quartile (52) = 24 years.

Measures of Location or Central Tendency for Grouped Data

The mean

$$\bar{X} = \frac{\sum_{i=1}^{8} f_i m_i}{n} \quad \text{where } m_i \text{ denotes the } i^{th} \text{ class mark}$$

$$m_i = \frac{LCL + UCL}{2} = \frac{LCB + UCB}{2}$$

The mode

$$\hat{X} = LCB + \left(\frac{\Delta_1}{\Delta_1 + \Delta_2} \right) \times W \quad \text{where}$$

The modal class is the class with the highest frequency

LCB = Lower Class Boundary of modal class

Δ_1 = frequency of the modal class – frequency of class that lies just before the modal class

Δ_1 = frequency of the modal class – frequency of class that lies just after the modal class

W = UCB – LCB = Width of modal class

The median

$$X_{med} = LCB + \left(\frac{\frac{n}{2} - \left(\Sigma f_i \right)_l}{f_m} \right) \times W$$ where

The median class is the $\left(\frac{n}{2}\right)^{th}$ class where n is even. (If n is odd, $\frac{n}{2}$ is replaced by $\frac{n+1}{2}$ in the above expression.)

LCB = Lower Class Boundary of median class

$(\Sigma f_i)_l$ = Sum of frequencies of classes that lie before the median class

W = UCB – LCB = Width of median class

Example:

Determine the mean, mode, and median for the following artificial grouped data set:

Class interval	**Frequency**
1 - 5	2
6 – 10	1
11 – 15	4
16 – 20	3

Solution:

Class	Limit	Boundary	m_i	f_i	$f_i m_i$	m_i^2	$f_i m_i^2$
1	1 – 5	0.5-5.5	3	2	6	9	18
2	6 – 10	5.5-10.5	8	1	8	64	64
3	11 – 15	10.5-15.5	13	4	52	169	676
4	16 – 20	15.5-20.5	18	3	54	324	972
Total				n=10	120		1730

K = 4 = number of distinct class intervals

n = 10 = total frequency

$$\bar{X} = \frac{\sum_{i=1}^{4} f_i m_i}{n} = \frac{120}{10} = 12$$

The modal class is 11 – 15.

$$\hat{X} = LCB + \left(\frac{\Delta_1}{\Delta_1 + \Delta_2}\right) \times W = 10.5 + \left(\frac{3}{3+1}\right) \times 5 = 14.25$$

The median class is the 5th class: 11 – 15.

$$X_{med} = LCB + \left(\frac{\frac{n}{2} - \left(\sum f_i\right)_l}{f_m}\right) \times W = 10.5 + \left(\frac{5-3}{4}\right) \times 5 = 13$$

Measures of Variation for Grouped Data

The variance is given by: $S^2 = \frac{\sum_{i=1}^{k} f_i (m_i - \bar{X})^2}{n-1} = \frac{\sum_{i=1}^{k} f_i m_i^2 - n\bar{X}^2}{n-1}$

The standard deviation is given by: $S = \sqrt{Variance}$

The coefficient of variation is given by: CV = $\frac{S}{\bar{X}}$

The range is given by: R = UCB of last class – LCB of first class

Example:

For the data set shown above,

The variance is given by:

$$S^2 = \frac{\sum_{i=1}^{k} f_i m_i^{\,2} - n\overline{X}^2}{n-1} = \frac{1730-1440}{9} = 32.22$$

The standard deviation is given by: $S = \sqrt{Variance} = 5.67$

The coefficient of variation is given by: CV = $\frac{S}{\overline{X}} = \frac{5.67}{12} = 0.47$

The range is given by:

R = UCB of last class – LCB of first class = 20.5 – 0.5 = 20

Sturge's Formula

Sturge's formula is a formula for transforming raw data into grouped data with the minimum possible loss of information.

K = 1 + 3.3Log(n)

n = the total number of observations in the raw data set

R = Maximum observation – Minimum observation

$l = \frac{R}{K}$ = class length = class width

Notations:

L	=	Class limit
B	=	Class boundary
UM	=	Unit of measurement
LCB	=	Lower Class Boundary
UCB	=	Upper Class Boundary
LCL	=	Lower Class Limit
UCL	=	Upper Class Limit

Remark:

Class boundaries are wider than class limits by half of the unit of measurement on both sides. For example, in a data set in which the unit of measurement is 1, let a class limit be given by 1 to 5. Then, the corresponding class boundary becomes 0.5 to 5.5.

The ith class limit is given by:

$$l_i = UCB_i - LCB_i = UCL_i - LCL_i + UM$$

$$l_1 = 40.5 - 32.5 = 8$$

$$LCB_1 = X_{\min} - \frac{UM}{2} = 33 - 0.5 = 32.5$$

$$UCB_1 = LCB_1 + l = 32.5 + 8 = 40.5$$

$$LCL_1 = LCB_1 + 0.5 = 32.5 + 0.5 = 33$$

$$UCL_1 = UCB_1 - 0.5 = 40.5 - 0.5 = 40$$

Example:

The weights in kg of 100 people selected for a nutrition study from a rural village at Kwa-Zulu Natal are shown below:

82, 64, 44, 85, 52, 48, 47, 33, 47, 49,

60, 59, 52, 49, 49, 62, 91, 88, 71, 48,

62, 61, 76, 44, 67, 75, 82, 91, 88, 78,

72, 74, 40, 59, 52, 78, 59, 60, 67, 69,

60, 51, 45, 58, 47, 58, 79, 56, 49, 68,

61, 54, 58, 54, 67 66, 77, 79, 56, 72,

60, 41, 52, 49, 49, 62, 91, 88, 71, 67,

82, 61, 76, 44, 67, 75, 82, 91, 88, 81,

82, 74, 40, 59, 52, 78, 59, 60, 67, 79,

80, 57, 65, 58, 47, 58, 79, 56, 49, 73

Transform the raw data set to grouped data set. Determine the number of class intervals using **Sturge's formula.**

Solution:

K = 1 + 3.3Log(n) where n is the total number of observations

n = 100

$K = 1 + 3.3\text{Log}(100) = 1 + 3.3(2) = 1 + 6.6 = 7.6 \approx 8$ class intervals

R = 91 – 33 = 58

$l = \frac{R}{K} = \frac{58}{8} = 7.25 \approx 8$ = class length = class width

Unit of measurement = UM = 1

$\frac{UM}{2} = \frac{1}{2} = 0.5$

$l_i = UCB_i - LCB_i = UCL_i - LCL_i + UM$

$l_1 = 40.5 - 32.5 = 8$

$LCB_1 = X_{\min} - \frac{UM}{2} = 33 - 0.5 = 32.5$

$UCB_1 = LCB_1 + l = 32.5 + 8 = 40.5$

$LCL_1 = LCB_1 + 0.5 = 32.5 + 0.5 = 33$

$UCL_1 = UCB1 - 0.5 = 40.5 - 0.5 = 40$

Class	Limit	Boundary	m_i	f_i	$f_i m_i$	m_i^2	$f_i m_i^2$
1	33-40	32.5-40.5	36.5	3	109.5	1332.25	3996.75
2	41-48	40.5-48.5	44.5	11	489.50	1980.25	21782.75
3	49-56	48.5-56.5	52.5	18	945.0	2756.25	49612.5
4	57-64	56.5-64.5	60.5	23	1391.5	3660.25	84185.75

(Contd.)

Class	Limit	Boundary	m_i	f_i	$f_i m_i$	m_i^2	$f_i m_i^2$
5	65-72	64.5-72.5	68.5	14	959.0	4692.25	65691.5
6	73-80	72.5-80.5	76.5	16	1224.0	5852.25	93636
7	81-88	80.5-88.5	84.5	11	929.50	7140.25	78542.75
8	89-96	88.5-96.5	92.5	4	370.0	8556.25	34225
Total				100	6418		431673

K = 8, n = 100

$$\overline{X} = \frac{\sum_{i=1}^{8} f_i m_i}{n} = \frac{6418}{100} = 64.18$$

$$n\overline{X}^2 = 100(4119.07) = 411907.24$$

$$S^2 = \frac{\sum_{i=1}^{8} f_i m_i^2 - n\overline{X}^2}{n-1} = \frac{431673 - 411907.24}{100-1} = \frac{19765.76}{99}$$

$= 199.65 =$ variance

$S = \sqrt{199.65} = 14.13 =$ standard deviation

The Quartiles or Percentiles

The quartiles or percentiles are used to split a data set into 4 or 100 equal parts. The 3 quartiles Q1, Q2, and Q3 are more often used than the 99 percentiles P1, P2, …., P99.

First, re-arrange the given data set in an increasing order of magnitude. A quarter of the observations in the data set lie to the left of Q1 or P25. Half of the observations in the data set lie to the left of Q2 or P50. 75% of the observations in the data set lie to the left of Q3 or P75.

Q2 = P50 = Median.

The inter-quartile range is given by: IQR = Q3 – Q1

The Coefficients of Skewness

The coefficient of skewness indicates whether the data is skewed to the left or to the right of the centre of distribution. The Pearson coefficient of skewness is given as follows:

$$SK_p = \frac{3(Mean - Median)}{S}$$

or, alternatively

$$SK_p = \frac{3(Mean - Mode)}{S}$$

For a symmetrical distribution, $SK_p = 0$

For a positively skewed distribution, $SK_p > 0$

For a negatively skewed distribution, $SK_p < 0$

Example:

Consider a set of data for which the mean, median, and standard deviation are respectively equal to 18.5, 18.89, and 6.627. Determine the magnitude of Pearson's coefficient of skewness, and comment on the shape of the distribution.

Solution:

$$SK_p = \frac{3(Mean - Median)}{S} = \frac{3(18.5 - 18.89)}{6.627} = -0.1766$$

The distribution is slightly negatively skewed.

The coefficient of kurtosis indicates whether the data is peaked or flat-topped.

A normally distributed data set is neither skewed nor peaked. That is, for a normally distributed data set, the coefficients of skewness and kurtosis are both close to 0.

The Coefficient of Kurtosis

The coefficient of kurtosis indicates whether the data is peaked or flat-topped. For a raw data set consisting of a random sample of n observations, the coefficient of kurtosis is given by:

$$K = \frac{\sum_{i=1}^{n}\left(x - \bar{x}\right)^4}{(n-1)S^4}$$

The coefficient of kurtosis is equal to 3 for the standard normal distribution. K=3 for the standard normal distribution. If K<3, the distribution is said to be flat-topped (negative kurtosis). If K>3, the distribution is said to be peaked (positive kurtosis).

The Kolmogorov-Smirnov test for normality

A test for normality can be done using the Kolmogorov-Smirnov test for normality. The null hypothesis states that we have no reason to doubt that the distribution is normally distributed. The alternative hypothesis states that the distribution is not normally distributed. At the 5% level of significance, the null hypothesis is rejected if the P-value is less than 0.05. Otherwise, the null hypothesis is accepted at the same level of significance.

Example:

Consider the raw data set with n=100 observations shown in the above example.

Enter the 100 observations in SPSS and save the data set as data1.sav. Use the variable name weight and label Weight in kg. Save the data set using the file name data1.sav.

Solution from SPSS

Go to SPSS and open up the SPSS data set c:\bos\data1.sav

Click on Analyze

Click on Descriptive statistics

Click on Explore

Select the variable weight as Dependent list

Click on Plots

Click on Normal plots with tests

Click on Histogram

Click on Continue

Click on OK

SPSS will produce the following computer printout.

Descriptive statistics from SPSS

			Statistic	Std. Error
Weight in kg	Mean		63.98	1.415
	95% Confidence Interval for Mean	Lower Bound	61.17	
		Upper Bound	66.79	
	5% Trimmed Mean		63.87	
	Median		61.00	
	Variance		200.202	
	Std. Deviation		14.149	
	Minimum		33	
	Maximum		91	
	Range		58	
	Interquartile Range		24	
	Skewness		0.177	0.241
	Kurtosis		-0.882	0.478

Percentiles from SPSS are shown below:

Percentiles	25	50	75
Weighted Average	52.00	61.00	76.00
Tukey's Hinges	52.00	61.00	76.00

A stem-and-leaf plot from SPSS

```
Weight in kg Stem-and-Leaf Plot

 Frequency    Stem &  Leaf
     1.00        3 .  3
      .00        3 .
     6.00        4 .  001444
    14.00        4 .  57777889999999
     8.00        5 .  12222244
    14.00        5 .  66678888899999
    12.00        6 .  000001112224
    10.00        6 .  5677777789
     7.00        7 .  1122344
    12.00        7 .  556678889999
     7.00        8 .  0122222
     5.00        8 .  58888
     4.00        9 .  1111

 Stem width:        10
ach leaf:        1 case(s)
```

A histogram from SPSS

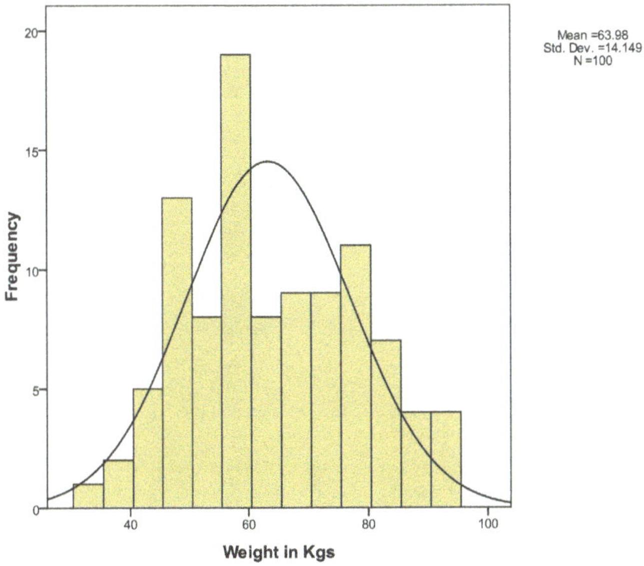

The Kolmogorov-Smirnov test for normality from SPSS

Tests of Normality

	Kolmogorov-Smirnova			Shapiro-Wilk		
	Statistic	**df**	**P-value**	**Statistic**	**df**	**P-value**
Weight in kg	0.096	100	0.025	0.969	100	0.019

a. Lilliefors Significance Correction

Null hypothesis: The 100 observations in the data set are distributed normally with mean 0 and constant variance

Alternative hypothesis: The 100 observations in the data set are not distributed normally with mean 0 and constant variance

Decision rule:

At the 5% level of significance,

Reject the null hypothesis if $P < 0.05$

Do not reject the null hypothesis if P is greater than or equal to 0.05

The P-value is equal to 0.025 < 0.05. Hence, the null hypothesis can be rejected at the 5% level of significance. We conclude that the distribution is not normal.

A box plot from SPSS

The coefficient of variation (CV)

The coefficient of variation (CV) is a measure of variation, and is given by:

$$CV = \frac{S}{\overline{\overline{X}}} = \frac{Std.\ Dev.}{Mean}$$

Values of CV greater than 10% show that there is a significant variation among the observations constituting the data set.

For the above example,

$$CV = \frac{S}{\overline{\overline{X}}} = \frac{14.4245}{112.7778} = 0.1279 = 12.79\%$$

UNIT 4

PROBABILITY DISTRIBUTIONS FOR BUSINESS STUDIES

The Probability of an Event

The probability of event A is the number of ways event A can occur divided by the total number of possible outcomes.

$P(A) = \dfrac{N(A)}{N(S)}$ where

N(A) = Number of outcomes favourable to event A

N(S) = Total number of outcomes

The probability of an event is the measure of the chance that the event will occur as a result of an experiment. The probability of an event A is the number of ways event A can occur divided by the total number of possible outcomes. The probability of an event A, symbolized by P(A), is a number between 0 and 1, inclusive, that measures the likelihood of an event in the following way:

If P(A) > P(B) then event A is more likely to occur than event B.

If P(A) = P(B) then events A and B are equally likely to occur.

The probability of an impossible event is 0.

The probability of a sure event is 1.

$0 \leq P(A) \leq 1$

The **complement** of an event A is the set of all outcomes in the sample space that are not included in the outcomes of $\bar{A}$ of event A is represented by $\bar{A}$ and the probability of $\bar{A}$ is given by

$P(\bar{A}) = 1 - P(A)$

Experiment 1:

A spinner with 4 possible colours (yellow, green, red and blue)

Experiment 1:	A spinner has 4 equal sectors, coloured yellow, blue, green, and red. After spinning the spinner, what is the probability of landing on each colour?	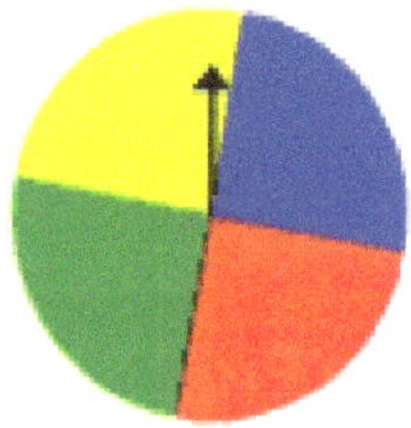
Outcomes:	The possible outcomes of this experiment are yellow, blue, green, and red.	

$$P(\text{Yellow}) = \frac{N(Yellow)}{4} = \frac{1}{4}$$

$$P(\text{Blue}) = \frac{N(Blue)}{4} = \frac{1}{4}$$

$$P(\text{Green}) = \frac{N(Green)}{4} = \frac{1}{4}$$

$$P(\text{Red}) = \frac{N(\text{Re}\,d)}{4} = \frac{1}{4}$$

Experiment 2:

A die with 6 possible faces (1, 2, 3, 4, 5, and 6)

Experiment 2:	A single 6-sided die is rolled. What is the probability of rolling an even number?	
Outcomes:	The possible outcomes of this experiment are 1, 2, 3, 4, 5, and 6.	Top of Form Bottom of Form

$$P(\text{Even number}) = \frac{N(Even\ Numbers)}{6} = \frac{3}{6} = 0.50$$

The Venn Diagram

The Venn Diagram is made up of two or more overlapping circles. It is often used in mathematics to show relationships between sets. In language arts instruction, Venn Diagrams are useful for examining similarities and differences in characters, stories, poems, etc. It is frequently used as a prewriting activity to enable students to organize thoughts or textual quotations prior to writing a compare/contrast essay. This activity enables students to organize similarities and differences visually.

The Venn Diagram shown below illustrates the relationship expressed in 2 overlapping circles. The two overlapping circles represent 3 distinct areas. These 3 areas represent 3 probabilities P(A), P(B), and P(A and B). In the Venn Diagram, the probability of event A is denoted by A. The probability of event B is denoted by B. The probability of events A and B is denoted by C.

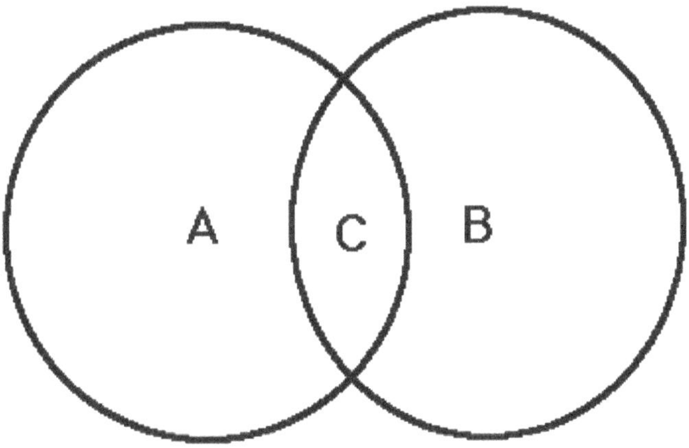

Definition of Independent Events:

Two events, A and B, are **independent** if the fact that A occurs does not affect the probability of B occurring.

Examples of independent events are:

- Landing on heads after tossing a coin **AND** rolling a 5 on a single 6-sided die.
- Choosing a marble from a jar **AND** landing on heads after tossing a coin.
- Choosing a 3 from a deck of cards, replacing it, **AND** then choosing an ace as the second card.
- Rolling a 4 on a single 6-sided die, **AND** then rolling a 1 on a second roll of the die.

When 2 events, A and B, are independent, the probability of both events occurring is given by:

$$\text{P(A and B)} = P(A \cap B) = P(A).P(B|A)$$

The conditional probability of an event B in relationship to an event A is the probability that event B occurs given that event A has already occurred. The notation for conditional probability is P(B|A),

$$P(B|A) = \frac{P(A \cap B)}{P(A)}$$

A math teacher gave her class two tests; 25% of the class passed both tests and 42% of the class passed the first test. What percent of those who passed the first test also passed the second test?

$$P(second \mid first) = \frac{P(first\, and\, second)}{P(first)} = \frac{0.25}{0.42} = 0.60 = 60\%$$

A jar contains black and white marbles. Two marbles are chosen without replacement. The probability of selecting a black marble and a white marble is 0.34, and the probability of selecting a black marble on the first draw is 0.47. What is the probability of selecting a white marble on the second draw, given that the first marble drawn was black?

$$P(white \mid black) = \frac{P(black\, and\, white)}{P(black)} = \frac{0.34}{0.47} = 0.72 = 72\%$$

The probability that it is Friday and that a student is absent is 0.03. Since there are 5 school days in a week, the probability that it is Friday is 0.2. What is the probability that a student is absent given that today is Friday?

$$P(Absent \mid Friday) = \frac{P(Friday\, and\, absent)}{P(Friday)} = \frac{0.03}{0.20} = 0.15 = 15\%$$

Conditional Probability

Let A and B denote 2 events with P(B) > 0. The probability that event A occurs given that event B has occurred is given by:

$$P(A \mid B) = \frac{P(A \cap B)}{P(B)} \quad \text{or} \quad P(A \cap B) = P(A \mid B)P(B)$$

Likewise, for event A such that P(A) > 0, the probability that event B occurs given that event A has occurred is given by:

$$P(B \mid A) = \frac{P(A \cap B)}{P(A)} \quad \text{or} \quad P(A \cap B) = P(B \mid A)P(A)$$

Hence, $P(A \cap B) = P(A|B)P(B) = P(B|A)P(A)$

Remark: If A and B are independent events, $P(A \cap B) = P(A)P(B)$

If A and B are independent, P(A|B) = P(A) and P(B|A) = P(B)

Example:

A vaccination box contains 12 vials, of which 3 are defective. If 2 vials are selected at random from the box one after another, what is the probability that both vials are defective?

Let A denote the event that the first vial is defective.

Let B denote the event that the second vial is defective.

$$P(A \cap B) = P(A)P(B \mid A) = \frac{3}{12} \times \frac{2}{11} = \frac{1}{22}$$

The Total Probability Theorem

$$P(A) = P(A|B_1)P(B_1) + P(A|B_2)P(B_2) + \ldots + P(A|B_n)P(B_n)$$
$$= \sum_{i=1}^{n} P(A \mid B_i)P(B_i)$$

Bayes theorem

$$P(A \mid B) = \frac{P(B \mid A)P(A)}{\sum_{i=1}^{n} P(B \mid A_i)P(A_i)}$$

Example:

A certain company has 3 engineers A, B, and C. Each day, on average, engineers A, B, and C assemble 37%, 42%, and 21% of machines sold by the company to customers respectively. It is known that 0.6% of all machines assembled by engineer A are faulty. The corresponding figures for engineers B and C are 0.4% and 1.2%, respectively.

a) What is the probability that a machine sold by the company is faulty?

b) What is the probability that a machine assembled by engineer A is faulty?

Let A denote the event that a machine sold by the company is faulty

Let B_1 denote the proportion of machines assembled by engineer A

Let B_2 denote the proportion of machines assembled by engineer B

Let B_3 denote the proportion of machines assembled by engineer C

$P(A \mid B_1)$ = the probability that a machine assembled by engineer A is faulty

$P(A \mid B_2)$ = the probability that a machine assembled by engineer B is faulty

$P(A \mid B_3)$ = the probability that a machine assembled by engineer C is faulty

$P(B_1) = 0.37$

$P(B_2) = 0.42$

$P(B_3) = 0.21$

$P(A \mid B_1) = 0.006$

$P(A \mid B_2) = 0.004$

$P(A \mid B_3) = 0.012$

a) $P(A) = P(A \mid B_1)P(B_1) + P(A \mid B_2)P(B_2) + P(A \mid B_3)P(B_3)$

$$= (0.006)(0.37) + (0.004)(0.42) + (0.012)(0.21)$$

$$= 0.0022 + 0.0017 + 0.0025$$

$$= 0.0064$$

b) $P(B_1 \mid A) = \dfrac{P(A \mid B_1)P(B_1)}{P(A)} = \dfrac{0.0022}{0.0064} = 0.3438 = 34.38\%$

Probability Distributions

In business-related studies, certain probability distributions are crucially important for statistical analyses. The most commonly used probability distributions are the Bernoulli distribution, the binomial distribution, the normal distribution, the Poisson distribution, and the Student's t-distribution.

The Bernoulli Distribution

When a coin is flipped, the outcome is either heads or tails; when a magician guesses the card selected from a deck, the magician can either be correct or incorrect; when a baby is born, the baby is either born in the month of March or is not. In each of these examples, an event has two mutually exclusive possible outcomes. For convenience, one of the outcomes can be labelled "success" and the other outcome "failure." A probability distribution that has only 2 possible outcomes (success or failure) is called the Bernoulli distribution.

$P(X = x) = p^x (1 - p)^{1-x}$ where x = 1 for a success, and x = 0 for a failure

The Binomial Probability Distribution

The binomial probability distribution arises from the Bernoulli probability distribution. The sum of n independently and identically distributed Bernoulli random variables follows the binomial probability distribution.

A random variable X is said to have the Bernoulli probability distribution if its probability distribution is given by:

$P(X = x) = p^x (1 - p)^{1-x}$ where $x = 0, 1$

X is a discrete random variable that can only have one of 2 possible values: either the event occurs, or it fails to occur.

$$x = \begin{cases} 1 \ \textit{if the event occurs} \\ 0 \ \textit{otherwise} \end{cases}$$

p = probability of success

1 – p = probability of failure = q

The expected value of X is equal to p

The variance of X is equal to p(1 – p) = pq

Example:

Suppose that a fair coin is tossed once, and the face-up is noted.

$$x = \begin{cases} 1 \ \textit{if a Head occurs} \\ 0 \ \textit{otherwise} \end{cases}$$

What is the probability that a Head appears?

Required: The probability that a Head appears = P(X=1)

$P(X=x)=p^x(1-p)^{1-x}$ where $x = 0, 1$

$P(X=1)=p^1(1-p)^{1-1}=p(1-p)^0=p$

The Binomial Random Variable

A random variable X is said to have the binomial probability distribution if its probability distribution is given by:

$$P(X=x)=\binom{n}{x}p^x(1-p)^{n-x} \quad \text{where} \quad x = 0, 1, \ldots\ldots, n$$

X is a discrete random variable.

n = total number of trials = sample size

x = number of successes in the experiments

p = probability of success

1-p = probability of failure = q

The expected value of the random variable X is equal to np

The variance of the random variable X is equal to $np(1-p)=npq$

Example:

According to the South African Chamber of Commerce, the proportion of small businesses that default on their bank loans is known to be 30%. A random sample of 10 small businesses is examined by a researcher working for the South African Chamber of Commerce. Assuming that the distribution of small businesses is independent,

a) What is the probability that exactly 3 of the 10 small businesses have defaulted on their loan?

P(X=3)

b) What is the probability that at least 5 of the 10 small businesses have defaulted on their loan?

P(X=5) + P(X=6) + P(X=7) + P(X=8) + P(X=9) + P(X=10)

c) What is the probability that between 4 and 6 businesses have defaulted on their loan?

P(X=4) + P(X=5) + P(X=6)

What is the probability that at most 4 of the 10 applicant default?

P(X=0) + P(X=1) + P(X=2) + P(X=3) + P(X=4)

What is the probability that fewer than 4 of the 10 applicants default?

P(X=0) + P(X=1) + P(X=2) + P(X=3)

d) What is the expected value of small businesses defaulting on their loans?

e) What is the standard error of estimation?

f) What is the probability that at most 2 applicants default?

P(X=0) + P(X=1) + P(X=2)

Solution:

n = 10

p = 30% = 0.3 = probability of success

1 – p = 70% = 0.70 = probability of failure

a) $P(X=3) = \binom{10}{3}(0.3)^3(0.7)^7 = 0.267$ where

$$\binom{10}{3} = 10C_3 = \frac{10!}{(10-3)!3!} = \frac{10!}{7!3!} = \frac{10\times9\times......\times3\times2\times1}{(7\times6\times...\times1)(3\times2\times1)}$$

$$= \frac{3628800}{5040 \times 6} = \frac{3628800}{30240} = 120$$

$(0.3)^3 = 0.0270$

$(0.7)^7 = 0.0824$

$10! = 10(9)(8)(7)(6)(5)(4)(3)(2)(1) = 3,628,800$

$(10\text{-}3)! = 7! = 7(6)(5)(4)(3)(2)(1) = 5,040$

$3! = 3(2)(1) = 6$

b) $P(X \geq 5) = \sum_{x=5}^{10} \binom{10}{x} (0.3)^x (0.7)^{10-x}$

$= P(X=5) + P(X=6) + \ldots.. + P(X=10) = 0.1500$

where

$$P(X = 5) = \binom{10}{5} (0.3)^5 (0.7)^5 = 0.103$$

$$P(X = 6) = \binom{10}{6} (0.3)^6 (0.7)^4 = 0.037$$

$$P(X = 7) = \binom{10}{7} (0.3)^7 (0.7)^3 = 0.009$$

$$P(X = 8) = \binom{10}{8} (0.3)^8 (0.7)^2 = 0.001$$

$$P(X = 9) = \binom{10}{9} (0.3)^9 (0.7)^1 = 0.000$$

c) $P(4 \leq X \leq 6) = \sum_{x=4}^{6} \binom{10}{x} (0.3)^x (0.7)^{10-x}$

P(X=4) + P(X=5) + P(X=6) = 0.200 + 0.103 + 0.037 = 0.34

d) E(X) = np = 10(0.3) = 3 = Expected value of X

e) V(X) = np(1 – p) = 10(0.3)(0.7) = 2.1 = Variance of X

Std.Dev(X) = $\sqrt{2.1}$

Std.Err(X) = $\frac{S}{\sqrt{n}} = \frac{\sqrt{2.1}}{10}$

The Poisson Distribution

A random variable X has a Poisson distribution with parameter λ if the probability density function is given by

$P(X = x) = \frac{e^{-\lambda} \lambda^x}{x!}$ where $x = 0, 1, 2, \ldots..$ and $\lambda > 0$.

The mean and variance of the Poisson random variable are both equal to λ.

$E(X) = \lambda$

$V(X) = \lambda$

The Poisson distribution is used to estimate the probability of rare events.

Example:

The number of businesses filing for bankruptcy protection, the number of people committing suicide in a day, the number of traffic accidents per day occurring on a particular stretch of road, etc.

Solution:

It is known that the N3 experiences an average of 6 major road accidents each day. What is the probability that 4 major road accidents occur on any given day?

$$P(X=4)=\frac{e^{-6}6^{x}}{x!}=\frac{e^{-6}6^{4}}{4!}=\frac{(0.0025)(1296)}{24}=0.135=13.5\%$$

where

$$4!=4(3)(2)(1)=24$$

$$e^{-6}=\frac{1}{e^{6}}=\frac{1}{403.43}=0.0025$$

The Binomial Table

$$P(X=x)=\binom{n}{x}p^{x}(1-p)^{n-x} \text{ where } x=0, 1, 2, \ldots.., n$$

- The following table lists the probability of attaining **x** successes out of **n** trials, where the probability of success in any one trial is **p**
- To find the probability of obtaining **x or more** successes in **n** trials, add the probabilities corresponding to **x**, **x+1**, **x+2**, ... together. For example, the probability of obtaining **1 or more** heads in two coin flips is 0.500 + 0.250 = 0.750
- If **p** is greater than 0.5, then use **1-p** as the probability and **n-x** as the desired number of successes (i.e., look up the probability of obtaining **n-x** *failures* rather than x *successes*).

The Binomial Table is shown below:

		p																				
n	**x**	**.01**	**.02**	**.04**	**.05**	**.06**	**.08**	**.10**	**.12**	**.14**	**.15**	**.16**	**.18**	**.20**	**.22**	**.24**	**.25**	**.30**	**.35**	**.40**	**.45**	**.50**
2	0	.980	.960	.922	.903	.884	.846	.810	.774	.740	.723	.706	.672	.640	.608	.578	.563	.490	.423	.360	.303	.250
2	1	.020	.039	.077	.095	.113	.147	.180	.211	.241	.255	.269	.295	.320	.343	.365	.375	.420	.455	.480	.495	.500
2	2			.002	.003	.004	.006	.010	.014	.020	.023	.026	.032	.040	.048	.058	.063	.090	.123	.160	.203	.250
3	0	.970	.941	.885	.857	.831	.779	.729	.681	.636	.614	.593	.551	.512	.475	.439	.422	.343	.275	.216	.166	.125
3	1	.029	.058	.111	.135	.159	.203	.243	.279	.311	.325	.339	.363	.384	.402	.416	.422	.441	.444	.432	.408	.375
3	2		.001	.005	.007	.010	.018	.027	.038	.051	.057	.065	.080	.096	.113	.131	.141	.189	.239	.288	.334	.375
3	3						.001	.001	.002	.003	.003	.004	.006	.008	.011	.014	.016	.027	.043	.064	.091	.125
4	0	.961	.922	.849	.815	.781	.716	.656	.600	.547	.522	.498	.452	.410	.370	.334	.316	.240	.179	.130	.092	.063
4	1	.039	.075	.142	.171	.199	.249	.292	.327	.356	.368	.379	.397	.410	.418	.421	.422	.412	.384	.346	.299	.250
4	2	.001	.002	.009	.014	.019	.033	.049	.067	.087	.098	.108	.131	.154	.177	.200	.211	.265	.311	.346	.368	.375
4	3					.001	.002	.004	.006	.009	.011	.014	.019	.026	.033	.042	.047	.076	.111	.154	.200	.250
4	4										.001	.001	.001	.002	.002	.003	.004	.008	.015	.026	.041	.063
		.01	.02	.04	.05	.06	.08	.10	.12	.14	.15	.16	.18	.20	.22	.24	.25	.30	.35	.40	.45	.50
5	0	.951	.904	.815	.774	.734	.659	.590	.528	.470	.444	.418	.371	.328	.289	.254	.237	.168	.116	.078	.050	.031
5	1	.048	.092	.170	.204	.234	.287	.328	.360	.383	.392	.398	.407	.410	.407	.400	.396	.360	.312	.259	.206	.156
5	2	.001	.004	.014	.021	.030	.050	.073	.098	.125	.138	.152	.179	.205	.230	.253	.264	.309	.336	.346	.337	.313
5	3			.001	.001	.002	.004	.008	.013	.020	.024	.029	.039	.051	.065	.080	.088	.132	.181	.230	.276	.313
5	4								.001	.002	.002	.003	.004	.006	.009	.013	.015	.028	.049	.077	.113	.156
5	5														.001	.001	.001	.002	.005	.010	.018	.031
		.01	.02	.04	.05	.06	.08	.10	.12	.14	.15	.16	.18	.20	.22	.24	.25	.30	.35	.40	.45	.50
6	0	.941	.886	.783	.735	.690	.606	.531	.464	.405	.377	.351	.304	.262	.225	.193	.178	.118	.075	.047	.028	.016
6	1	.057	.108	.196	.232	.264	.316	.354	.380	.395	.399	.401	.400	.393	.381	.365	.356	.303	.244	.187	.136	.094
6	2	.001	.006	.020	.031	.042	.069	.098	.130	.161	.176	.191	.220	.246	.269	.288	.297	.324	.328	.311	.278	.234
6	3			.001	.002	.004	.008	.015	.024	.035	.041	.049	.064	.082	.101	.121	.132	.185	.235	.276	.303	.313
6	4						.001	.001	.002	.004	.005	.007	.011	.015	.021	.029	.033	.060	.095	.138	.186	.234
6	5											.001	.001	.002	.002	.004	.004	.010	.020	.037	.061	.094
6	6																	.001	.002	.004	.008	.016
		.01	.02	.04	.05	.06	.08	.10	.12	.14	.15	.16	.18	.20	.22	.24	.25	.30	.35	.40	.45	.50
7	0	.932	.868	.751	.698	.648	.558	.478	.409	.348	.321	.295	.249	.210	.176	.146	.133	.082	.049	.028	.015	.008
7	1	.066	.124	.219	.257	.290	.340	.372	.390	.396	.396	.393	.383	.367	.347	.324	.311	.247	.185	.131	.087	.055
7	2	.002	.008	.027	.041	.055	.089	.124	.160	.194	.210	.225	.252	.275	.293	.307	.311	.318	.298	.261	.214	.164
7	3			.002	.004	.006	.013	.023	.036	.053	.062	.071	.092	.115	.138	.161	.173	.227	.268	.290	.292	.273
7	4						.001	.003	.005	.009	.011	.014	.020	.029	.039	.051	.058	.097	.144	.194	.239	.273
7	5									.001	.001	.002	.003	.004	.007	.010	.012	.025	.047	.077	.117	.164
7	6														.001	.001	.001	.004	.008	.017	.032	.055
7	7																		.001	.002	.004	.008
		.01	.02	.04	.05	.06	.08	.10	.12	.14	.15	.16	.18	.20	.22	.24	.25	.30	.35	.40	.45	.50
8	0	.923	.851	.721	.663	.610	.513	.430	.360	.299	.272	.248	.204	.168	.137	.111	.100	.058	.032	.017	.008	.004
8	1	.075	.139	.240	.279	.311	.357	.383	.392	.390	.385	.378	.359	.336	.309	.281	.267	.198	.137	.090	.055	.031
8	2	.003	.010	.035	.051	.070	.109	.149	.187	.222	.238	.252	.276	.294	.305	.311	.311	.296	.259	.209	.157	.109
8	3			.003	.005	.009	.019	.033	.051	.072	.084	.096	.121	.147	.172	.196	.208	.254	.279	.279	.257	.219
8	4					.001	.002	.005	.009	.015	.018	.023	.033	.046	.061	.077	.087	.136	.188	.232	.263	.273
8	5								.001	.002	.003	.003	.006	.009	.014	.020	.023	.047	.081	.124	.172	.219
8	6												.001	.001	.002	.003	.004	.010	.022	.041	.070	.109
8	7																	.001	.003	.008	.016	.031
8	8																			.001	.002	.004
9	0	.914	.834	.693	.630	.573	.472	.387	.316	.257	.232	.208	.168	.134	.107	.085	.075	.040	.021	.010	.005	.002
9	1	.083	.153	.260	.299	.329	.370	.387	.388	.377	.368	.357	.331	.302	.271	.240	.225	.156	.100	.060	.034	.018
9	2	.003	.013	.043	.063	.084	.129	.172	.212	.245	.260	.272	.291	.302	.306	.304	.300	.267	.216	.161	.111	.070
9	3		.001	.004	.008	.013	.026	.045	.067	.093	.107	.121	.149	.176	.201	.224	.234	.267	.272	.251	.212	.164
9	4				.001	.001	.003	.007	.014	.023	.028	.035	.049	.066	.085	.106	.117	.172	.219	.251	.260	.246
9	5							.001	.002	.004	.005	.007	.011	.017	.024	.033	.039	.074	.118	.167	.213	.246
9	6										.001	.001	.002	.003	.005	.007	.009	.021	.042	.074	.116	.164
9	7														.001	.001	.001	.004	.010	.021	.041	.070

9	8																		.001	.004	.008	.018
9	9																				.001	.002
		.01	.02	.04	.05	.06	.08	.10	.12	.14	.15	.16	.18	.20	.22	.24	.25	.30	.35	.40	.45	.50
10	0	.904	.817	.665	.599	.539	.434	.349	.279	.221	.197	.175	.137	.107	.083	.064	.056	.028	.013	.006	.003	.001
10	1	.091	.167	.277	.315	.344	.378	.387	.380	.360	.347	.333	.302	.268	.235	.203	.188	.121	.072	.040	.021	.010
10	2	.004	.015	.052	.075	.099	.148	.194	.233	.264	.276	.286	.298	.302	.298	.288	.282	.233	.176	.121	.076	.044
10	3		.001	.006	.010	.017	.034	.057	.085	.115	.130	.145	.174	.201	.224	.243	.250	.267	.252	.215	.166	.117
10	4				.001	.002	.005	.011	.020	.033	.040	.048	.067	.088	.111	.134	.146	.200	.238	.251	.238	.205
10	5						.001	.001	.003	.006	.008	.011	.018	.026	.037	.051	.058	.103	.154	.201	.234	.246
10	6									.001	.001	.002	.003	.006	.009	.013	.016	.037	.069	.111	.160	.205
10	7													.001	.001	.002	.003	.009	.021	.042	.075	.117
10	8																	.001	.004	.011	.023	.044
10	9																		.001	.002	.004	.010
10	10																					.001
		.01	.02	.04	.05	.06	.08	.10	.12	.14	.15	.16	.18	.20	.22	.24	.25	.30	.35	.40	.45	.50
11	0	.895	.801	.638	.569	.506	.400	.314	.245	.190	.167	.147	.113	.086	.065	.049	.042	.020	.009	.004	.001	
11	1	.099	.180	.293	.329	.355	.382	.384	.368	.341	.325	.308	.272	.236	.202	.170	.155	.093	.052	.027	.013	.005
11	2	.005	.018	.061	.087	.113	.166	.213	.251	.277	.287	.293	.299	.295	.284	.268	.258	.200	.140	.089	.051	.027
11	3		.001	.008	.014	.022	.043	.071	.103	.135	.152	.168	.197	.221	.241	.254	.258	.257	.225	.177	.126	.081
11	4			.001	.001	.003	.008	.016	.028	.044	.054	.064	.086	.111	.136	.160	.172	.220	.243	.236	.206	.161
11	5						.001	.002	.005	.010	.013	.017	.027	.039	.054	.071	.080	.132	.183	.221	.236	.226
11	6								.001	.002	.002	.003	.006	.010	.015	.022	.027	.057	.099	.147	.193	.226
11	7												.001	.002	.003	.005	.006	.017	.038	.070	.113	.161
11	8															.001	.001	.004	.010	.023	.046	.081
11	9																	.001	.002	.005	.013	.027
11	10																			.001	.002	.005
11	11																					
		.01	.02	.04	.05	.06	.08	.10	.12	.14	.15	.16	.18	.20	.22	.24	.25	.30	.35	.40	.45	.50
12	0	.886	.785	.613	.540	.476	.368	.282	.216	.164	.142	.123	.092	.069	.051	.037	.032	.014	.006	.002	.001	
12	1	.107	.192	.306	.341	.365	.384	.377	.353	.320	.301	.282	.243	.206	.172	.141	.127	.071	.037	.017	.008	.003
12	2	.006	.022	.070	.099	.128	.183	.230	.265	.286	.292	.296	.294	.283	.266	.244	.232	.168	.109	.064	.034	.016
12	3		.001	.010	.017	.027	.053	.085	.120	.155	.172	.188	.215	.236	.250	.257	.258	.240	.195	.142	.092	.054
12	4			.001	.002	.004	.010	.021	.037	.057	.068	.080	.106	.133	.159	.183	.194	.231	.237	.213	.170	.121
12	5						.001	.004	.008	.015	.019	.025	.037	.053	.072	.092	.103	.158	.204	.227	.222	.193
12	6								.001	.003	.004	.005	.010	.016	.024	.034	.040	.079	.128	.177	.212	.226
12	7										.001	.001	.002	.003	.006	.009	.011	.029	.059	.101	.149	.193
12	8													.001	.001	.002	.002	.008	.020	.042	.076	.121
12	9																	.001	.005	.012	.028	.054
12	10																		.001	.002	.007	.016
12	11																				.001	.003
12	12																					
		.01	.02	.04	.05	.06	.08	.10	.12	.14	.15	.16	.18	.20	.22	.24	.25	.30	.35	.40	.45	.50
13	0	.878	.769	.588	.513	.447	.338	.254	.190	.141	.121	.104	.076	.055	.040	.028	.024	.010	.004	.001		
13	1	.115	.204	.319	.351	.371	.382	.367	.336	.298	.277	.257	.216	.179	.145	.116	.103	.054	.026	.011	.004	.002
13	2	.007	.025	.080	.111	.142	.199	.245	.275	.291	.294	.293	.285	.268	.245	.220	.206	.139	.084	.045	.022	.010
13	3		.002	.012	.021	.033	.064	.100	.138	.174	.190	.205	.229	.246	.254	.254	.252	.218	.165	.111	.066	.035
13	4			.001	.003	.005	.014	.028	.047	.071	.084	.098	.126	.154	.179	.201	.210	.234	.222	.184	.135	.087
13	5					.001	.002	.006	.012	.021	.027	.033	.050	.069	.091	.114	.126	.180	.215	.221	.199	.157
13	6							.001	.002	.004	.006	.008	.015	.023	.034	.048	.056	.103	.155	.197	.217	.209
13	7									.001	.001	.002	.003	.006	.010	.015	.019	.044	.083	.131	.177	.209
13	8												.001	.001	.002	.004	.005	.014	.034	.066	.109	.157
13	9															.001	.001	.003	.010	.024	.050	.087
13	10																	.001	.002	.006	.016	.035
13	11																			.001	.004	.010
13	12																					.002
13	13																					
		.01	.02	.04	.05	.06	.08	.10	.12	.14	.15	.16	.18	.20	.22	.24	.25	.30	.35	.40	.45	.50
14	0	.869	.754	.565	.488	.421	.311	.229	.167	.121	.103	.087	.062	.044	.031	.021	.018	.007	.002	.001		
14	1	.123	.215	.329	.359	.376	.379	.356	.319	.276	.254	.232	.191	.154	.122	.095	.083	.041	.018	.007	.003	.001
14	2	.008	.029	.089	.123	.156	.214	.257	.283	.292	.291	.287	.272	.250	.223	.195	.180	.113	.063	.032	.014	.006
14	3		.002	.015	.026	.040	.074	.114	.154	.190	.206	.219	.239	.250	.252	.246	.240	.194	.137	.085	.046	.022
14	4			.002	.004	.007	.018	.035	.058	.085	.100	.115	.144	.172	.195	.214	.220	.229	.202	.155	.104	.061

(Contd.)

14	5					.001	.003	.008	.016	.028	.035	.044	.063	.086	.110	.135	.147	.196	.218	.207	.170	.122
14	6							.001	.003	.007	.009	.012	.021	.032	.047	.064	.073	.126	.176	.207	.209	.183
14	7								.001	.001	.002	.003	.005	.009	.015	.023	.028	.062	.108	.157	.195	.209
14	8												.001	.002	.004	.006	.008	.023	.051	.092	.140	.183
14	9														.001	.001	.002	.007	.018	.041	.076	.122
14	10																	.001	.005	.014	.031	.061
14	11																		.001	.003	.009	.022
14	12																			.001	.002	.006
14	13																					.001
14	14																					
		.01	.02	.04	.05	.06	.08	.10	.12	.14	.15	.16	.18	.20	.22	.24	.25	.30	.35	.40	.45	.50
15	0	.860	.739	.542	.463	.395	.286	.206	.147	.104	.087	.073	.051	.035	.024	.016	.013	.005	.002			
15	1	.130	.226	.339	.366	.378	.373	.343	.301	.254	.231	.209	.168	.132	.102	.077	.067	.031	.013	.005	.002	
15	2	.009	.032	.099	.135	.169	.227	.267	.287	.290	.286	.279	.258	.231	.201	.171	.156	.092	.048	.022	.009	.003
15	3		.003	.018	.031	.047	.086	.129	.170	.204	.218	.230	.245	.250	.246	.234	.225	.170	.111	.063	.032	.014
15	4			.002	.005	.009	.022	.043	.069	.100	.116	.131	.162	.188	.208	.221	.225	.219	.179	.127	.078	.042
15	5				.001	.001	.004	.010	.021	.036	.045	.055	.078	.103	.129	.154	.165	.206	.212	.186	.140	.092
15	6						.001	.002	.005	.010	.013	.017	.029	.043	.061	.081	.092	.147	.191	.207	.191	.153
15	7								.001	.002	.003	.004	.008	.014	.022	.033	.039	.081	.132	.177	.201	.196
15	8										.001	.001	.002	.003	.006	.010	.013	.035	.071	.118	.165	.196
15	9													.001	.001	.003	.003	.012	.030	.061	.105	.153
15	10																.001	.003	.010	.024	.051	.092
15	11																	.001	.002	.007	.019	.042
15	12																			.002	.005	.014
15	13																				.001	.003
15	14																					
15	15																					

The Poisson table

For values of λ and x = 0, 1, 2, ….

The likeliest number of occurrences (which is λ, rounded down to the nearest whole number) is shown in **bold**. For any whole number λ, $P(\lambda) = P(\lambda - 1)$.

For values of $\lambda > 20$, the Poisson distribution is approximated by the normal distribution.

The Poisson table for small values of λ

λ	0.1	0.2	0.3	0.4	0.5	0.6	0.7	0.8	0.9
P(X=0)	**0.9048**	**0.8187**	**0.7408**	**0.6703**	**0.6065**	**0.5488**	**0.4966**	**0.4493**	**0.4066**
P(X=1)	0.0905	0.1637	0.2222	0.2681	0.3033	0.3293	0.3476	0.3595	0.3659
P(X=2)	0.0045	0.0164	0.0333	0.0536	0.0758	0.0988	0.1217	0.1438	0.1647
P(X=3)	0.0002	0.0011	0.0033	0.0072	0.0126	0.0198	0.0284	0.0383	0.0494
P(X=4)		0.0001	0.0003	0.0007	0.0016	0.0030	0.0050	0.0077	0.0111
P(X=5)				0.0001	0.0002	0.0004	0.0007	0.0012	0.0020
P(X=6)							0.0001	0.0002	0.0003

The Poisson table for moderate values of λ

λ	1.0	1.5	2.0	2.5	3.0	3.5	4.0	4.5	5.0
P(X=0)	0.3679	0.2231	0.1353	0.0821	0.0498	0.0302	0.0183	0.0111	0.0067
P(X=1)	0.3679	0.3347	0.2707	0.2052	0.1494	0.1057	0.0733	0.0500	0.0337
P(X=2)	0.1839	0.2510	0.2707	0.2565	0.2240	0.1850	0.1465	0.1125	0.0842
P(X=3)	0.0613	0.1255	0.1804	0.2138	0.2240	0.2158	0.1954	0.1687	0.1404
P(X=4)	0.0153	0.0471	0.0902	0.1336	0.1680	0.1888	0.1954	0.1898	0.1755
P(X=5)	0.0031	0.0141	0.0361	0.0668	0.1008	0.1322	0.1563	0.1708	0.1755
P(X=6)	0.0005	0.0035	0.0120	0.0278	0.0504	0.0771	0.1042	0.1281	0.1462
P(X=7)	0.0001	0.0008	0.0034	0.0099	0.0216	0.0385	0.0595	0.0824	0.1044
P(X=8)		0.0001	0.0009	0.0031	0.0081	0.0169	0.0298	0.0463	0.0653
P(X=9)			0.0002	0.0009	0.0027	0.0066	0.0132	0.0232	0.0363
P(X=10)				0.0002	0.0008	0.0023	0.0053	0.0104	0.0181
P(X=11)					0.0002	0.0007	0.0019	0.0043	0.0082
P(X=12)					0.0001	0.0002	0.0006	0.0016	0.0034
P(X=13)						0.0001	0.0002	0.0006	0.0013
P(X=14)							0.0001	0.0002	0.0005
P(X=15)								0.0001	0.0002

The Poisson table for large values of λ

λ	5	6	7	8	9	10	15	20
P(X=0)	0.0067	0.0025	0.0009	0.0003	0.0001	0.0000	0.0000	0.0000
P(X=1)	0.0337	0.0149	0.0064	0.0027	0.0011	0.0005	0.0000	0.0000
P(X=2)	0.0842	0.0446	0.0223	0.0107	0.0050	0.0023	0.0000	0.0000
P(X=3)	0.1404	0.0892	0.0521	0.0286	0.0150	0.0076	0.0002	0.0000
P(X=4)	0.1755	0.1339	0.0912	0.0573	0.0337	0.0189	0.0006	0.0000
P(X=5)	0.1755	0.1606	0.1277	0.0916	0.0607	0.0378	0.0019	0.0001
P(X=6)	0.1462	0.1606	0.1490	0.1221	0.0911	0.0631	0.0048	0.0002
P(X=7)	0.1044	0.1377	0.1490	0.1396	0.1171	0.0901	0.0104	0.0005
P(X=8)	0.0653	0.1033	0.1304	0.1396	0.1318	0.1126	0.0194	0.0013
P(X=9)	0.0363	0.0688	0.1014	0.1241	0.1318	0.1251	0.0324	0.0029
P(X=10)	0.0181	0.0413	0.0710	0.0993	0.1186	0.1251	0.0486	0.0058
P(X=11)	0.0082	0.0225	0.0452	0.0722	0.0970	0.1137	0.0663	0.0106
P(X=12)	0.0034	0.0113	0.0264	0.0481	0.0728	0.0948	0.0829	0.0176
P(X=13)	0.0013	0.0052	0.0142	0.0296	0.0504	0.0729	0.0956	0.0271
P(X=14)	0.0005	0.0022	0.0071	0.0169	0.0324	0.0521	0.1024	0.0387
P(X=15)	0.0002	0.0009	0.0033	0.0090	0.0194	0.0347	0.1024	0.0516
P(X=16)		0.0003	0.0014	0.0045	0.0109	0.0217	0.0960	0.0646

(Contd.)

P(X=17)		0.0001	0.0006	0.0021	0.0058	0.0128	0.0847	0.0760
P(X=18)			0.0002	0.0009	0.0029	0.0071	0.0706	0.0844
P(X=19)			0.0001	0.0004	0.0014	0.0037	0.0557	**0.0888**
P(X=20)				0.0002	0.0006	0.0019	0.0418	**0.0888**
P(X=21)				0.0001	0.0003	0.0009	0.0299	0.0846
P(X=22)					0.0001	0.0004	0.0204	0.0769
P(X=23)						0.0002	0.0133	0.0669
P(X=24)						0.0001	0.0083	0.0557
P(X=25)							0.0050	0.0446
P(X=26)							0.0029	0.0343
P(X=27)							0.0016	0.0254
P(X=28)							0.0009	0.0181
P(X=29)							0.0004	0.0125
P(X=30)							0.0002	0.0083
P(X=31)							0.0001	0.0054
P(X=32)							0.0001	0.0034
P(X=33)								0.0020
P(X=34)								0.0012
P(X=35)								0.0007
P(X=36)								0.0004
P(X=37)								0.0002
P(X=38)								0.0001
P(X=39)								0.0001

The Standard Normal Distribution and Applications

Normal distributions are a family of distributions that have the shape shown below.

Normal distributions are symmetrical with regards to the vertical axis. The majority of observations lie in the middle of the distribution. The tails of the distribution represent fewer observations. Normal distributions are defined by two parameters.

These are the mean $\mu$and variance σ^2. The normal distribution is the most commonly used probability distribution because most variables of interest are distributed normally. For example, there are as many exceptionally fast runners as there are exceptionally slow runners in the world. This example could be extended to the height of trees, the lifetimes of animals, the ages of people, the weights of people, etc. As the sample size keeps increasing, all probability distributions ultimately reduce to the normal distribution. Let X denote a random variable. Let x denote a specific value of the random variable. The mathematical expression for the normal probability distribution is given as follows:

$$f\left(x;\mu,\sigma^2\right)=\frac{1}{\sqrt{2\pi\sigma^2}}e^{-\frac{1}{2}\left(\frac{x-\mu}{\sigma}\right)^2} \quad \text{where } -\infty < X < +\infty$$

Definition of the Normal Probability Distribution

A random variable X is said to have a normal distribution with mean μ and variance σ^2 if its probability density function is given by:

$$f\left(x;\mu,\sigma^2\right)=\frac{1}{\sqrt{2\pi\sigma^2}}e^{-\frac{1}{2}\left(\frac{x-\mu}{\sigma}\right)^2} \quad \text{where } -\infty < X < +\infty$$

$E(X) = \mu$ (the true mean or average value of the distribution)

$V(X) = \sigma^2$ (the true variance of the distribution)

Definition of the Standard Normal Random Variable Z

Let X be a random variable distributed normally with mean μ and variance σ^2. The standard normal random variable Z is a function of X, and is defined as follows:

$$Z=\frac{X-\mu}{\sigma}=\frac{\overline{X}-\mu}{\sigma/\sqrt{n}}\sim N(0,1)$$

Areas under the standard normal curve

The total area under the standard normal curve is 1.

The area to the left of 0 under the standard normal curve is 0.5.

The area to the right of 0 under the standard normal curve is 0.5.

The area that lies under the standard normal curve is symmetrical with respect to the Y-axis.

Example:

Suppose that test scores in an exam are normally distributed with a mean of 60 and a standard deviation of 10. What is the proportion of scores that are above 85?

Solution:

Let X denote a random score obtained by a student in the class.

The random variable X is distributed normally with mean 60 and standard deviation 10.

We need to find the probability that X is greater than 85.

Required: $P(X > 85)$

$Z = \frac{X-\mu}{\sigma}$ where $\mu = 60$ and $\sigma = 10$

$$P(X > 85) = P\left(\frac{X-\mu}{\sigma} > \frac{85-\mu}{\sigma}\right) = P\left(Z > \frac{85-60}{10}\right) =$$

$$P\left(Z > \frac{25}{10}\right) = P(Z > 2.5) = 1 - P(Z \leq 2.5)$$

To find $P(Z \leq 2.5)$, follow the following steps.

Under the standard normal curve, the area that lies between 0 and 2.5 is equal to 0.4938. (See the standard normal table below under Z=2.5).

The area that lies to the left of 0 under the standard normal curve is equal to 0.5.

Thus, $P(Z \leq 2.5) = 0.4938 + 0.5 = 0.9938$

Hence,

$P(X > 85) = 1 - P(Z \leq 2.5) = 1 - 0.9938 = 0.0.0062 = 0.62\%$.

Thus, the percentage of students whose scores are above 85 is equal to 0.62%.

The Z-table (The standard normal table)

The Z-table shows the area that lies under the standard normal curve between 0 and a positive number Z that lies to the right of 0.

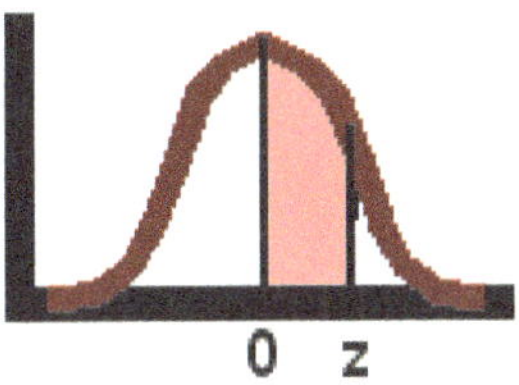

The area that lies under the standard normal curve is symmetrical. The area to the left of 0 is 0.5. The area to the right of 0 is also equal to 0.5. These 2 properties can be used to determine any area that lies under the standard normal curve between any two points a and b.

Table 1 (Areas under the standard normal curve between 0 and Z)

Z	0.00	0.01	0.02	0.03	0.04	0.05	0.06	0.07	0.08	0.09
0.0	0.0000	0.0040	0.0080	0.0120	0.0160	0.0199	0.0239	0.0279	0.0319	0.0359
0.1	0.0398	0.0438	0.0478	0.0517	0.0557	0.0596	0.0636	0.0675	0.0714	0.0753
0.2	0.0793	0.0832	0.0871	0.0910	0.0948	0.0987	0.1026	0.1064	0.1103	0.1141
0.3	0.1179	0.1217	0.1255	0.1293	0.1331	0.1368	0.1406	0.1443	0.1480	0.1517

(Contd.)

Z	0.00	0.01	0.02	0.03	0.04	0.05	0.06	0.07	0.08	0.09
0.4	0.1554	0.1591	0.1628	0.1664	0.1700	0.1736	0.1772	0.1808	0.1844	0.1879
0.5	0.1915	0.1950	0.1985	0.2019	0.2054	0.2088	0.2123	0.2157	0.2190	0.2224
0.6	0.2257	0.2291	0.2324	0.2357	0.2389	0.2422	0.2454	0.2486	0.2517	0.2549
0.7	0.2580	0.2611	0.2642	0.2673	0.2704	0.2734	0.2764	0.2794	0.2823	0.2852
0.8	0.2881	0.2910	0.2939	0.2967	0.2995	0.3023	0.3051	0.3078	0.3106	0.3133
0.9	0.3159	0.3186	0.3212	0.3238	0.3264	0.3289	0.3315	0.3340	0.3365	0.3389
1.0	0.3413	0.3438	0.3461	0.3485	0.3508	0.3531	0.3554	0.3577	0.3599	0.3621
1.1	0.3643	0.3665	0.3686	0.3708	0.3729	0.3749	0.3770	0.3790	0.3810	0.3830
1.2	0.3849	0.3869	0.3888	0.3907	0.3925	0.3944	0.3962	0.3980	0.3997	0.4015
1.3	0.4032	0.4049	0.4066	0.4082	0.4099	0.4115	0.4131	0.4147	0.4162	0.4177
1.4	0.4192	0.4207	0.4222	0.4236	0.4251	0.4265	0.4279	0.4292	0.4306	0.4319
1.5	0.4332	0.4345	0.4357	0.4370	0.4382	0.4394	0.4406	0.4418	0.4429	0.4441
1.6	0.4452	0.4463	0.4474	0.4484	0.4495	0.4505	0.4515	0.4525	0.4535	0.4545
1.7	0.4554	0.4564	0.4573	0.4582	0.4591	0.4599	0.4608	0.4616	0.4625	0.4633
1.8	0.4641	0.4649	0.4656	0.4664	0.4671	0.4678	0.4686	0.4693	0.4699	0.4706
1.9	0.4713	0.4719	0.4726	0.4732	0.4738	0.4744	0.4750	0.4756	0.4761	0.4767
2.0	0.4772	0.4778	0.4783	0.4788	0.4793	0.4798	0.4803	0.4808	0.4812	0.4817
2.1	0.4821	0.4826	0.4830	0.4834	0.4838	0.4842	0.4846	0.4850	0.4854	0.4857
2.2	0.4861	0.4864	0.4868	0.4871	0.4875	0.4878	0.4881	0.4884	0.4887	0.4890
2.3	0.4893	0.4896	0.4898	0.4901	0.4904	0.4906	0.4909	0.4911	0.4913	0.4916
2.4	0.4918	0.4920	0.4922	0.4925	0.4927	0.4929	0.4931	0.4932	0.4934	0.4936
2.5	0.4938	0.4940	0.4941	0.4943	0.4945	0.4946	0.4948	0.4949	0.4951	0.4952
2.6	0.4953	0.4955	0.4956	0.4957	0.4959	0.4960	0.4961	0.4962	0.4963	0.4964
2.7	0.4965	0.4966	0.4967	0.4968	0.4969	0.4970	0.4971	0.4972	0.4973	0.4974
2.8	0.4974	0.4975	0.4976	0.4977	0.4977	0.4978	0.4979	0.4979	0.4980	0.4981
2.9	0.4981	0.4982	0.4982	0.4983	0.4984	0.4984	0.4985	0.4985	0.4986	0.4986
3.0	0.4987	0.4987	0.4987	0.4988	0.4988	0.4989	0.4989	0.4989	0.4990	0.4990
3.1	0.4990	0.4991	0.4991	0.4991	0.4992	0.4992	0.4992	0.4992	0.4993	0.4993
3.2	0.4993	0.4993	0.4994	0.4994	0.4994	0.4994	0.4994	0.4995	0.4995	0.4995
3.3	0.4995	0.4995	0.4995	0.4996	0.4996	0.4996	0.4996	0.4996	0.4996	0.4997
3.4	0.4997	0.4997	0.4997	0.4997	0.4997	0.4997	0.4997	0.4997	0.4997	0.4998
3.5	0.4998	0.4998	0.4998	0.4998	0.4998	0.4998	0.4998	0.4998	0.4998	0.4998
3.6	0.4998	0.4998	0.4999	0.4999	0.4999	0.4999	0.4999	0.4999	0.4999	0.4999
3.7	0.4999	0.4999	0.4999	0.4999	0.4999	0.4999	0.4999	0.4999	0.4999	0.4999
3.8	0.4999	0.4999	0.4999	0.4999	0.4999	0.4999	0.4999	0.4999	0.4999	0.4999

Table 2 (Areas under the standard normal curve to the left of Z)

Z	0.00	0.01	0.02	0.03	0.04	0.05	0.06	0.07	0.08	0.09
0.0	0.5000	0.5040	0.5080	0.5120	0.5160	0.5199	0.5239	0.5279	0.5319	0.5359
0.1	0.5398	0.5438	0.5478	0.5517	0.5557	0.5596	0.5636	0.5675	0.5714	0.5753
0.2	0.5793	0.5832	0.5871	0.5910	0.5948	0.5987	0.6026	0.6064	0.6103	0.6141
0.3	0.6179	0.6217	0.6255	0.6293	0.6331	0.6368	0.6406	0.6443	0.6480	0.6517
0.4	0.6554	0.6591	0.6628	0.6664	0.6700	0.6736	0.6772	0.6808	0.6844	0.6879
0.5	0.6915	0.6950	0.6985	0.7019	0.7054	0.7088	0.7123	0.7157	0.7190	0.7224
0.6	0.7257	0.7291	0.7324	0.7357	0.7389	0.7422	0.7454	0.7486	0.7517	0.7549
0.7	0.7580	0.7611	0.7642	0.7673	0.7704	0.7734	0.7764	0.7794	0.7823	0.7852
0.8	0.7881	0.7910	0.7939	0.7967	0.7995	0.8023	0.8051	0.8078	0.8106	0.8133
0.9	0.8159	0.8186	0.8212	0.8238	0.8264	0.8289	0.8315	0.8340	0.8365	0.8389
1.0	0.8413	0.8438	0.8461	0.8485	0.8508	0.8531	0.8554	0.8577	0.8599	0.8621
1.1	0.8643	0.8665	0.8686	0.8708	0.8729	0.8749	0.8770	0.8790	0.8810	0.8830
1.2	0.8849	0.8869	0.8888	0.8907	0.8925	0.8944	0.8962	0.8980	0.8997	0.9015
1.3	0.9032	0.9049	0.9066	0.9082	0.9099	0.9115	0.9131	0.9147	0.9162	0.9177
1.4	0.9192	0.9207	0.9222	0.9236	0.9251	0.9265	0.9279	0.9292	0.9306	0.9319
1.5	0.9332	0.9345	0.9357	0.9370	0.9382	0.9394	0.9406	0.9418	0.9429	0.9441
1.6	0.9452	0.9463	0.9474	0.9484	0.9495	0.9505	0.9515	0.9525	0.9535	0.9545
1.7	0.9554	0.9564	0.9573	0.9582	0.9591	0.9599	0.9608	0.9616	0.9625	0.9633
1.8	0.9641	0.9649	0.9656	0.9664	0.9671	0.9678	0.9686	0.9693	0.9699	0.9706
1.9	0.9713	0.9719	0.9726	0.9732	0.9738	0.9744	0.9750	0.9756	0.9761	0.9767
2.0	0.9772	0.9778	0.9783	0.9788	0.9793	0.9798	0.9803	0.9808	0.9812	0.9817
2.1	0.9821	0.9826	0.9830	0.9834	0.9838	0.9842	0.9846	0.9850	0.9854	0.9857
2.2	0.9861	0.9864	0.9868	0.9871	0.9875	0.9878	0.9881	0.9884	0.9887	0.9890
2.3	0.9893	0.9896	0.9898	0.9901	0.9904	0.9906	0.9909	0.9911	0.9913	0.9916
2.4	0.9918	0.9920	0.9922	0.9925	0.9927	0.9929	0.9931	0.9932	0.9934	0.9936
2.5	0.9938	0.9940	0.9941	0.9943	0.9945	0.9946	0.9948	0.9949	0.9951	0.9952
2.6	0.9953	0.9955	0.9956	0.9957	0.9959	0.9960	0.9961	0.9962	0.9963	0.9964
2.7	0.9965	0.9966	0.9967	0.9968	0.9969	0.9970	0.9971	0.9972	0.9973	0.9974
2.8	0.9974	0.9975	0.9976	0.9977	0.9977	0.9978	0.9979	0.9979	0.9980	0.9981
2.9	0.9981	0.9982	0.9982	0.9983	0.9984	0.9984	0.9985	0.9985	0.9986	0.9986
3.0	0.9987	0.9987	0.9987	0.9988	0.9988	0.9989	0.9989	0.9989	0.9990	0.9990

Example 1:

How large is the area that lies under the standard normal curve to the left of 1.53?

In **Table 2**, look for 1.5 under Column Z, and go to the right to the 0.03 column to find the value 0.9370.

Example 2:

How large is the area that lies under the standard normal curve to the left of –1.53?

By symmetry, the area to the left of –1.53 is equal to the area to the right of 1.53. That is, –

$P(Z < -1.53) = P(Z > 1.53) = 1 - P(Z \leq 1.53)$

$= 1 - 0.9370 = 0.0630$ **(Table 2)**

Example 3:

How large is the area that lies under the standard normal curve between the numbers –1.00 and 0.50?

Solution

$P(-1 \leq Z \leq 0.50) = P(-1 \leq Z \leq 0) + P(0 \leq Z \leq 0.50)$

$= P(0 \leq Z \leq 1) + P(0 \leq Z \leq 0.50)$ by symmetry

$= 0.3413 + 0.1915$ (Both values are obtained from Table 1)

$= 0.5328$

Exercise 1:

Find the area that lies under the standard normal curve between 1.38 and 2.15

Area = Area to the left of 2.15 – Area to the left of 1.38
Use Table 2

Area to the left of 2.15 = 0.9842

Area to the left of 1.38 = 0.9162

Area = Area to the left of 2.15 – Area to the left of 1.38 = 0.9842 – 0.9162 = 0.0680

Exercise 2:

Find the area that lies under the standard normal curve between –2.15 and –1.38

Area between –2.15 and – 1.38 is equal to the Area between 1.38 and 2.15 by symmetry.

Area = Area to the left of 2.15 – Area to the left of 1.38

Use Table 2

Area to the left of 2.15 = 0.9842

Area to the left of 1.38 = 0.9162

Area = Area to the left of 2.15 – Area to the left of 1.38 = 0.9842 – 0.9162 = 0.0680

Exercise 3:

Find the area that lies under the standard normal curve between -2.15 and 1.38

Area between – 2.15 and 1.38 is equal to the Area between – 2.15 and 0 plus Area between 0 and 1.38

Area between – 2.15 and 0 = Area between 0 and 2.15 by symmetry

Use Table 1

Area 1 = Area between 0 and 2.15 = 0.4842

Area 2 = Area between 0 and 1.38 = 0.4162

Total area = Area 1 + Area 2 = 0.4842 + 0.4162 = 0.9004

Exercise 4:

Find the area under the standard normal curve that lies to the right of 2.39.

Area to the right of 2.39 = 1 – Area to the left of 2.39
= 1 – 0.9916 = 0.0084

Use Table 2

Exercise 5:

Find the area under the standard normal curve that lies to the right of the number –1.25.

The area that lies to the right of –1.25 is the sum of the Area between the number – 1.25 and 0 and the area to the right of 0.

Area 1 = Area between – 1.25 and 0 = Area between 0 and 1.25
= 0.3944 (Use Table 1)

Area 2 = Area to the right of 0 = 0.5

Thus, Area to the right of –1.25 = Area 1 + Area 2
= 0.3944 + 0.5 = 0.8944

Example 4:

The number of CD4+ cells among a large number of terminal HIV patients at a certain home-based care centre is distributed normally with mean 425 and variance 90, 000.

a) What is the probability that a randomly identified patient in the group has less than 800 CD4+ cells?

$$P(X < 800) = P\left(\frac{X-\mu}{\sigma} < \frac{800-\mu}{\sigma}\right)$$

$$= P\left(Z < \frac{800-425}{300}\right) = P(Z < 1.25) = 0.8944$$

b) What is the probability that a randomly identified patient in the group has between 500 and 600 CD4+ cells?

$$P(500 < X < 600) = P\left(\frac{500-\mu}{\sigma} < \frac{X-\mu}{\sigma} < \frac{600-\mu}{\sigma}\right)$$

$$= P\left(\frac{500-425}{300} < Z < \frac{600-425}{300}\right)$$

$$= P(0.25 < Z < 0.58) = \mathrm{P(Z<0.58)} - \mathrm{P(Z<0.25)} = 0.7190 - 0.5987$$

$$= 0.1203 = 12.03\%$$

Examples:

1) Why is the normal distribution the most important probability distribution in inferential statistics?

Because most events in the real world are distributed normally with mean μ and variance σ^2.

2) How is the central limit theorem related to sample sizes of studies?

As the sample size of study approaches the size of the population of study, the probability distribution being used reduces to the normal distribution.

3) How large is the area that lies under the standard normal curve

   a) to the left of 1.25
   b) to the right of 2.34
   c) between 1.25 and 2.02
   d) to the right of –2.55
   e) between –2.23 and –1.25

Solution:

a) Look for 1.2 in the X column, go right to the 0.05 column to find the value 0.3944. Now add 0.5 (for the probability less than zero) to obtain the final result of 0.8944.

b) How large is the area that lies to the right of 2.34?

$P(Z > 2.34) = 1 - P(Z \leq 2.34) = 1 - 0.9904 = 0.0096$ **(Table 2)**

c) How large is the area that lies between 1.25 and 2.02?

$P(1.25 < Z < 2.02) = P(Z < 2.02) - P(Z < 1.25)$

$= 0.9783 - 0.8944 = 0.0839$

(Table 2)

d) How large is the area that lies to the right of –2.55?

$P(Z > -2.55) = 1 - P(Z \leq -2.55)$ where $P(Z \leq -2.55) = P(Z \geq 2.55)$

$= 1 - P(Z \leq 2.55) = 1 - 0.9946 = 0.0054$ **(Table 2)**

Hence, $P(Z > -2.55) = 1 - 0.0054 = 0.9946$

e) How large is the area that lies between –2.23 and –1.25?

$P(-2.23 < Z < -1.25) = P(1.25 < Z < 2.23)$ by symmetry

$= P(Z < 2.23) - P(Z < 1.25) = 0.9871 - 0.8944 = 0.0927$ **(Table 2)**

4) The number of boxes of syringes produced daily by a small pharmaceutical plant in Durban is normally distributed with mean 250 and variance 900.

a) What is the probability that more than 300 boxes of syringes are produced on a randomly selected day?

$$P(X > 300) = 1 - P(X \leq 300)$$

$$= 1 - P\left(\frac{X-\mu}{\sigma} \le \frac{300-\mu}{\sigma}\right) = 1 - P\left(Z \le \frac{300-250}{30}\right)$$

$= 1 - P(Z \le 1.67) = 1 - 0.9525 = 0.0475 = 4.75\%$ **(Table 2)**

b) What is the probability that between 275 and 300 boxes of syringes are produced on a randomly selected day?

$$P(275 < X < 300) = P\left(\frac{275-\mu}{\sigma} < \frac{X-\mu}{\sigma} < \frac{300-\mu}{\sigma}\right)$$

$$= P\left(\frac{275-250}{30} < Z < \frac{300-250}{30}\right)$$

$= P(0.83 < Z < 1.67) = P(Z<1.67) - P(Z<0.83) = 0.9525 - 0.7967$

$= 0.1558 = 15.58\%$. **(Table 2)**

Critical Values of the Standard Normal Random Variable Z

A few particularly important values of Z derived from the standard normal table are shown below. These values are commonly used for hypothesis testing and the construction of confidence intervals for the mean μ.

$1-\frac{\alpha}{2}$	**0.999**	**0.995**	**0.990**	**0.975**	**0.950**	**0.900**
$Z_{1-\frac{\alpha}{2}}$	**3.09**	**2.58**	**2.33**	**1.96**	**1.65**	**1.28**

At the 5% level of significance,

$$z_{0.975} = 1.961 - \frac{\alpha}{2} = 1 - \frac{0.05}{2}$$

$$= 1 - 0.025 = 0.975 Z_{0.975} = 1.96$$

UNIT 5

THE PEARSON CHI-SQUARE TEST OF ASSOCIATION

The Pearson chi-square test of association (Beh and Lombardo, 2021) is used to test the strength of association between factors that are related to each other. The factors being tested could have any number of rows and any number of columns. The most commonly used version of the test is the two-by-two test. The Pearson chi-square statistic produces theoretically reliable results when the sample size of study is large (Example: 120 observations or more). An association between two categorical variables A and B is said to be significant at the 5% level of significance if the probability value (P-value) obtained from the Pearson chi-square test of association is less than 0.05. A probability value which is 0.05 or more indicates that there is no statistically significant association between factors A and B at the 5% level of significance.

The Pearson chi-square test of association becomes unreliable when the expected cell frequency falls below 5. In such cases, it is necessary to reduce the number of categories of factors A and B, increase the sample size of study, or use Fisher's exact test of association.

Assumptions needed for the Pearson chi-square test of association

The data used for analysis comes from a random sample.

The size of the sample is large. At small sample sizes, the Pearson chi-square test of association exposes the researcher to an unacceptable rate of Type 2 errors (the mistake of accepting a false null hypothesis). While using two-by-two Pearson chi-square tests, in the fields of business, management, socioeconomic, and behavioural studies, it is highly beneficial to set the minimum sample size of study at 120 or more. Doing so enables the researcher to obtain theoretically reliable probability values and large expected cell frequencies (5 or above).

All expected cell frequencies must be at least 5 in magnitude. For example, in a two-by-two test of association, all 4 expected cell frequencies must be 5 or more in magnitude. When this assumption is not met, Yates' correction is applied.

Observations are assumed to be independent of each other. That is, an observation can only appear in one cell. The chi-square random variable cannot be used to assess the strength of association between correlated variables. Example: Paired observations (before and after), matched pairs, and panel data sets.

The observations must come from the same underlying distribution. That is, the hypothesised distribution is known or specified in advance, so that the number of observations that are expected to appear in each cell in the table can be calculated without reference to the observed values. Normally this expected value is the cross-product of the row and column marginals divided by the sample size.

It is assumed that chi-square tests the hypothesis that two variables are related only by chance. If a significant relationship is found, this is not equivalent to establishing the researcher's hypothesis that A causes B, or that B causes A.

It is assumed that values are finite. Observations must be grouped in categories.

A normal distribution of deviations (observed minus expected values) is assumed.

The Pearson chi-square test allows the researcher to use variables that are nominal, ordinal, or interval in nature.

How to calculate the Pearson chi-square statistic

The calculated value of the Pearson chi-square statistic is given by:

$$X^2_{cal} = \frac{\sum_{i=1}^{r}\sum_{j=1}^{c}\left(O_{ij} - E_{ij}\right)^2}{E_{ij}}$$

where

$$E_{ij} = \frac{n_{i.} \times n_{.j}}{n}$$

O_{ij} is the observed cell frequency in cell i, j

E_{ij} is the expected frequency in cell i, j

n_i is the sum of observations in row i

n_j is the sum of observations in column j

r is the number of rows (i = 1, 2, …, r)

c is the number of columns (j = 1, 2, …, c)

$X^2_{tab} = X^2_{\alpha}[(r-1)(c-1)]$

α is the level of significance of test

When the row and column variables are independent, the calculated value of the chi-square statistic follows an asymptotic chi-squared distribution with (r–1)(c–1) degrees of freedom. The null hypothesis gets rejected when the calculated value of the statistic is large. The null hypothesis cannot be rejected when the calculated value of the statistic is small.

Let H0 and H1 denote the null hypothesis and alternative hypothesis respectively. In a two-by-two Pearson chi-square test of association, the hypotheses H0 and H1 are expressed as follows:

H0: There is no significant association between factors A and B

H1: There is a significant association between factors A and B

Decision rule:

Reject H0 if the calculated chi-square value is greater than the tabulated chi-square value. Alternatively, reject H0 if $P < \alpha$.

Do not reject H0 if the calculated chi-square value is less than or equal to the tabulated chi-square value. Alternatively, do not reject H0 if $P \geq \alpha$.

The tabulated value of chi-square has (r–1)(c–1) degrees of freedom, and is read from the chi-square table. The letter r denotes the number of rows. The letter c denotes the number of columns.

The following table gives values of the chi-square random variable for degrees of freedom varying from 1 to 100 and for levels of significance 0.05, 0.01, and 0.001. For a simple two-by-two test of association at the 5% level of significance, the degrees of freedom are (2–1)(2–1) = (1)(1) = 1. The tabulated value of the chi-square statistic is seen under df=1 and $\alpha = 0.05$. It is 3.84.

Table 1: Tabulated values of the chi-square statistic

df = (r–1)(c–1)	α = 0.05	α = 0.01	α = 0.01
1	3.84	6.64	10.83
2	5.99	9.21	13.82
3	7.82	11.35	16.27
4	9.49	13.28	18.47
5	11.07	15.09	20.52
6	12.59	16.81	22.46
7	14.07	18.48	24.32

df = (r–1)(c–1)	α = 0.05	α = 0.01	α = 0.01
8	15.51	20.09	26.13
9	16.92	21.67	27.88
10	18.31	23.21	29.59
11	19.68	24.73	31.26
12	21.03	26.22	32.91
13	22.36	27.69	34.53
14	23.69	29.14	36.12
15	25.00	30.58	37.70
16	26.30	32.00	39.25
17	27.59	33.41	40.79
18	28.87	34.81	42.31
19	30.14	36.19	43.82
20	31.41	37.57	45.32
21	32.67	38.93	46.80
22	33.92	40.29	48.27
23	35.17	41.64	49.73
24	36.42	42.98	51.18
25	37.65	44.31	52.62
26	38.89	45.64	54.05
27	40.11	46.96	55.48
28	41.34	48.28	56.89
29	42.56	49.59	58.30
30	43.77	50.89	59.70
31	44.99	52.19	61.10
32	46.19	53.49	62.49
33	47.40	54.78	63.87
34	48.60	56.06	65.25
35	49.80	57.34	66.62
36	51.00	58.62	67.99
37	52.19	59.89	69.35
38	53.38	61.16	70.71

(Contd.)

df = (r–1)(c–1)	α = 0.05	α = 0.01	α = 0.01
39	54.57	62.43	72.06
40	55.76	63.69	73.41
41	56.94	64.95	74.75
42	58.12	66.21	76.09
43	59.30	67.46	77.42
44	60.48	68.71	78.75
45	61.66	69.96	80.08
46	62.83	71.20	81.40
47	64.00	72.44	82.72
48	65.17	73.68	84.03
49	66.34	74.92	85.35
50	67.51	76.15	86.66
51	68.67	77.39	87.97
52	69.83	78.62	89.27
53	70.99	79.84	90.57
54	72.15	81.07	91.88
55	73.31	82.29	93.17
56	74.47	83.52	94.47
57	75.62	84.73	95.75
58	76.78	85.95	97.03
59	77.93	87.17	98.34
60	79.08	88.38	99.62
61	80.23	89.59	100.88
62	81.38	90.80	102.15
63	82.53	92.01	103.46
64	83.68	93.22	104.72
65	84.82	94.42	105.97
66	85.97	95.63	107.26
67	87.11	96.83	108.54
68	88.25	98.03	109.79
69	89.39	99.23	111.06

df = (r–1)(c–1)	α = 0.05	α = 0.01	α = 0.01
70	90.53	100.42	112.31
71	91.67	101.62	113.56
72	92.81	102.82	114.84
73	93.95	104.01	116.08
74	95.08	105.20	117.35
75	96.22	106.39	118.60
76	97.35	107.58	119.85
77	98.49	108.77	121.11
78	99.62	109.96	122.36
79	100.75	111.15	123.60
80	101.88	112.33	124.84
81	103.01	113.51	126.09
82	104.14	114.70	127.33
83	105.27	115.88	128.57
84	106.40	117.06	129.80
85	107.52	118.24	131.04
86	108.65	119.41	132.28
87	109.77	120.59	133.51
88	110.90	121.77	134.74
89	112.02	122.94	135.96
90	113.15	124.12	137.19
91	114.27	125.29	138.45
92	115.39	126.46	139.66
93	116.51	127.63	140.90
94	117.63	128.80	142.12
95	118.75	129.97	143.32
96	119.87	131.14	144.55
97	120.99	132.31	145.78
98	122.11	133.47	146.99
99	123.23	134.64	148.21
100	124.34	135.81	149.48

Decision rule based on calculated and tabulated values of the chi-square statistic

The calculated value of the Pearson chi-square statistic is shown in the printout from data analysis. The number of rows is denoted by r. The number of columns is denoted by c. The degrees of freedom of the chi-square statistic are $(r - 1) \times (c - 1)$. At the 5% level of significance, the null hypothesis is rejected if the calculated value of the chi-square statistic is greater than the tabulated value of the chi-square statistic.

Null hypothesis: There is no significant association between factors A and B

Alternative hypothesis: There is a significant association between factors A and B

At the 5% level of significance, the null hypothesis cannot be rejected if the calculated value of the chi-square statistic is less than or equal to the tabulated value of the chi-square statistic.

Rejecting the null hypothesis means that there is a statistically significant association between the two factors. Failing to reject the null hypothesis means that there is no statistically significant association between the two factors.

The basic two-by-two contingency table for exposure and outcome

		Outcome		
		Ill	Not ill	
	Yes	a	b	a+b = total exposed
Exposure				
	No	c	d	c+d = total unexposed
		a+c	b+d	a+b+c+d = n
		(total ill)	(total not ill)	

Notations for the basic two-by-two contingency table

a = Number of businesses exposed to fraud that are bankrupt

b = Number of businesses exposed to fraud that are not bankrupt

c = Number of businesses not exposed to fraud that are bankrupt

d = Number of businesses that are not exposed to fraud and not bankrupt

$$X^2{}_{cal} = \frac{\left(|ad-bc|-\frac{n}{2}\right)^2 n}{(a+b)(a+c)(c+d)(b+d)}$$ = the calculated value of

the Pearson chi-square statistic

$$\text{Absolute risk} = \frac{a+c}{a+b+c+d}$$

$$\text{Attack rate} = \text{Exposure specific risk} = \frac{a}{a+b}$$

$$\text{Relative risk} = \frac{\frac{a}{(a+b)}}{\frac{c}{(c+d)}}$$

$$\text{Odds ratio} = \frac{a/b}{c/d} = \frac{d}{b}$$

Example 1:

The STATA data set **c:\bos\smme.dta** contains the variables **capital** (1 if high, 2 if moderate, 3 if low) and **bankruptcy** (1 if bankrupt, 0 otherwise). Use the Pearson chi-square test of association in STATA to test the strength of association between the 2 variables at the 5% level of significance.

Note that r = 3 = Number of rows; and
c = 2 = Number of columns

Factor A: Capital amount

1) High
2) Moderate
3) Low

Factor B: Bankruptcy of business

1. Yes
0. No

```
. use c:\bos\smme.dta, clear
. tab2   capital  bankrupt,    cell   exp   chi2
-> tabulation of capital by bankruptcy
+--------------------+
| Key                |
|--------------------|
|     frequency      |
| expected frequency |
|  cell percentage   |
+--------------------+


   Capital |       Bankruptcy
    amount |         0          1 |     Total
-----------+----------------------+----------
         1 |        14          7 |        21
           |      17.0        4.0 |      21.0
           |      7.29       3.65 |     10.94
-----------+----------------------+----------
         2 |        40          0 |        40
           |      32.3        7.7 |      40.0
           |     20.83       0.00 |     20.83
-----------+----------------------+----------
         3 |       101         30 |       131
           |     105.8       25.2 |     131.0
           |     52.60      15.63 |     68.23
-----------+----------------------+----------
     Total |       155         37 |       192
           |     155.0       37.0 |     192.0
           |     80.73      19.27 |    100.00

          Pearson chi2(2) =  13.3273   Pr = 0.001
```

The calculated value of the Pearson chi-square statistic is 13.33. The degrees of freedom are equal to (3-1)(2-1) = 2(1) = 2. At the 5% level of significance, the tabulated value of the chi-square statistic is 5.99.

Since 13.33 > 5.99, there is a significant association between the two variables at the 5% level.

The two-tailed P-value for the same test is 0.001 < 0.05. Since the P-value is smaller than the level of significance of test, the null hypothesis is rejected at the 5% level of significance. We conclude that there is a significant association between capital amount and bankruptcy at the 5% level.

Example 2

A survey is conducted by gathering data from a random sample size of 212 rural households. The aim of the survey was to assess the strength of association between the practice of boiling drinking water regularly (Yes, No) and diarrhoeal sickness (Yes, No). The STATA data set c:\bos\cholera.dta shows the raw data set. At the 5% level of significance, test the strength of association between the 2 variables.

```
. use c:\bos\cholera.dta, clear
. tab2 boil sickness, chi2
-> tabulation of boil by sickness
           |       sickness
      boil |        No        Yes |     Total
-----------+----------------------+----------
        No |         4         32 |        36
       Yes |       159         17 |       176
-----------+----------------------+----------
     Total |       163         49 |       212

          Pearson chi2(1) = 105.5710   Pr = 0.000
```

The above table is a **two-by-two contingency table.** Factor A is the exposure variable (exposed, not exposed). Factor B is the outcome variable (sick, not sick). For Factors A and B, STATA calculates an estimate for the crude odds ratio (OR) by using the **CSI** command as shown below:

. csi a b c d, or

where

a = Number of respondents exposed and sick = 32

b = Number of respondents exposed and not sick = 4

c = Number of respondents not exposed and sick = 17

d = Number of respondents not exposed and not sick = 159

```
. use c:\bos\cholera.dta, clear

. csi  32  4  17  159, or

                 |   Exposed   Unexposed  |      Total
-----------------+------------------------+-----------
           Cases |        32           4  |         36
        Noncases |        17         159  |        176
-----------------+------------------------+-----------
           Total |        49         163  |        212
                 |                        |
            Risk |  .6530612    .0245399  |   .1698113
                 |                        |
                 |      Point estimate    |    [95% conf. interval]
                 |------------------------+------------------------
 Risk difference |         .6285213       |    .493145    .7638977
      Risk ratio |         26.61224       |   9.896758    71.55996
 Attr. frac. ex. |         .9624233       |   .8989568    .9860257
 Attr. frac. pop |         .8554874       |
      Odds ratio |         74.82353       |   24.37853    226.9039 (Cornfield)
                 +-------------------------------------------------
                               chi2(1) =   105.57  Pr>chi2 = 0.0000
```

From the STATA printout shown above, it can be seen that the calculated value of the Pearson chi-square statistic is equal to 105.57. The crude odds ratio is equal to 74.82. The 95% confidence interval for the true odds ratio is (24.38, 226.90).

Interpretation of Odds Ratio

A respondent who does not boil drinking water regularly is 74.82 times as likely to have diarrhoeal diseases in comparison with a respondent who boils drinking water regularly. The calculated value of the Pearson chi-square statistic is equal to 105.57. The degrees of freedom of the chi-square statistic are (2 – 1)(2 – 1) = 1. The level of significance of test is 5% or 0.05. The tabulated value of the Pearson chi-square statistic is 3.84. Note that 105.57 is greater than 3.84. Thus, the null hypothesis can be rejected at the 5% level. We conclude that there is a significant association between the variables boil (boiling drinking water regularly) and sickness (diarrhoeal sickness) at the 5% level.

How to perform the Pearson chi-square test of association in STATA

Go to STATA and open up the STATA data set c:\bos\cholera.dta

Steps to follow in STATA

Go to the main menu of STATA

Open the STATA data file c:\bos\cholera.dta

Click on Statistics

Click on summaries, tables, and tests

Click on tables

Click on two-way tables with measures of association

Row variable? Select the variable boil from the list of variables

Column variable? Select the variable sickness from the list of variables

Click on Pearson's chi-squared test, relative frequencies, expected frequencies

Click on OK

STATA will produce the following printout:

```
. use c:\bos\cholera.dta, clear
. tab2 boil sickness, exp  chi2
-> tabulation of boil by sickness

+--------------------+
| Key                |
|--------------------|
|     frequency      |
| expected frequency |
+--------------------+

           |       sickness
      boil |        No        Yes |     Total
-----------+----------------------+----------
        No |         4         32 |        36
           |      27.7        8.3 |      36.0
-----------+----------------------+----------
       Yes |       159         17 |       176
           |     135.3       40.7 |     176.0
-----------+----------------------+----------
     Total |       163         49 |       212
           |     163.0       49.0 |     212.0

          Pearson chi2(1) = 105.5710   Pr = 0.000
```

Null hypothesis: There is no statistically significant association between the 2 variables boil and sickness

Alternative hypothesis: There is a statistically significant association between the 2 variables boil and sickness

Decision rule:

At the 5% level of significance, reject the null hypothesis if P is less than 0.05.

At the 5% level of significance, do not reject the null hypothesis if P is greater than or equal to 0.05.

Note that each one of the 4 expected cell frequencies (27.7, 8.3, 135.3 and 40.7) is greater than 5. This fact shows that results obtained from the Pearson chi-square test of association are theoretically valid.

Decision rule based on calculated and tabulated values of the chi-square statistic

The calculated value of the Pearson chi-square statistic is equal to 105.5710. The number of rows (r) is equal to 2. The number of columns (c) is equal to 2. The degrees of freedom of the chi-square statistic are $(r - 1) \times (c - 1) = (2 - 1) \times (2 - 1) = 1 \times 1 = 1$. At the 5% level of significance, the tabulated value of the chi-square statistic is equal to 3.84. The tabulated value of the chi-square statistic can be read from the chi-square table. Since 105.5710 is greater than 3.84, the null hypothesis can be rejected at the 5% level of significance. Thus, there is a statistically significant association between the 2 factors (boil and sickness) at the 5% level of significance.

How to obtain cell percentages, row percentages, and column percentages in STATA

```
. use c:\bos\cholera.dta, clear
. tab2 boil sickness, cell row col exp chi2
-> tabulation of boil by sickness

+--------------------+
| Key                |
|--------------------|
|     frequency      |
| expected frequency |
|   row percentage   |
| column percentage  |
|  cell percentage   |
+--------------------+

           |       sickness
      boil |        No        Yes |     Total
-----------+----------------------+----------
        No |         4         32 |        36
           |      27.7        8.3 |      36.0
           |     11.11      88.89 |    100.00
           |      2.45      65.31 |     16.98
           |      1.89      15.09 |     16.98
-----------+----------------------+----------
       Yes |       159         17 |       176
           |     135.3       40.7 |     176.0
           |     90.34       9.66 |    100.00
           |     97.55      34.69 |     83.02
           |     75.00       8.02 |     83.02
-----------+----------------------+----------
     Total |       163         49 |       212
           |     163.0       49.0 |     212.0
           |     76.89      23.11 |    100.00
           |    100.00     100.00 |    100.00
           |     76.89      23.11 |    100.00

          Pearson chi2(1) = 105.5710   Pr = 0.000
```

How to obtain row, column frequencies in STATA

Go to the main menu of STATA

Open the STATA data file c:\bos\cholera.dta

Click on Statistics

Click on summaries, tables, and tests

Click on Frequency tables

Click on Two-way tables with measures of association

Row variable? Select the variable *boil* from the list of variables

Column variable? Select the variable *sickness* from the list of variables

Click on Pearson's chi-squared test, Within column relative frequencies, Within row relative frequencies, Relative frequencies, Expected frequencies

Click on OK

```
. use c:\bos\cholera.dta, clear
. tabulate boil sickness, cell chi2 column expected row

+--------------------+
| Key                |
|--------------------|
|     frequency      |
| expected frequency |
|   row percentage   |
| column percentage  |
|  cell percentage   |
+--------------------+

           |       sickness
      boil |        No        Yes |     Total
-----------+----------------------+----------
        No |         4         32 |        36
           |      27.7        8.3 |      36.0
           |     11.11      88.89 |    100.00
           |      2.45      65.31 |     16.98
           |      1.89      15.09 |     16.98
-----------+----------------------+----------
       Yes |       159         17 |       176
           |     135.3       40.7 |     176.0
           |     90.34       9.66 |    100.00
           |     97.55      34.69 |     83.02
           |     75.00       8.02 |     83.02
-----------+----------------------+----------
     Total |       163         49 |       212
           |     163.0       49.0 |     212.0
           |     76.89      23.11 |    100.00
           |    100.00     100.00 |    100.00
           |     76.89      23.11 |    100.00

          Pearson chi2(1) = 105.5710   Pr = 0.000
```

The following STATA commands are equivalent:

```
. tabulate boil sickness, cell chi2 column expected row

. tab2 boil sickness, cell col row exp chi2
```

Null hypothesis: There is no statistically significant association between the 2 variables *boil* and *sickness*

Alternative hypothesis: There is a statistically significant association between the 2 variables *boil* and *sickness*

Decision rule:

At the 5% level of significance, reject the null hypothesis if P is less than 0.05.

At the 5% level of significance, do not reject the null hypothesis if P is greater than or equal to 0.05.

Now, since P=0.000 < 0.05, the null hypothesis is rejected at the 5% level. We conclude that there is a statistically significant association between the 2 variables *boil* and *sickness*.

Decision rule based on calculated and tabulated values of the chi-square statistic

The calculated value of the Pearson chi-square statistic is equal to 105.5710. The number of rows (r) is equal to 2. The number of columns (c) is equal to 2. The degrees of freedom of the chi-square statistic are $(r - 1) \times (c - 1) = (2 - 1) \times (2 - 1) = 1 \times 1 = 1$. At the 5% level of significance, the tabulated value of the chi-square statistic is equal to 3.84. The tabulated value of the chi-square statistic can be read from the chi-square table. Since 105.5710 is greater than 3.84, the null hypothesis can be rejected at the 5% level of significance.

How to Perform Pearson's chi-square test of association in SPSS

Open up the SPSS data set c:\bos\cholera.sav

Click on Analyze

Click on Descriptive statistics

Click on crosstabs

Select the variable *sickness* as row

Select the variable *boil* as column

Click on statistics

Click on chi-square tests

Click on continue

Click on OK

SPSS will produce the following computer printout:

boil * sickness Crosstabulation

Count

		sickness		
		No	Yes	Total
boil	No	4	32	36
	Yes	159	17	176
Total		163	49	212

Chi-Square Tests

	Value	df	Asymptotic Significance (2-sided)	Exact Sig. (2-sided)	Exact Sig. (1-sided)
Pearson Chi-Square	105.571[a]	1	<.001		
Continuity Correction[b]	101.160	1	<.001		
Likelihood Ratio	92.346	1	<.001		
Fisher's Exact Test				<.001	<.001
N of Valid Cases	212				

a. 0 cells (0.0%) have expected count less than 5. The minimum expected count is 8.32.

b. Computed only for a 2x2 table

Example 3:

The following table provides data from a case-control study in which the association between the history of gambling by business owners and defaulting on bank loans in a random sample of 582 small enterprises was studied:

Gambling	Default on loan	No default on loan	Total
Yes	31	69	100
No	17	465	482
Total	48	534	582

Estimate the odds of defaulting on a loan for businesses that are owned by operators with a history of gambling.

Solution:

a = Number of businesses gambling and defaulted = 31

b = Number of businesses gambling and not defaulted = 69

c = Number of businesses not gambling and defaulted = 17

d = Number of businesses not gambling and not defaulted = 465

n = Sample size of study = 582

$$X^2_{cal} = \frac{\left(|ad - bc| - \frac{n}{2}\right)^2 n}{(a+b)(a+c)(c+d)(b+d)} = 82.60$$

= the calculated value of the Pearson chi-square statistic

Degrees of freedom of chi-square statistic = (2 – 1)(2 – 1) = 1

Tabulated value of chi-square statistic = $X^2_{0.05}(1) = 3.84$

Since 82.60 > 3.84, we conclude that there is a significant association between the history of gambling and defaulting on bank loans at the 0.05 level of significance.

$$\text{Odds ratio} = \frac{a/b}{c/d} = \frac{d}{b} = 12.29$$

The odds of defaulting on bank loans in businesses with a history of gambling are 12.29 in comparison with businesses with no past history of gambling.

This exercise is solved in STATA by using the following STATA command:

```
. csi  31   69   17  465,  or


                 |   Exposed   Unexposed  |      Total
-----------------+------------------------+------------
           Cases |        31          69  |        100
        Noncases |        17         465  |        482
-----------------+------------------------+------------
           Total |        48         534  |        582
                 |                        |
            Risk |  .6458333    .1292135  |   .1718213
                 |                        |
                 |      Point estimate    |    [95% Conf. Interval]
                 |------------------------+------------------------
 Risk difference |         .5166199       |    .3783629    .6548768
      Risk ratio |         4.998188       |    3.688264    6.773346
 Attr. frac. ex. |         .7999275       |    .7288697    .8523625
 Attr. frac. pop |         .2479775       |
      Odds ratio |           12.289       |     6.50082     23.2202 (Cornfield)
                 +-------------------------------------------------
                               chi2(1) =    82.60  Pr>chi2 = 0.0000
```

The odds ratio is equal to 12.289. The 95% confidence interval for the true odds ratio is (6.50, 23.22).

How to obtain multiple frequency tables and two-by-two Pearson's chi-square tests of association in STATA

Example:

The STATA data set **c:\bos\marcia.dta** contains raw data gathered from a stratified random sample size of 208 small retail businesses in Pretoria. The data set shows that 159 of the 208 businesses were operated by the owners themselves, whereas the remaining 49 businesses were operated by employed managers.

The data set contains data on the following 9 variables of study:

profit: Profitability of retail business (Yes, No)

ownership: Ownership of retail business (Yes, No)

rent: Renting business premises (Yes, No)

duration: Duration of business operation (5 years or less, More than 5 years)

freelabour: Using free labour from family members (Yes, No)

wholesale: Ability to order merchandise in bulk from wholesalers (Yes, No)

bankaccount: Ownership of bank account (Yes, No)

socialmedia: Use of social media for marketing (Yes, No)

businessplan: Ability to write up a business plan (Yes, No)

Open up the STATA data set c:\bos\marcia.dta

Click on Statistics

Click on Summaries, tables and tests, Frequency tables, Multiple one-way tables

Categorical variables?

Click on each one of the variables of study to select them

Click on OK

STATA will produce the following printout consisting of 9 frequency tables corresponding to the 9 categorical variables of study in the data set.

```
. use c:\bos\marcia.dta, clear

. tabl profit ownership rent duration freelabour wholesale bankaccount
socialmedia businessplan


-> tabulation of profit

     profit |      Freq.     Percent        Cum.
------------+-----------------------------------
         No |         40       19.23       19.23
        Yes |        168       80.77      100.00
------------+-----------------------------------
      Total |        208      100.00
```

-> tabulation of ownership

ownership	Freq.	Percent	Cum.
No	49	23.56	23.56
Yes	159	76.44	100.00
Total	208	100.00	

-> tabulation of rent

rent	Freq.	Percent	Cum.
No	39	18.75	18.75
Yes	169	81.25	100.00
Total	208	100.00	

-> tabulation of duration

duration	Freq.	Percent	Cum.
5 years or less	29	13.94	13.94
More than 5 years	179	86.06	100.00
Total	208	100.00	

-> tabulation of freelabour

freelabour	Freq.	Percent	Cum.
No	39	18.75	18.75
Yes	169	81.25	100.00
Total	208	100.00	

-> tabulation of wholesale

wholesale	Freq.	Percent	Cum.
No	40	19.23	19.23
Yes	168	80.77	100.00
Total	208	100.00	

-> tabulation of bankaccount

bankaccount	Freq.	Percent	Cum.
No	41	19.71	19.71
Yes	167	80.29	100.00
Total	208	100.00	

-> tabulation of socialmedia

socialmedia	Freq.	Percent	Cum.
No	47	22.60	22.60
Yes	161	77.40	100.00
Total	208	100.00	

```
-> tabulation of businessplan

businessplan |      Freq.     Percent        Cum.
-------------+-----------------------------------
          No |         38       18.27       18.27
         Yes |        170       81.73      100.00
-------------+-----------------------------------
       Total |        208      100.00
```

To obtain multiple two-by-two tests of association,

Open up the STATA data set c:\bos\marcia.dta

Click on Statistics

Click on Summaries, tables and tests, Frequency tables, All possible two-way tables

Categorical variables?

Click on each one of the variables of study to select them (The first variable to be selected should be the outcome variable of study, profit)

Click on Pearson's chi-squared test, Within column relative frequencies, Within row relative frequencies, Relative frequencies, Expected frequencies

Click on Show only tables that include the first variable

Click on OK

```
. use c:\bos\fp1.dta, clear
. tab2 profit ownership rent duration freelabour wholesale bankaccount socialme-
dia businessplan, chi2 column expected row firstonly
```

Remark:

The above STATA command is equivalent to the following command:

```
. for var ownership rent duration freelabour wholesale bankaccount socialmedia
businessplan: tab2  profit  X,   cell row col exp  chi2
```

How to obtain multiple one-way tables in SPSS

Go to SPSS and open up the data set c:\bos\marcia.sav

Click on Analyze, Descriptive statistics, Frequency tables

Highlight and select all 9 categorical variables by clicking on the selection bar

Click on OK

SPSS will display 9 frequency tables corresponding to the 9 categorical variables of study

How to obtain multiple two-by-two tables in SPSS

Go to SPSS and open up the data set c:\bos\marcia.sav

Click on Analyze, Descriptive statistics, Crosstabs

Select the variable profit as a row variable

Highlight and select the remaining 8 categorical variables as column variables by clicking on the selection bar

Click on Statistics, Chi-square

Click on Continue

Click on OK

SPSS will display 9 frequency tables corresponding to the 9 categorical variables of study

UNIT 6

ONE-SAMPLE TESTS AND CONFIDENCE INTERVALS

When the population variance σ^2 is known, the one-sample Z-test on the mean μ is used to test the null hypothesis that the true average of the observations constituting the population of study is equal to a hypothesised value μ_0 In cases where the population variance σ^2 is unknown, however, the one-sample t-test on the mean μ is used to test the null hypothesis that the true average of the observations constituting the population of study is equal to a hypothesised value μ_0. When the sample size of study is large ($n \geq 30$), the normal distribution and the Student's t-distribution become theoretically equivalent.

Suppose that the population variance σ^2 is unknown.

$H_0 : \mu = \mu_0$ (Null hypothesis)

$H_1 : \mu \neq \mu_0$ (Two-sided alternative hypothesis)

α = Level of significance of test

$$t_{cal} = \frac{\overline{X} - \mu_0}{S / \sqrt{n}} = \text{the calculated value of the Student's t-statistic}$$

$$t_{tab} = t_{1-\frac{\alpha}{2}}(n-1) = \text{the tabulated value of the t-statistic}$$

Decision rule

At the α level of significance,

Reject the null hypothesis if $|t_{cal}| > t_{tab}$ or if $P < \alpha$

Do not reject the null hypothesis if $|t_{cal}| \leq t_{tab}$ or if $P \geq \alpha$

Confidence interval for μ

A confidence interval for the true average μ is given by:

$\mu \in (\bar{x} - L, \bar{x} + L)$ where

$\bar{x} - L$= Lower confidence limit

$\bar{x} + L$= Upper confidence limit

$$L = t_{1-\frac{\alpha}{2}}(n-1) \times \frac{S}{\sqrt{n}} = \text{Margin of error}$$

Remark

The confidence interval for μ can be used to test the null hypothesis $H_0 : \mu = \mu_0$.

At the 5% level of significance, the null hypothesis $H_0 : \mu = \mu_0$ is accepted if the 95% confidence interval for μ contains μ_0.

The Student's t-table (two-tailed tabulated values)

Two-tailed tabulated values of the Student's t-statistic with degrees of freedom (df)

df	1.00	0.50	0.40	0.30	0.20	0.10	0.05	0.02	0.01	0.002	0.001
1	0.000	1.000	1.376	1.963	3.078	6.314	12.71	31.82	63.66	318.31	636.62
2	0.000	0.816	1.061	1.386	1.886	2.920	4.303	6.965	9.925	22.327	31.599
3	0.000	0.765	0.978	1.250	1.638	2.353	3.182	4.541	5.841	10.215	12.924
4	0.000	0.741	0.941	1.190	1.533	2.132	2.776	3.747	4.604	7.173	8.610
5	0.000	0.727	0.920	1.156	1.476	2.015	2.571	3.365	4.032	5.893	6.869
6	0.000	0.718	0.906	1.134	1.440	1.943	2.447	3.143	3.707	5.208	5.959
7	0.000	0.711	0.896	1.119	1.415	1.895	2.365	2.998	3.499	4.785	5.408
8	0.000	0.706	0.889	1.108	1.397	1.860	2.306	2.896	3.355	4.501	5.041
9	0.000	0.703	0.883	1.100	1.383	1.833	2.262	2.821	3.250	4.297	4.781
10	0.000	0.700	0.879	1.093	1.372	1.812	2.228	2.764	3.169	4.144	4.587
11	0.000	0.697	0.876	1.088	1.363	1.796	2.201	2.718	3.106	4.025	4.437
12	0.000	0.695	0.873	1.083	1.356	1.782	2.179	2.681	3.055	3.930	4.318
13	0.000	0.694	0.870	1.079	1.350	1.771	2.160	2.650	3.012	3.852	4.221
14	0.000	0.692	0.868	1.076	1.345	1.761	2.145	2.624	2.977	3.787	4.140
15	0.000	0.691	0.866	1.074	1.341	1.753	2.131	2.602	2.947	3.733	4.073
16	0.000	0.690	0.865	1.071	1.337	1.746	2.120	2.583	2.921	3.686	4.015
17	0.000	0.689	0.863	1.069	1.333	1.740	2.110	2.567	2.898	3.646	3.965
18	0.000	0.688	0.862	1.067	1.330	1.734	2.101	2.552	2.878	3.610	3.922
19	0.000	0.688	0.861	1.066	1.328	1.729	2.093	2.539	2.861	3.579	3.883
20	0.000	0.687	0.860	1.064	1.325	1.725	2.086	2.528	2.845	3.552	3.850

df	1.00	0.50	0.40	0.30	0.20	0.10	0.05	0.02	0.01	0.002	0.001
21	0.000	0.686	0.859	1.063	1.323	1.721	2.080	2.518	2.831	3.527	3.819
22	0.000	0.686	0.858	1.061	1.321	1.717	2.074	2.508	2.819	3.505	3.792
23	0.000	0.685	0.858	1.060	1.319	1.714	2.069	2.500	2.807	3.485	3.768
24	0.000	0.685	0.857	1.059	1.318	1.711	2.064	2.492	2.797	3.467	3.745
25	0.000	0.684	0.856	1.058	1.316	1.708	2.060	2.485	2.787	3.450	3.725
26	0.000	0.684	0.856	1.058	1.315	1.706	2.056	2.479	2.779	3.435	3.707
27	0.000	0.684	0.855	1.057	1.314	1.703	2.052	2.473	2.771	3.421	3.690
28	0.000	0.683	0.855	1.056	1.313	1.701	2.048	2.467	2.763	3.408	3.674
29	0.000	0.683	0.854	1.055	1.311	1.699	2.045	2.462	2.756	3.396	3.659
30	0.000	0.683	0.854	1.055	1.310	1.697	2.042	2.457	2.750	3.385	3.646
31	0.000	0.681	0.851	1.050	1.303	1.684	2.021	2.423	2.704	3.307	3.551
32	0.000	0.679	0.848	1.045	1.296	1.671	2.000	2.390	2.660	3.232	3.460
33	0.000	0.678	0.846	1.043	1.292	1.664	1.990	2.374	2.639	3.195	3.416
34	0.000	0.677	0.845	1.042	1.290	1.660	1.984	2.364	2.626	3.174	3.390
35	0.000	0.675	0.842	1.037	1.282	1.646	1.962	2.330	2.581	3.098	3.300

Example:

Let n = 15. Thus, n –1 = 14.

Let $\alpha = 5\% = 0.05$ = level of significance

$$t_{tab} = t_{1-\frac{\alpha}{2}}(n-1)$$

$t_{0.975}(14) = 2.145$ (two-tailed tabulated value of the t-statistic)

Example 1:

A drug was tested on 15 cats, and the variation in the rate of heartbeat of each cat was measured as follows. A positive reading indicates an increase in the rate of heartbeat while a negative reading indicates a decrease in the rate of heartbeat.

–4, –8, +2, –1, –5, –9, –8, –6, –3, –7, +1, +2, –2, –3, +3

a) At the 5% level of significance, test the null hypothesis that $\mu = -4$ against the alternative hypothesis that $\mu \neq -4$.

b) Construct a 95% confidence interval for the true average heartbeat μ

Solution:

a) n $= 15 =$ sample size of study

$\bar{x} = -3.2 =$ sample mean

$S^2 = 15.88 =$ sample variance

S $= 3.99 =$ sample standard deviation

$\mu_0 = -4 =$ hypothesized value of mean

$$t_{cal} = \frac{\bar{X} - \mu_0}{S/\sqrt{n}} = 0.78 = \text{the calculated value of the t-statistic}$$

$$t_{tab} = t_{1-\frac{\alpha}{2}}(n-1) = t_{0.975}(14) = 2.145$$

Now, since $0.78 < 2.145$, the null hypothesis cannot be rejected at the 5% level of significance. We conclude that the true average variation in the rate of heartbeat is –4, an average decrease of 4 units.

b) $1-\alpha = 95\% =$ confidence coefficient

$\alpha = 5\% = 0.05 =$ level of significance

$$L = t_{1-\frac{\alpha}{2}}(n-1) \times \frac{S}{\sqrt{n}} = t_{0.975}(14) \times \frac{3.99}{\sqrt{15}} = 2.145(1.031)$$

$= 2.21 =$ Margin of error

$\bar{x} - L = -3.2 - 2.21 = -5.41 =$ Lower confidence limit

$\bar{x} + L = -3.2 + 2.21 = -0.99 =$ Upper confidence limit

$\mu \in (\bar{x} - L, \bar{x} + L) = (-5.41, -0.99) =$ *95% confidence interval for* μ

Note that the 95% confidence interval for μ contains –4.

Thus, the null hypothesis cannot be rejected at the 5% level.

A STATA printout of the above result is shown below:

```
. use c:\bos\onet.dta, clear

. ttest  heartbeat=-4, level(95)

One-sample t test
------------------------------------------------------------------------------
Variable |     Obs        Mean    Std. Err.   Std. Dev.   [95% Conf. Interval]
---------+--------------------------------------------------------------------
heartb~t |      15        -3.2      1.0291    3.985689   -5.407201   -.9927992
------------------------------------------------------------------------------
Degrees of freedom: 14

                         Ho: mean(heartbeat) = -4

     Ha: mean < -4           Ha: mean != -4            Ha: mean > -4
       t =   0.7774            t =   0.7774              t =   0.7774
   P < t =   0.7751      P > |t| =   0.4499          P > t =   0.2249
```

P = 0.4499

$\alpha = 0.05$

Since P > 0.05, the null hypothesis cannot be rejected at the 5% level. That is, we do not have enough reason to doubt the accuracy of the null hypothesis.

The calculated value of the t-statistic is equal to 0.7774.

The degrees of freedom of the t-statistic are equal to n – 1 = 15 – 1 = 14.

The tabulated value of the t-statistic is read from the Student's t-table with a level of significance of 0.05 and 14 degrees of freedom as 2.145.

Since 0.7774 is less than 2.145, the null hypothesis cannot be rejected at the 5% level. That is, we do not have enough reason to doubt the accuracy of the null hypothesis. We conclude that the true average value is equal to –4 at the 5% level.

The 95% confidence interval for the true mean is given by (–5.41, –0.99). Note that this 95% confidence interval contains –4. Thus, the null hypothesis $\mu_0 = -4$ cannot be rejected at the 5% level of significance.

How to perform the one-sample t-test in SPSS

Open up the SPSS data set c:\bos\onet.sav

Click on Analyze

Click on Compare means

Click on One-sample t-test

Select the variable heartbeat by clicking on the selection bar

Test value? –4

Click on OK

SPSS will produce the following computer printout:

One-Sample Test							
	Test Value = –4						
			Significance			95% Confidence Interval of the Difference	
	t	df	One-Sided p	Two-Sided p	Mean Difference	Lower	Upper
Heartbeat	0.777	14	0.225	0.450	0.800	–1.41	3.01

The 95% confidence interval for the true mean is given by (–5.41, –0.99). Note that this 95% confidence interval contains –4. Thus, the null hypothesis $\mu_0 = -4$ cannot be rejected at the 5% level of significance.

A 95% confidence interval for the true mean is given by:

$\mu \in$ (Hypothesised value of mean + "lower", Hypothesised value of mean + "upper")

$$\mu \in (-4 + \text{"lower"},\ -4 + \text{"upper"})$$

$$= (-4 + (-1.41),\ -4 + (3.01))$$

$$= (-5.41,\ -0.99)$$

Examples in STATA and SPSS

Exercises 1 and 2 are to be solved using the data sets **data1.dta** and **data1.sav** in STATA and SPSS respectively. The data set contains the weights of a random sample of size 100 people chosen for a survey in kilograms.

Exercise 1

1) The STATA data set **data1.dta** contains a variable called **weight** in kg. Obtain all measures of location and variation for the weight variable.
2) Test the null hypothesis $H_0 : \mu = 65$ kg at the 5% level of significance by using the one-sample t-test.
3) Obtain a 95% confidence interval for the true average μ by using the one-sample t-test.
4) Repeat (1), (2) and (3) in SPSS using the data set **data1.sav**.

Solutions in STATA and SPSS

Steps to be followed in STATA to obtain detailed summary statistics

Go to STATA and open up the STATA data set c:\bos\data1.dta

Click on Statistics

Click on Summaries, tables and tests

Click on Summary and descriptive statistics

Click on Summary statistics

Variable? Select the variable *weight* by using the selection bar

Click on Display additional statistics

Click on OK

STATA will produce the following printout:

```
. use c:\bos\data1.dta, clear
. su weight, detail

                          weight
. su weight, detail

                        weight in kg
-------------------------------------------------------------
      Percentiles      Smallest
 1%        36.5             33
 5%          44             40
10%          47             40       Obs                 100
25%          52             41       Sum of wgt.         100

50%          61                      Mean              63.98
                        Largest      Std. dev.      14.14926
75%          76             91
90%          82             91       Variance       200.2016
95%          88             91       Skewness       .1745792
99%          91             91       Kurtosis        2.10218
```

Steps to be followed in STATA to perform the one-sample t-test

Go to the main menu of STATA

Open the STATA data file c:\bos\data1.dta

Click on Statistics

Click on summaries, tables, and tests

Click on classical tests of hypotheses

Click on t-test (mean comparison tests)

Click on One-sample test

Variable name? Select the variable weight from the list of variables

Hypothesised value of mean? 65

Confidence level? 95 (default value)

Click on OK

STATA will produce the following printout:

```
. use c:\bos\data1.dta, clear
. ttest weight=65, level(95)

One-sample t test
------------------------------------------------------------------------------
Variable |     Obs        Mean    Std. err.   Std. dev.   [95% conf. interval]
---------+--------------------------------------------------------------------
  weight |     100       63.98    1.414926    14.14926    61.17248    66.78752
------------------------------------------------------------------------------
    mean = mean(weight)                                           t =   6.3466
H0: mean = 55                                    Degrees of freedom =       99

    Ha: mean < 55               Ha: mean != 55                Ha: mean > 55
 Pr(T < t) = 1.0000         Pr(|T| > |t|) = 0.0000          Pr(T > t) = 0.0000
```

A 95% confidence interval for the true average weight is given by:

$\mu \in (61.17, \quad 66.79)$ kg

Note that the 95% confidence interval for μ contains 65 (the hypothesised value of the mean). Thus, the null hypothesis $H_0 : \mu = 65$ kg cannot be rejected at the 5% level of significance.

Results from SPSS

Enter SPSS

Open up the SPSS data set c:\bos\data1.sav

Click on Analyze

Click on Descriptive Statistics

Click on Explore

Select the variable weight

Click on Statistics, Mean estimators, Outliers, Percentiles

Click on Plots, Normal plots with tests, histogram

Click on OK

The following results are obtained from SPSS

Explore

Descriptives

			Statistic	Std. Error
Weight in kg	Mean		63.98	1.415
	95% Confidence Interval for Mean	Lower Bound	61.17	
		Upper Bound	66.79	
	5% Trimmed Mean		63.87	
	Median		61.00	
	Variance		200.202	
	Std. Deviation		14.149	
	Minimum		33	
	Maximum		91	
	Range		58	
	Interquartile Range (IQR)		24	
	Skewness		0.177	0.241
	Kurtosis		–0.882	0.478

Percentiles

	Percentiles						
	5	10	25	50	75	90	95
Weighted Average	44.00	47.00	52.00	61.00	76.00	82.00	88.00

The Kolmogorov-Smirnov and Shapiro-Wilk tests of normality

Tests of Normality

	Kolmogorov-Smirnova			Shapiro-Wilk		
	Statistic	df	P-value	Statistic	df	P-value
Weight in kg	0.096	100	0.025	0.969	100	0.019

a. Lilliefors Significance Correction

Null hypothesis: The 100 observations in the data set are distributed normally with mean 0 and constant variance

Alternative hypothesis: The 100 observations in the data set are not distributed normally with mean 0 and constant variance

Decision rule:

At the 5% level of significance,

Reject the null hypothesis if $P < 0.05$.

Do not reject the null hypothesis if P is greater than or equal to 0.05.

The P-value is equal to 0.025 < 0.05. Hence, the null hypothesis can be rejected at the 5% level of significance. We conclude that the distribution is not normal.

A stem-and-leaf plot from SPSS

```
Weight in kg Stem-and-Leaf Plot

 Frequency    Stem &  Leaf

     1,00        3 .  3
      ,00        3 .
     6,00        4 .  001444
    14,00        4 .  57777889999999
     8,00        5 .  12222244
    14,00        5 .  66678888899999
    12,00        6 .  000001112224
    10,00        6 .  5677777789
     7,00        7 .  1122344
    12,00        7 .  556678889999
     7,00        8 .  0122222
     5,00        8 .  58888
     4,00        9 .  1111

 Stem width:       10
 Each leaf:       1 case(s)
```

A histogram from SPSS is shown below:

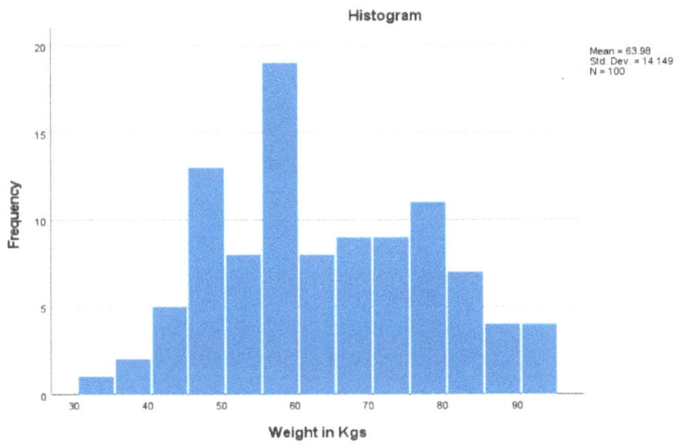

A box plot from SPSS is shown below:

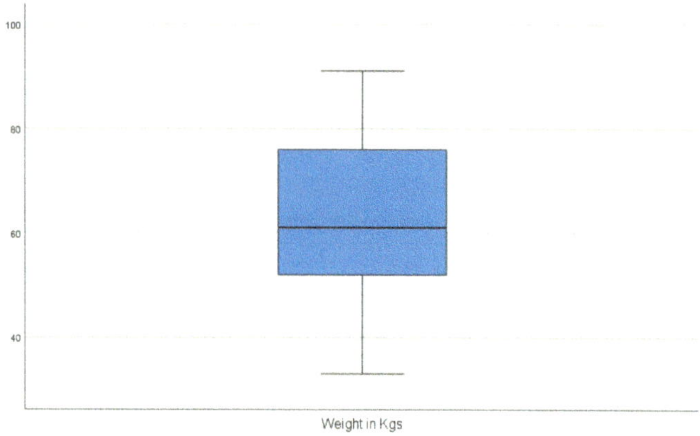

Interpretation of box plot

The bottom of the box plot represents the minimum observation (32.87).

The lower end of the inner box denotes the first quartile (Q1 = 47.67).

The solid line in the middle of the inner box denotes the median or second quartile (Q2 = 54.78).

The upper end of the inner box denotes the third quartile (Q3 = 62.12).

The inter-quartile range is given by: IQR = Q3 – Q1 = 62.12 – 47.67 = 14.45.

The top of the box plot represents the maximum observation (78.23).

The one-sample test in SPSS

Open up the SPSS data set c:\bos\data1.sav

Click on Analyze

Click on Compare means

Click on one-sample t-test

Select the weight variable

Test value? Type 65

Click on OK

SPSS will give the following result:

One-Sample Test							
	Test Value = 65						
			Significance			95% Confidence Interval of the Difference	
	t	df	One-Sided p	Two-Sided p	Mean Difference	Lower	Upper
Weight in kg	–0.721	99	0.236	0.473	–1.020	–3.83	1.79

H0: $\mu = 65$ (Null hypothesis)

H1: $\mu \neq 65$ (Alternative hypothesis)

$\alpha = 0.05$ = Level of significance of test

$P = 0.473 > 0.05$

Since $P > \alpha = 0.05$, the null hypothesis cannot be rejected at the 5% level of significance.

A 95% confidence interval for the true mean is given by:

$$\mu \in (65 + \text{“lower”},\quad 65 + \text{“upper”})$$

$$= (65 + (-3.83),\quad 65 + (1.79))$$

$$= (65 - 3.83,\quad 65 + 1.79)$$

$$= (61.17,\quad 66.79)$$

UNIT 7

TWO-SAMPLE T-TESTS AND CONFIDENCE INTERVALS

The two-sample unpaired t-test is used to compare two independent or unpairedgroups with each other. Before comparing means, it is necessary to compare the variances of the populations from which the samples are drawn. In cases where the population variances differ significantly, comparison of means does not help much.

$H_0 : \mu_1 = \mu_2$ (null hypothesis)

$H_1 : \mu_1 \neq \mu_2$ (a two-sided alternative hypothesis)

Decision rule:

1) Reject H_0 if $p < \alpha$
2) Do not reject H_0 if $p \geq \alpha$

Where α is the level of significance of test. In most studies, the value of α is fixed at the 0.05 level of significance.

Alternative decision rule:

1) Reject H_0 if $|t_{cal}| > t_{tab}$
2) Do not reject H_0 if $|t_{cal}| \leq t_{tab}$ where

$$t_{cal} = \frac{\overline{X}_1 - \overline{X}_2}{S_P\sqrt{\frac{1}{n_1} + \frac{1}{n_2}}} = \text{the calculated value of the t-statistic where}$$

$$S^2{}_P = \frac{(n_1 - 1)S_1{}^2 + (n_2 - 1)S_2{}^2}{n_1 + n_2 - 2} = \text{pooled error variance}$$

S_p = pooled error standard deviation

$t_{tab} = t_{1-\frac{\alpha}{2}}(n_1 + n_2 - 2)$ = the tabulated value of the t-statistic for a two-sided alternative hypothesis

A 100(1-α)% confidence interval for $\mu_1 - \mu_2$ is given as follows:

$\mu_1 - \mu_2 \in [(\bar{X}_1 - \bar{X}_2) - L, (\bar{X}_1 - \bar{X}_2) + L$ where

$$L = t_{1-\frac{\alpha}{2}}(n_1 + n_2 - 2) \times S_P \times \sqrt{\frac{1}{n_1} + \frac{1}{n_2}} = \text{margin of error}$$

Assumptions:

1) $X_{1_1}, \ldots\ldots, X_{1n_1}$ is a random sample drawn from a parent population distributed normally with mean μ_1 and variance σ_1^2
2) $X_{2_1}, \ldots\ldots, X_{2n_2}$ is a random sample drawn from a parent population distributed normally with mean μ_2 and variance σ_2^2
3) Samples 1 and 2 are independent of each other
4) The equality of the population variances must be tested before the equality of the population means is tested. Most statistical packages give two sets of results (the first on the basis of equal variances, and the second on the basis of unequal variances).

Levene's test for the equality of variances is used to compare populations 1 and 2 with respect to cost.

$H_0 : \sigma_1^2 = \sigma_2^2$ (Null hypothesis) (Assumption of equal variances)

$H_1 : \sigma_1^2 \neq \sigma_2^2$ (Two-sided alternative hypothesis) (Assumption of unequal variances)

Decision rule:

1) Reject H_0 if $p < \alpha$
2) Do not reject H_0 if $p \geq \alpha$

Rejecting the null hypothesis indicates that the two populations being compared are significantly different from each other with respect to the variable of comparison. In this case, the unequal variances assumption must be made.

Failing to reject the null hypothesis indicates that the two populations being compared are similar to each other with respect to the variable of comparison. In this case, the equal variances assumption must be made.

Example in STATA

The STATA data file **c:\bos\bos1.dta** contains data on 181 respondents and 30 variables. The variable *sickness* (1 if yes, 0 otherwise) denotes the presence or absence of sickness. The variable *age* gives the age of each participant in the study. Use the two-sample unpaired t-test to compare the ages of healthy and sick respondents in the study. Before comparing means, compare variances. Assume that sick and healthy respondents are independent of each other.

How to perform the two-sample unpaired t-test in STATA

Comparison of variances of two independent groups

Go to the main menu of STATA

Open the STATA data file c:\bos\bos1.dta

Click on Statistics

Click on summaries, tables, and tests

Click on classical tests of hypotheses

Click on variance comparison test

Click on Two samples using groups

Variable name? Select the variable *age* from the list of variables

Group variable name? Select the variable *sickness* from the list of variables

Confidence level? 95 (default value)

Click on OK

```
. use c:\bos\bos1.dta, clear

. sdtest  age, by(sickness)  level(95)

Variance ratio test
------------------------------------------------------------------------------
   Group |     Obs        Mean    Std. Err.   Std. Dev.   [95% Conf. Interval]
---------+--------------------------------------------------------------------
       0 |     140    41.45714    .7560901    8.946179    39.96222    42.95207
       1 |      41    40.26829    1.363292    8.729331    37.51298    43.02361
---------+--------------------------------------------------------------------
combined |     181    41.18785    .6605988    8.887448    39.88433    42.49136
------------------------------------------------------------------------------
    ratio = sd(0) / sd(1)                                         f =   1.0503
Ho: ratio = 1                                    degrees of freedom =  139, 40

    Ha: ratio < 1               Ha: ratio != 1                 Ha: ratio > 1
  Pr(F < f) = 0.5576         2*Pr(F > f) = 0.8847           Pr(F > f) = 0.4424
```

Bartlett's test for the equality of variances

H0: The two variances are equal

H1: The two variances are not equal

Since the P-value is 0.8847 > 0.05, the null hypothesis cannot be rejected at the 5% level. We conclude that the two populations being compared are similar with regard to variable age.

Remark: Since the variances of the two groups are equal, comparison of averages of the 2 groups becomes appropriate.

Comparison of the average ages of sick and healthy respondents

Comparison of averages of two independent (unpaired) groups

Go to the main menu of STATA

Open the STATA data file c:\bos\bos1.dta

Click on Statistics

Click on summaries, tables, and tests

Click on classical tests of hypotheses

Click on t-test (mean comparison test)

Click on Two samples using groups

Variable name? Select the variable *age* from the list of variables

Group variable name? Select the variable *sickness* from the list of variables

Confidence level? 95 (default value)

Click on OK

```
. use c:\bos\bos1.dta, clear

. ttest  age, by(sickness)  level(95)

Two-sample t test with equal variances
------------------------------------------------------------------------------
   Group |     Obs        Mean    Std. Err.   Std. Dev.   [95% Conf. Interval]
---------+--------------------------------------------------------------------
       0 |     140    41.45714    .7560901    8.946179    39.96222    42.95207
       1 |      41    40.26829    1.363292    8.729331    37.51298    43.02361
---------+--------------------------------------------------------------------
combined |     181    41.18785    .6605988    8.887448    39.88433    42.49136
---------+--------------------------------------------------------------------
    diff |            1.18885      1.5801                -1.929169     4.30687
------------------------------------------------------------------------------
    diff = mean(0) - mean(1)                                      t =   0.7524
Ho: diff = 0                                     degrees of freedom =      179

    Ha: diff < 0                 Ha: diff != 0                 Ha: diff > 0
 Pr(T < t) = 0.7736         Pr(|T| > |t|) = 0.4528          Pr(T > t) = 0.2264
```

H0: The two means are equal

H1: The two means are not equal

Since the P-value is 0.4528 > 0.05, the null hypothesis cannot be rejected at the 5% level. We conclude that the mean ages of sick respondents (sickness = 1) and healthy respondents (sickness = 2) are equal.

A 95% confidence interval for the true difference between mean ages is given by:

$$\mu_1 - \mu_2 \in (-1.929, \quad 4.307)$$

Since the 95% confidence interval shown above contains 0, the two mean ages are equal.

Solution from SPSS

Open up the SPSS data set c:\bos\bos1.sav

Click on Analyze

Compare means

Independent samples t-test

Test variable? Select the variable *age* by clicking on the selection bar

Grouping variable? Select the variable *sickness* by clicking on the selection bar

Define groups?

Group 1 is represented by 1 (Group 1 has 140 people)

Group 2 is represented by 0 (Group 2 has 41 people)

Click on OK

A computer printout obtained from SPSS is shown below:

T-Test (the two-sample independent or unpaired samples t-test)

Group Statistics					
	Sickness	N	Mean	Std. Deviation	Std. Error Mean
age	1	140	41.4571	8.94618	0.75609
	0	41	40.2683	8.72933	1.36329

		Levene's Test for Equality of Variances									
						Significance				95% Confidence Interval of the Difference	
		F	P	t	df	One-Sided P	Two-Sided P	Mean Difference	Std. Difference	Lower	Upper
age	Equal variances assumed	0.423	0.516	0.752	179	0.226	0.453	1.19	1.58	-1.93	4.31
	Equal variances not assumed			0.763	66.579	0.224	0.448	1.19	1.56	-1.91	4.30

Levene's test for the equality of variances

H0: The two variances are equal

H1: The two variances are not equal

Since the P-value is 0.516 > 0.05, the null hypothesis cannot be rejected at the 5% level. We conclude that the two populations have equal variances. That is, the two parent populations are similar with regard to the distribution of age.

SPSS gives 2 sets of results. Since the variances are shown to be equal, we should take the first set of results corresponding to "**Equal variances assumed**". The two-sided probability value for the comparison of means is equal to P=0.453. Since 0.453 > 0.05, the null hypothesis cannot be rejected at the 5% level. We conclude that the two means are equal at the 5% level.

H0: The two means are equal

H1: The two means are not equal

Since the P-value is 0.453 > 0.05, the null hypothesis cannot be rejected at the 5% level. We conclude that the mean ages of sick respondents (sickness = 1) and healthy respondents (sickness = 2) are equal. From the above SPSS output, it can be seen that a 95% confidence interval for the true difference between mean ages is given by:

$$\mu_1 - \mu_2 \in (-1.93, \quad 4.31)$$

Since the 95% confidence interval shown above contains 0, the two mean ages are equal.

The two-sample paired t-test

The two-sample paired t-test is used to compare two related or paired samples. A typical application of the two-sample paired t-test is when readings are taken before and after on the same group of patients.

$H_0 : \mu_D = 0$ (Null hypothesis)

$H_1 : \mu_D = 0$ (Alternative hypothesis)

$$t_{cal} = \frac{\bar{d} - \mu_d}{S_d / \sqrt{n}}$$ = the calculated value of the t-statistic

$$t_{tab} = t_{1-\frac{\alpha}{2}}(n-1)$$ = the tabulated value of the t-statistic

where

$d_i = X_i - Y_i$; i=1, ….., n

$$\bar{d} = \frac{\sum_{i=1}^{n} d_i}{n}$$ = sample mean of the d_i

$$S^2{}_d = \frac{\sum_{i=1}^{n} (d_i - \bar{d})^2}{n-1}$$ = sample variance of the d_i

S_d= sample standard deviation of the d_i

Decision rule:

Reject H_0 if $P < \alpha$

Do not reject H_0 if $P \geq \alpha$

Alternative decision rule

Reject H_0 if $|t_{cal}| > t_{tab}$

Do not reject H_0if $|t_{cal}| \leq t_{tab}$

A (1-α)100% confidence interval for the true average difference μ_d is given by:

$\mu_d \in (\bar{d} - L, \quad \bar{d} + L)$ where

$\bar{d}$ is the sample average difference

$$L = t_{1-\frac{\alpha}{2}}(n-1) \times \frac{S_d}{\sqrt{n}}$$ = margin of error

Example:

Ten army officers were given an intensive physical training, and the time in minutes taken by each officer to complete the exercise was recorded before (X) and after (Y) the training, as shown below:

	1	2	3	4	5	6	7	8	9	10
X	127	195	162	170	143	205	168	175	197	139
Y	135	200	160	182	147	200	172	186	194	140
X–Y	–8	–5	2	–12	–4	5	–4	–11	3	–1

At the 5% level of significance, test whether the training programme has significantly helped the trainees.

Solution:

$H_0 : \mu_D = 0$ (Null hypothesis)

$H_1 : \mu_D \neq 0$ (Alternative hypothesis)

n = 10 = number of paired observations

n – 1 = 9 = degrees of freedom

α = 5% = level of significance of test

$\bar{d} = -3.9$ = average difference

S_d = 5.74 = standard deviation of average differences

t_{cal} = –2.13 = the calculated value of the t-statistic

$t_{0'975}(9)$ = 2.262= the tabulated value of the t-statistic

Since 2.13 < 2.262, the null hypothesis cannot be rejected at the 5% level of significance. We conclude that the training programme has not helped the trainees.

The above exercise can be solved in **STATA** as follows:

Steps to perform the paired samples t-test in STATA

Open the STATA data file c:\bos\paired.dta

Click on Statistics, summaries, tables, and tests

Click on classical tests of hypotheses

Click on mean comparison test, paired data

First variable? Select the variable *before* from the list of variables

Second variable? Select the variable *after* from the list of variables

Confidence level? 95

Click on OK

STATA will produce the following printout:

```
. use c:\bos\paired.dta, clear

. ttest  before=after, level(95)

Paired t test
------------------------------------------------------------------------------
Variable |     Obs        Mean    Std. Err.   Std. Dev.   [95% Conf. Interval]
---------+--------------------------------------------------------------------
  before |      10       168.1    8.283115    26.19351    149.3623    186.8377
   after |      10       171.6    7.823327    24.73953    153.9024    189.2976
---------+--------------------------------------------------------------------
    diff |      10        -3.5    1.833333    5.797509   -7.647288    .6472881
------------------------------------------------------------------------------
     mean(diff) = mean(before - after)                            t =  -1.9091
 Ho: mean(diff) = 0                              degrees of freedom =        9

 Ha: mean(diff) < 0           Ha: mean(diff) != 0           Ha: mean(diff) > 0
 Pr(T < t) = 0.0443         Pr(|T| > |t|) = 0.0886          Pr(T > t) = 0.9557
```

P = 0.0886 > 0.05. Hence, the null hypothesis cannot be rejected at the 5% level of significance. We conclude that there is no significant decrease in the average length of time required by the trainees to complete their physical exercise.

A 95% confidence interval for the true average difference is given by:

$\mu_D \in (-7.65,\ 0.65)$. Note that this confidence interval contains 0.

Solution from SPSS

Open up the SPSS data set c:\bos\bos1.sav

Click on Analyze

Compare means

Independent samples t-test

Test variable? Select the variable *age* by clicking on the selection bar

Grouping variable? Select the variable *sickness* by clicking on the selection bar

Define groups?

Group 1 is represented by 1 (Group 1 has 140 people)

Group 2 is represented by 0 (Group 2 has 41 people)

Click on OK

A computer printout obtained from SPSS is shown below:

Paired Samples Statistics					
		Mean	**N**	**Std. Deviation**	**Std. Error Mean**
Pair 1	before	168.10	10	26.194	8.283
	after	171.60	10	24.740	7.823

Paired Samples Test									
	Paired Differences							**Significance**	
				95% Confidence Interval of the Difference					
	Mean	**Std. Dev**	**Std. Err**	**Lower**	**Upper**	**t**	**df**	**One-Sided p**	**Two-Sided p**
Pair 1: before - after	–3.5	5.79	1.83	–7.65	0.65	–1.91	9	0.044	0.089

UNIT 8

TESTS ON PROPORTIONS

Test of Hypothesis on a Single Proportion $H_0: P = P_0$

Suppose that $X_1, \ldots, X_n$ constitute a random sample of n observations drawn from a normal parent population. The sampling distribution of the sample proportion $\hat{p}$ is similar to the sampling distribution of the sample mean $\bar{X}$ where the sample mean and sample proportion are given by:

$$\bar{X} = \frac{\sum_{i=1}^{n} X_i}{n} = \text{the sample mean or average}$$

$$\hat{p} = \frac{\sum_{i=1}^{n} X_i}{n} \quad \text{where} \quad X_i = \begin{cases} 1 & \text{if attribute exists} \\ 0 & \text{otherwise} \end{cases}$$

To perform a test of hypothesis on the proportion P, the following null and alternative hypotheses are used:

$H_0 : P = P_0$ (Null hypothesis)

$H_1 : P \neq P_0$ (Two-sided alternative hypothesis)

Decision rule:

1) Reject H_0 if $p < \alpha$
2) Do not reject H_0 if $p \geq \alpha$

Alternative decision rule:

3) Reject H_0 if $|Z_{cal}| > Z_{1-\frac{\alpha}{2}}$

4) Do not reject H_0 if $|Z_{cal}| \leq Z_{1-\frac{\alpha}{2}}$ where

$$Z_{cal} = \frac{\hat{p} - P_0}{\sqrt{\frac{\hat{p}(1-\hat{p})}{n}}} \sim Z_{1-\frac{\alpha}{2}}$$

where P_0 is the hypothesized value of P.

Confidence Interval for a Single Proportion P

A $(1-\alpha)100\%$ confidence interval for the true proportion P is given by:

$$P \in \left(\hat{p} \pm Z_{1-\frac{\alpha}{2}} \sqrt{\frac{\hat{p}(1-\hat{p})}{n}} \right)$$

Example:

A home-based care facility contains 100 HIV-positive patients. At the facility, CD4+ cell counts are done regularly. A patient is said to be seriously sick if the CD4 cell count falls below 500.

CD4 cell counts at the facility are shown below:

482, 464, 444, 585, 652, 648, 547, 533, 547, 549,

660, 459, 352, 449, 549, 662, 791, 888, 771, 948,

362, 461, 476, 544, 667, 775, 882, 791, 788, 678,

572, 674, 540, 559, 552, 678, 859, 960, 867, 769,

360, 451, 445, 558, 467, 658, 679, 856, 849, 768,

361, 354, 458, 554, 667, 666, 677, 679, 756, 772,

560, 541, 612, 149, 349, 262, 291, 388, 371, 667,

382, 361, 476, 444, 467, 675, 782, 791, 888, 881,

682, 674, 640, 659, 852, 878, 859, 860, 867, 879,

880, 757, 685, 758, 747, 758, 679, 656, 749, 473

At the 5% level of significance, would it be correct to assume that the true average proportion of seriously sick patients at Facility 1 is equal to 50%?

Solution:

The hypothesised value of P is 50% = 0.50. The number of patients with CD4+ counts less than 500 at Facility 1 is equal to 28 out of 100. Hence, the proportion of patients that are seriously sick at Facility 1 is 28% = 0.28. The calculated value of Z is given by:

$$Z_{cal} = \frac{\hat{p}-0.50}{\sqrt{\frac{\hat{p}(1-\hat{p})}{n}}} \quad \frac{0.28-0.50}{\sqrt{\frac{0.28(0.72)}{100}}} = \frac{-0.22}{0.0449} = -4.9$$

At the 5% level of significance, $Z_{tab} = Z_{1-\frac{\alpha}{2}} = Z_{0.975} = 1.96$

Since $|Z_{cal}| = |-4.9| = 4.9 > 1.96$, the null hypothesis H0: P = 0.50 can be rejected at the 5% level of significance. Hence, it is not correct to assume that the true average proportion of seriously sick patients at Facility 1 is 50%. A 95% confidence interval for the true proportion of seriously sick patients at Facility 1 is given by:

$$P \in \left(\hat{p} \pm Z_{1-\frac{\alpha}{2}} \sqrt{\frac{\hat{p}(1-\hat{p})}{n}} \right) = (0.19, \quad 0.37) = (19\%, \quad 37\%)$$

Note that the above 95% confidence interval for P does not contain 50%.

Solution in STATA

Capture your data in STATA. Use the variable name **cd4**. Save your data file as **c:\bos\p1.dta**.

```
. use c:\bos\p1.dta, clear

. generate sick=.
(200 missing values generated)

. replace sick=1 if cd4 < 500
(70 real changes made)

. replace sick=0 if cd4 >= 500
(130 real changes made)

. save c:\bos\p1.dta, replace

. prtest sick=0.50, level(95)

One-sample test of proportion                    Number of obs      =        100

------------------------------------------------------------------------------
    Variable |       Mean   Std. err.                     [95% conf. interval]
-------------+----------------------------------------------------------------
        sick |        .28   .0448999                      .1919978    .3680022
------------------------------------------------------------------------------
    p = proportion(sick)                                          z =  -4.4000
H0: p = 0.5

     Ha: p < 0.5                 Ha: p != 0.5                 Ha: p > 0.5
 Pr(Z < z) = 0.0000         Pr(|Z| > |z|) = 0.0000          Pr(Z > z) = 1.0000
```

Since P = 0.0000 < 0.05, the null hypothesis can be rejected at the 5% level. The 95% confidence interval for the true average proportion of seriously sick patients at Facility 1 is given by $P \in (0.19, 0.37)$. Note that this 95% confidence interval does not contain 50%.

How to perform a test on a single proportion in STATA

Go to the main menu of STATA

Open the STATA data file c:\bos\p1.dta

Click on Statistics

Click on summaries, tables, and tests

Click on Classical tests of hypothesis

Click on proportion test

Click on One-sample test

Variables? Select variable *sick* from the list of variables

Hypothesized mean? 0.50

Click on OK

Solution from SPSS

Open up the SPSS data set c:\bos\p1.sav

Click on Analyze

Click on Compare means

Click on One sample proportions test

Test variable? Select the variable *sickness* by clicking on the selection bar

Click on Define success

Value of success? 1

Click on OK

A computer printout obtained from SPSS is shown below:

One-Sample Proportions Confidence Intervals							
	Interval Type	Observed			Asymptotic Standard Error	95% Confidence Interval	
		Successes	Trials	Proportion		Lower	Upper
sick = 1	Agresti-Coull	28	100	0.280	0.045	0.201	0.375
	Jeffreys	**28**	**100**	**0.280**	**0.045**	**0.199**	**0.373**
	Wilson Score	28	100	0.280	0.045	0.201	0.375

Observed			Observed Test Value*	Asymptotic Standard Error	Z	Significance	
Successes	Trials	Proportion				One-Sided p	Two-Sided p
28	100	0.280	–0.220	0.045	–4.4	<.001	<.001

* Test value = 0.5

Test of Hypothesis on Two Proportions

$H_0 : P_1 = P_2$ (Null hypothesis)

$H_1 : P_1 \neq P_2$ (Two-sided alternative hypothesis)

Decision rule:

1) Reject H_0 if $p < \alpha$
2) Do not reject H_0 if $p \geq \alpha$

Alternative decision rule:

1) Reject H_0 if $| Z_{cal} | > Z_{1-\frac{\alpha}{2}}$

2) Do not reject H_0 if $| Z_{cal} | \leq Z_{1-\frac{\alpha}{2}}$ where

$$Z_{cal} = \frac{\hat{p}_1 - \hat{p}_2}{\sqrt{\frac{\hat{p}_1(1-\hat{p}_1)}{n_1} + \frac{\hat{p}_2(1-\hat{p}_2)}{n_2}}} \sim Z_{1-\frac{\alpha}{2}}$$

A $(1-\alpha)100\%$ confidence interval for the difference between the true proportions of the two groups of mothers is given by:

$$P_1 - P_2 \in \left((\hat{p}_1 - \hat{p}_2) \pm Z_{1-\frac{\alpha}{2}} \sqrt{\frac{\hat{p}_1(1-\hat{p}_1)}{n_1} + \frac{\hat{p}_2(1-\hat{p}_2)}{n_2}} \right)$$

The width of the above confidence interval is equal to the distance between the lower confidence limit and the upper confidence limit (or twice the length from the center of the confidence interval to the upper confidence limit), and is given by:

$$W = 2 \times Z_{1-\frac{\alpha}{2}} \sqrt{\frac{\hat{p}_1(1-\hat{p}_1)}{n_1} + \frac{\hat{p}_2(1-\hat{p}_2)}{n_2}}$$

W denotes the effect size. The effect size is a measure of the difference between P_1 and P_2.

Example:

Two home-based care facilities contain 100 HIVpositive patients. At each facility, CD4 cell counts are done regularly. A patient is said to be seriously sick if the CD4 cell count falls below 500. The raw data set c:\bos\p2.dta shows raw data for Facilities 1 and 2, CD4+ counts and an indicator of serious sickness. It is desired to find out if Facilities 1 and 2 provide home based care to the same percentage of seriously sick patients at the 5% level of significance. To do so, one needs to use **the two-sample test on proportions**.

CD4 cell counts at Facility 1

482, 464, 444, 585, 652, 648, 547, 533, 547, 549,

660, 459, 352, 449, 549, 662, 791, 888, 771, 948,

362, 461, 476, 544, 667, 775, 882, 791, 788, 678,

572, 674, 540, 559, 552, 678, 859, 960, 867, 769,

360, 451, 445, 558, 467, 658, 679, 856, 849, 768,

361, 354, 458, 554, 667 666, 677, 679, 756, 772,

560, 541, 612, 149, 349, 262, 291, 388, 371, 667,

382, 361, 476, 444, 467, 675, 782, 791, 888, 881,

682, 674, 640, 659, 852, 878, 859, 860, 867, 879,

880, 757, 685, 758, 747, 758, 679, 656, 749, 473

CD4 cell counts at Facility 2

582, 564, 744, 855, 352, 666, 809, 452, 673, 347,

460, 659, 352, 449, 549, 662, 791, 888, 771, 848,

562, 561, 476, 555, 367, 751, 382, 491, 488, 708,

672, 474, 540, 559, 552, 678, 859, 960, 867, 267,

460, 351, 445, 558, 467, 658, 679, 856, 849, 467,

561, 554, 458, 554, 411, 469, 567, 379, 656, 863,

460, 441, 612, 149, 349, 362, 468, 479, 371, 458,

482, 461, 476, 444, 467, 675, 782, 791, 888, 881,

444, 574, 640, 659, 852, 878, 859, 860, 867, 879,

309, 623, 611, 803, 444, 459, 379, 356, 709, 877

a) At the $\alpha = 5\%$ level of significance, test the null hypothesis that the proportion of seriously sick HIV patients at the two facilities is equal.

b) Construct a 95% confidence interval for $P_1 - P_2$.

How to compare 2 proportions in STATA

Open the STATA data file c:\bos\p2.dta

Click on Statistics, summaries, tables, and tests

Click on classical tests of hypotheses

Click on Proportion test

Click on Two-group using groups

Variable? Select the variable *sick* from the list of variables

Group indicator? Select the variable *facility* from the list of variables

Confidence level? 95

Click on OK

```
. use c:\bos\p2.dta, clear

. prtest sick, by(facility) level(95)

Two-sample test of proportions                   1: Number of obs =       100
                                                 2: Number of obs =       100
------------------------------------------------------------------------------
    Variable |       Mean   Std. Err.      z    P>|z|     [95% Conf. Interval]
-------------+----------------------------------------------------------------
           1 |        .28   .0448999                      .1919978    .3680022
           2 |        .42   .0493559                      .3232643    .5167357
-------------+----------------------------------------------------------------
        diff |       -.14   .0667233                     -.2707753   -.0092247
             |  under Ho:   .0674537    -2.08   0.038
------------------------------------------------------------------------------
        diff = prop(1) - prop(2)                                  z =  -2.0755
    Ho: diff = 0

    Ha: diff < 0                 Ha: diff != 0                 Ha: diff > 0
 Pr(Z < z) = 0.0190         Pr(|Z| < |z|) = 0.0379          Pr(Z > z) = 0.9810
```

H0: The proportions of seriously sick people in Facilities 1 and 2 are equal

H1: The proportions of seriously sick people in Facilities 1 and 2 are not equal

Since P = 0.0379 < 0.05, we conclude that the two proportions are significantly different at the 5% level of significance.

A 95% confidence interval for the true difference between the 2 proportions is given by (–0.271, –0.009) or (0.009, 0.271) = (0.9%, 27.1%). Note that this confidence interval does not contain 0%.

Solution from SPSS

Open up the SPSS data set c:\bos\p2.sav

Click on Analyze

Click on Compare means

Click on Independent sample proportions test

Test variable? Select the variable sickness by clicking on the selection bar

Grouping variable? Select the variable facility by clicking on the selection bar

Define groups

Group 1? 1

Group 2? 2

Click on Continue

Click on OK

A computer printout obtained from SPSS is shown below:

Independent-Samples Proportions Group Statistics					
	Facility	Successes	Trials	Proportion	Asymptotic Standard Error
sick = 1	1	28	100	0.280	0.045
	2	42	100	0.420	0.049

Independent-Samples Proportions Confidence Intervals					
				95% Confidence Interval of the Difference	
	Interval Type	Difference in Proportions	Asymptotic Standard Error	Lower	Upper
sick = 1	Agresti-Caffo	–0.140	0.067	–0.267	-0.007
	Newcombe	–0.140	0.067	–0.266	-0.008

The alternative hypothesis is two-sided. As such, we need to take the value of P = 0.038 in the following printout from SPSS. Since P=0.038 < 0.05, the null hypothesis can be rejected at the 5% level. We conclude that the 2 proportions are not equal at the 5% level.

Independent-Samples Proportions Tests						
					Significance	
	Test Type	Difference in Proportions	Asymptotic Standard Error	Z	One-Sided p	Two-Sided p
sick = 1	Wald H0	–0.140	0.067	–2.075	0.019	0.038

UNIT 9

THE ONE-WAY ANALYSIS OF VARIANCE

The One-Way Analysis of Variance

The one-way analysis of variance is a technique used to compare 3 or more groups with each other. If the groups being compared are each drawn from normally distributed parent populations, the test becomes parametric. Otherwise, the test becomes non-parametric.

Assume that it is desired to compare k groups (treatments) that are mutually independent with each other using the one-way analysis of variance method. If the effects of treatments are fixed, the one-way ANOVA model becomes:

Model: $Y_{ij} = \mu + T_j + \varepsilon_{ij}$ where

j = 1, 2, ……. k = number of treatments

i = 1,2,……,n_j = number of observations per group (treatment)

Y_{ij} = observation in cell (i, j) or the ith row and jth column

μ = overall (common) effect

T_j = effect of the jth treatment

ε_{ij} = random error associated with observation Y_{ij}

The one-way ANOVA test is used to test the null hypothesis:

$H_0 : \mu_1 = \mu_2 = \ldots\ldots = \mu_k$ versus the alternative hypothesis

H_1 At least 2 means differ significantly from each other

Decision rule:

1. Reject H_0 if $F_{cal} > F_{tab}$ or if $p < \alpha$
2. Do not reject H_0 if $F_{cal} \leq F_{tab}$ where

$F_{tab} = F_{1-}\alpha(k-1, N-k)$ where

k is the number of distinct treatments or groups being compared

N = total sample size = $n_1 + n_2 + \ldots + n_k$

The following table shows the basic elements of the one-way ANOVA table.

Source of variation (SV)	Degrees of freedom (df)	Sum of squares (SS)	Mean of Squares (MS)	The calculated value of F (Fcal)	The tabulated value of F (Ftab)
Treatments	k – 1	SS(trt)	MS(trt)	$\frac{MS(trt)}{MS(err)}$	$F_{1-\alpha}(k-1, N-k)$
Error	N – k	SS(err)	MS(err)		
Total	N – 1	SS(total)			

$$SS(tot) = \sum_{j=1}^{k}\sum_{i=1}^{n_j} Y_{ij}^2 - \frac{T_{..}^2}{N} = \text{total sum of squares}$$

$$SS(trt) = \sum_{j=1}^{k}\frac{T_{.j}^2}{n_j} - \frac{T_{.}^2}{N} = \text{treatment sum of squares}$$

$$SS(error) = SS(tot) - SS(trt) = \sum_{j=1}^{k}\sum_{i=1}^{n_j} Y_{ij}^2 - \sum_{j=1}^{k}\frac{T_{.j}^2}{n_j} = \text{error}$$

sum of squares

$$MS(trt) = \frac{SS(trt)}{k-1} = \text{mean squares for treatments}$$

$$MS(err) = \frac{SS(err)}{N-k} = \text{mean squares for error terms}$$

$$F_{cal} = \frac{MS(trt)}{MS(err)} = \text{the calculated value of the F-statistic}$$

$$T_{..} = \sum_{j=1}^{k}\sum_{i=1}^{n_j} Y_{ij} = \text{the sum total of all observations}$$

α is the level of significance of test

Example:

Four brands of painkillers (treatments) were administered to 4 independent groups of patients, and the time taken to bring about relief from pain to each patient in the study was recorded. The purpose of the experiment is to find out whether or not there is any significant difference among the 4 brands of painkillers with respect to efficacy at the $\alpha = 0.05$ level of significance.

Brand 1	Brand 2	Brand 3	Brand 4
4.3	5.4	7.8	5.8
6.4	7.5	8.0	6.4
5.1	6.9	6.3	8.3
3.2	3.2	8.7	9.2
4.1	7.2	3.9	8.9
5.5	3.8	8.8	7.8
7.0	6.3	5.5	8.3
4.4	5.7	–	8.4
–	8.1	–	8.9
–	5.9	–	–

Solution:

K = 4 = number of treatments being compared

N = 34 = total number of observations

	Brand 1	Brand 2	Brand 3	Brand 4
	4.3	5.4	7.8	5.8
	6.4	7.5	8.0	6.4
	5.1	6.9	6.3	8.3
	3.2	3.2	8.7	9.2
	4.1	7.2	3.9	8.9
	5.5	3.8	8.8	7.8
	7.0	6.3	5.5	8.3
	4.4	5.7	–	8.4
	–	8.1	–	8.9
	–	5.9	–	–
$T_{.j}$	40	60	49	72
n_j	8	10	7	9
$T_{.j}^2$	1600	3600	2401	5184
$\frac{T_{.j}^2}{n_j}$	200	360	343	576

$$N = n_1 + n_2 + n_3 + n_4 = 8 + 10 + 7 + 9 = 34$$

$$T.. = T._1 + T._2 + T._3 + T._4 = 40 + 60 + 49 + 72 = 221$$

$$\sum_{j=1}^{k}\sum_{i=1}^{n_j} Y_{ij} = T_{..} = 221$$

$$\sum_{j=1}^{k}\sum_{i=1}^{n_j} Y_{ij}^2 = (4.3)^2 + (6.4)^2 + ... + (5.8)^2 + (6.4)^2 = 1543.2$$

$$\sum_{j=1}^{k}\frac{T_{.j}^2}{n_j} = \frac{T_{.1}^2}{n_1} + \frac{T_{.2}^2}{n_2} + \frac{T_{.3}^2}{n_3} + \frac{T_{.4}^2}{n_4}$$

$$= 200 + 360 + 343 + 576 = 1479$$

$$\frac{T_{..}^2}{N} = \frac{(221)^2}{34} = 1436.5$$

$$\text{SS(tot)} = \sum_{j=1}^{k}\sum_{i=1}^{n_j} Y_{ij}^2 - \frac{T_{..}^2}{N} = 1543.2 - 1436.5 = 106.7$$

$$\text{SS(trt)} = \sum_{j=1}^{k} \frac{T_{.j}^2}{n_j} - \frac{T_{.}^2}{N} = 1479 - 1436.5 = 42.5$$

$$\text{SS(error)} = \text{SS(tot)} - \text{SS(trt)} = 106.7 - 42.5 = 64.2$$

$K = 4$

$N = 34$

$N - K = 34 - 4 = 30$

$\alpha = 0.05$

$1 - \alpha = 0.95$

$$MS(trt) = \frac{SS(trt)}{k-1} = \frac{42.5}{3} = 14.17$$

$$MS(err) = \frac{SS(err)}{N-k} = \frac{64.2}{30} = 2.14$$

$$F_{cal} = \frac{MS(trt)}{MS(err)} = \frac{14.17}{2.14} = 6.62$$

$F_{tab} = F_{1-\alpha}\ (k - 1, N - k) = F_{0.95}(3,30) = 2.92$ (This tabulated value of the F (0.05) statistic can be read from the F-table shown in Appendix A for the 0.05 level of significance. Read under 3 degrees of freedom horizontally and 30 degrees of freedom vertically. The value that lies in the F (0.05) table at the intersection of the 2 degrees of freedom (3 and 30) is equal to 2.92.

Since $F_{cal} > F_{tab}$, the null hypothesis H_0 is rejected at the 5% level of significance. We conclude that there is a significance difference between the 4 brands.

ANOVA table

Source of variation (SV)	Degrees of freedom (df)	Sum of squares (SS)	Mean of Squares (MS)	The calculated value of F (Fcal)	The tabulated value of F (Ftab)
Treatments	k – 1 = 3	42.5	14.17	6.62	2.92*
Error	N – k = 30	64.2	2.14		
Total	N – 1 = 33	106.7			

* indicates significance at the $\alpha = 0.05$ level of significance

The STATA data set **c:\bos\anova1.dta** contains the data for the example.

The above results could be obtained from STATA as follows:

Open up the STATA data set c:\bos\anova1.dta

Click on Statistics

Click on Linear models and related, ANOVA/MANOVA, One-way ANOVA

Response variable? Select the variable *time*

Factor variable? Select the variable *group*

Click on Bonferroni Multiple Comparison test

Click on Produce summary table

Click on OK

```
. use c:\bos\anova1.dta, clear

. oneway time group, bonferroni tabulate

            |         Summary of time
      group |        Mean   Std. dev.       Freq.
------------+------------------------------------
          1 |           5   1.2603854           8
          2 |           6   1.5684388          10
          3 |   7.0000001   1.8312109           7
          4 |   7.9999999   1.1640445           9
------------+------------------------------------
      Total |         6.5   1.7983157          34

                        Analysis of variance
    Source              SS         df      MS            F     Prob > F
------------------------------------------------------------------------
Between groups     42.4999979      3   14.166666      6.62     0.0015
 Within groups     64.2199976     30   2.14066659
------------------------------------------------------------------------
    Total          106.719995     33   3.23393926
```

```
Bartlett's equal-variances test: chi2(3) =   1.7050    Prob>chi2 = 0.636

           Comparison of time by group

                                    (Bonferroni)
Row Mean-|
Col Mean |          1           2           3
---------+-----------------------------------
       2 |          1
         |      0.960
         |
       3 |          2           1
         |      0.078       1.000
         |
       4 |          3           2           1
         |      0.001       0.034       1.000
```

H_0: There is no significant difference among the 4 brands of painkillers

H_1: There is a significant difference among the 4 brands of painkillers

Since P=0.0015 < 0.05, the null hypothesis H_0 is rejected at the 5% level of significance. We conclude that there is a significance difference between the 4 brands.

We have shown above that the 4 types of brands differ significantly. Multiple comparison tests enable us to pin point which pairs of drugs differ significantly at the 5% level. A P-value which is smaller than 0.05 indicates a significant difference. A P-value which is greater than or equal to 0.05 indicates similarity. The following table provides a summary of pairs that differ significantly at the 5% level.

Interactions among drug types	**Probability values**	**Interpretation of probability value at the 5% level of significance**
1 and 2	0.960	Similar
1 and 3	0.078	Similar
1 and 4	**0.001**	**Different**
2 and 3	1.000	Similar
2 and 4	**0.034**	**Different**
3 and 4	1.000	Similar

The rejection of the null hypothesis is attributed to the significant differences among the pairs 1 and 4 and 2 and 4.

Solution from SPSS

Open up the SPSS data set c:\bos\anova1.sav

Click on Analyze

Click on General Linear Model

Click on Univariate

Dependent variable? Select the variable *Sita* by using the selection bar

Fixed factor? Select the variable *group* by clicking on the selection bar

Click on Post Hoc multiple comparison tests

Click on Group

Click on LSD (Least Significant Difference)

Click on Continue

Click on OK

A computer printout obtained from SPSS is shown below:

Between-Subjects Factors		
		N
Group	1	8
	2	10
	3	7
	4	9

Tests of Between-Subjects Effects					
Dependent Variable: time					
Source	Type III Sum of Squares	df	Mean Square	F	P-value
Corrected Model	42.500[a]	3	14.167	6.618	.001
Intercept	1411.367	1	1411.367	659.312	<0.001
group	42.500	3	14.167	6.618	0.001
Error	64.220	30	2.141		
Total	1543.220	34			
Corrected Total	106.720	33			

a. R Squared = 0.398 (Adjusted R Squared = 0.338)

Multiple Comparisons						
Dependent Variable: time						
LSD						
(I) group	(J) group	Mean Difference (I – J)	Std. Error	P-value	95% Confidence Interval Lower Bound	Upper Bound
1	2	–1.0000	0.69401	0.160	–2.4174	0.4174
	3	–2.0000*	0.75723	0.013	–3.5465	–0.4535
	4	–3.0000*	0.71094	<0.001	–4.4519	–1.5481
2	1	1.0000	0.69401	0.160	–0.4174	2.4174
	3	–1.0000	0.72102	0.176	–2.4725	0.4725
	4	–2.0000*	0.67225	0.006	–3.3729	–0.6271
3	1	2.0000*	0.75723	0.013	0.4535	3.5465
	2	1.0000	0.72102	0.176	–0.4725	2.4725
	4	–1.0000	0.73733	0.185	–2.5058	0.5058
4	1	3.0000*	0.71094	<0.001	1.5481	4.4519
	2	2.0000*	0.67225	0.006	0.6271	3.3729
	3	1.0000	0.73733	0.185	–0.5058	2.5058

Based on observed means.
The error term is Mean Square(Error) = 2.141.

*. The mean difference is significant at the 0.05 level.

Repeated measures univariate ANOVA

The SPSS data set **c:\bos\anova2.sav** contains the following variables:

4 types of drugs per method of treatment
5 concentration levels per drug
4 readings per concentration level

The objective of the study is to find out if there is a significant difference among:

a) the 4 types of drugs
b) the 5 levels of concentration
c) the 4 readings taken per concentration level.

The statistical model for the experiment is given as follows:

$$
\begin{aligned}
Y_{ijkl} = \ & \mu \ + \\
& A_i + B_j + C_k + \\
& A_iB_j + A_iC_k + B_jC_k + \\
& A_iB_jC_k + \\
& \varepsilon
\end{aligned}
$$

where

μ denotes the overall or common effect

A_i denotes the effect of drugs; i = 1, 2, 3, 4 = number of drugs

B_j denotes the effect of concentration levels; j = 1, 2, 3, 4, 5 = number of concentration levels per drug

C_k denotes the effect of readings; k = 1, 2, 3, 4 = number of readings per concentration level

ε denotes the error term

Total number of rows = 4 × 5 × 4 = 80

We need to test the significance of the overall (common) effect, the 2 main effects (drugs and concentration levels), as well as the interaction effect between drugs and concentration levels. In addition to this, the significance of associations between the various levels of drugs and concentration levels will be tested using the LSD (least significant difference) statistic.

The structure of the data set is as follows:

#	drug	conc	reading	#	drug	conc	reading
1.	1	1	6	27.	2	2	1
2.	1	1	2	28.	2	2	10
3.	1	1	0	29.	2	3	10
4.	1	1	8	30.	2	3	11
5.	1	2	10	31.	2	3	6
6.	1	2	9	32.	2	3	7
7.	1	2	7	33.	2	4	5
8.	1	2	12	34.	2	4	10
9.	1	3	0	35.	2	4	8
10.	1	3	0	36.	2	4	3
11.	1	3	5	37.	2	5	6
12.	1	3	5	38.	2	5	7
13.	1	4	11	39.	2	5	0
14.	1	4	0	40.	2	5	3
15.	1	4	6	41.	3	1	1
16.	1	4	4	42.	3	1	10
17.	1	5	1	43.	3	1	0
18.	1	5	4	44.	3	1	6
19.	1	5	7	45.	3	2	4
20.	1	5	9	46.	3	2	1
21.	2	1	13	47.	3	2	7
22.	2	1	3	48.	3	2	9
23.	2	1	9	49.	3	3	8
24.	2	1	8	50.	3	3	5
25.	2	2	2	51.	3	3	0
26.	2	2	1	52.	3	3	7

(Contd.)

#	drug	conc	reading	#	drug	conc	reading
53.	3	4	1	67.	4	2	4
54.	3	4	8	68.	4	2	1
55.	3	4	9	69.	4	3	7
56.	3	4	4	70.	4	3	2
57.	3	5	3	71.	4	3	5
58.	3	5	0	72.	4	3	4
59.	3	5	2	73.	4	4	0
60.	3	5	2	74.	4	4	8
61.	4	1	7	75.	4	4	6
62.	4	1	4	76.	4	4	5
63.	4	1	7	77.	4	5	3
64.	4	1	9	78.	4	5	7
65.	4	2	0	79.	4	5	4
66.	4	2	3	80.	4	5	0

In SPSS,

Open the data file **c:\bos\anova2.sav**

Click on Analyze

Go to general linear models

Go to univariate

Select readings as dependent

Select drug and conc as fixed factors

Click on options

Display means for? Select all variables to the right including the overall mean

Click on descriptives

Click on continue

Click on post hoc tests

Select drug, conc and all other interaction effects

Click on LSD

Click on continue

Click on OK

Univariate Analysis of Variance

Between-Subjects Factors

		N
Drug	1	20
	2	20
	3	20
	4	20
Conc	1	16
	2	16
	3	16
	4	16
	5	16

Descriptive Statistics

Dependent Variable: reading

drug	conc	Mean	Std. Deviation	N
1	1	4.00	3.651	4
	2	9.50	2.082	4
	3	2.50	2.887	4
	4	5.25	4.573	4
	5	5.25	3.500	4
	Total	5.30	3.881	20
2	1	8.25	4.113	4
	2	3.50	4.359	4
	3	8.50	2.380	4
	4	6.50	3.109	4
	5	4.00	3.162	4
	Total	6.15	3.774	20
3	1	4.25	4.646	4
	2	5.25	3.500	4
	3	5.00	3.559	4
	4	5.50	3.697	4
	5	1.75	1.258	4
	Total	4.35	3.422	20

(Contd.)

Descriptive Statistics				
Dependent Variable: reading				
drug	**conc**	**Mean**	**Std. Deviation**	**N**
4	1	6.75	2.062	4
	2	2.00	1.826	4
	3	4.50	2.082	4
	4	4.75	3.403	4
	5	3.50	2.887	4
	Total	4.30	2.755	20
Total	1	5.81	3.816	16
	2	5.06	4.024	16
	3	5.13	3.344	16
	4	5.50	3.406	16
	5	3.63	2.849	16
	Total	5.02	3.504	80

Tests of Between-Subjects Effects						
Dependent Variable: reading						
Source	**Type III Sum of Squares**	**df**	**Mean Square**	**F**	**P-value**	**Partial Eta Squared**
Corrected Model	327.950[a]	19	17.261	1.613	0.082	0.338
Intercept	2020.050	1	2020.050	188.790	<0.001	0.759
drug	46.450	3	15.483	1.447	0.238	0.067
conc	45.075	4	11.269	1.053	0.388	0.066
drug * conc	236.425	12	19.702	1.841	0.061	0.269
Error	642.000	60	10.700			
Total	2990.000	80				
Corrected Total	969.950	79				

a. R Squared = 0.338 (Adjusted R Squared = 0.129)

Conclusion

The effect of drugs is insignificant at the 5% level because 0.238 > 0.05. Thus, there is no significant difference between the 4 types of drugs used.

The effect of concentration levels is insignificant at the 5% level because 0.388 > 0.05. Thus, there is no significant difference between the 5 levels of concentration.

There is no significant interaction effect between drugs and concentration levels at the 5% level because 0.061 > 0.05.

Estimated Marginal Means

1. Grand Mean

Dependent Variable: reading

		95% Confidence Interval	
Mean	Std. Error	Lower Bound	Upper Bound
5.025	0.366	4.293	5.757

2. drug

Dependent Variable: reading

			95% Confidence Interval	
drug	Mean	Std. Error	Lower Bound	Upper Bound
1	5.300	0.731	3.837	6.763
2	6.150	0.731	4.687	7.613
3	4.350	0.731	2.887	5.813
4	4.300	0.731	2.837	5.763

3. conc				
Dependent Variable: reading				
conc	Mean	Std. Error	95% Confidence Interval	
			Lower Bound	Upper Bound
1	5.813	0.818	4.177	7.448
2	5.063	0.818	3.427	6.698
3	5.125	0.818	3.489	6.761
4	5.500	0.818	3.864	7.136
5	3.625	0.818	1.989	5.261

4. drug * conc					
Dependent Variable: reading					
drug	conc	Mean	Std. Error	95% Confidence Interval	
				Lower Bound	Upper Bound
1	1	4.000	1.636	0.728	7.272
	2	9.500	1.636	6.228	12.772
	3	2.500	1.636	-0.772	5.772
	4	5.250	1.636	1.978	8.522
	5	5.250	1.636	1.978	8.522
2	1	8.250	1.636	4.978	11.522
	2	3.500	1.636	0.228	6.772
	3	8.500	1.636	5.228	11.772
	4	6.500	1.636	3.228	9.772
	5	4.000	1.636	0.728	7.272
3	1	4.250	1.636	0.978	7.522
	2	5.250	1.636	1.978	8.522
	3	5.000	1.636	1.728	8.272
	4	5.500	1.636	2.228	8.772
	5	1.750	1.636	-1.522	5.022
4	1	6.750	1.636	3.478	10.022
	2	2.000	1.636	-1.272	5.272
	3	4.500	1.636	1.228	7.772
	4	4.750	1.636	1.478	8.022
	5	3.500	1.636	0.228	6.772

Multiple Comparisons						
Dependent Variable: reading						
LSD						
(I) drug	(J) drug	Mean Difference (I – J)	Std. Error	P-value	95% Confidence Interval	
					Lower Bound	Upper Bound
1	2	–0.85	1.034	0.414	–2.92	1.22
	3	0.95	1.034	0.362	–1.12	3.02
	4	1.00	1.034	0.338	–1.07	3.07
2	1	0.85	1.034	0.414	–1.22	2.92
	3	1.80	1.034	0.087	–0.27	3.87
	4	1.85	1.034	0.079	–0.22	3.92
3	1	–0.95	1.034	0.362	–3.02	1.12
	2	–1.80	1.034	0.087	–3.87	0.27
	4	0.05	1.034	0.962	–2.02	2.12
4	1	–1.00	1.034	0.338	–3.07	1.07
	2	–1.85	1.034	0.079	–3.92	0.22
	3	–0.05	1.034	0.962	–2.12	2.02

Based on observed means.

The error term is Mean Square (Error) = 10.700.

Multiple Comparisons						
Dependent Variable: reading						
LSD						
(I) conc	(J) conc	Mean Difference (I – J)	Std. Error	P-value	95% Confidence Interval Lower Bound	95% Confidence Interval Upper Bound
1	2	0.75	1.157	0.519	–1.56	3.06
	3	0.69	1.157	0.554	–1.63	3.00
	4	0.31	1.157	0.788	–2.00	2.63
	5	2.19	1.157	0.063	–0.13	4.50
2	1	–0.75	1.157	0.519	–3.06	1.56
	3	–0.06	1.157	0.957	–2.38	2.25
	4	–0.44	1.157	0.707	–2.75	1.88
	5	1.44	1.157	0.219	–0.88	3.75
3	1	–0.69	1.157	0.554	–3.00	1.63
	2	0.06	1.157	0.957	–2.25	2.38
	4	–0.37	1.157	0.747	–2.69	1.94
	5	1.50	1.157	0.200	–0.81	3.81
4	1	–0.31	1.157	0.788	–2.63	2.00
	2	0.44	1.157	0.707	–1.88	2.75
	3	0.38	1.157	0.747	–1.94	2.69
	5	1.87	1.157	0.110	–0.44	4.19
5	1	–2.19	1.157	0.063	–4.50	0.13
	2	–1.44	1.157	0.219	–3.75	0.88
	3	–1.50	1.157	0.200	–3.81	0.81
	4	–1.87	1.157	0.110	–4.19	0.44

Based on observed means.

The error term is Mean Square (Error) = 10.700.

The result obtained from SPSS can be obtained from **STATA** by using the **sequential anova** procedure as follows. Note that the variable **drugconc** is the product of the variables **drug** and conc.

Open up the STATA data set c:\bos\anova2.dta

Click on Statistics, Linear models and related, ANOVA/MANOVA, Analysis of variance and covariance

Dependent variable? Select the variable *reading*

Model? Select the variables *reading drug conc drugconc*

Click on repeated measures variables

Select conc reading

Click on Sequential

Click on OK

```
. use c:\bos\anova2.dta, clear

. anova reading drug conc drugconc, sequential

                  Number of obs =         80     R-squared     =  0.2906
                  Root MSE      =    3.30494     Adj R-squared =  0.1104

              Source |    Seq. SS        df        MS           F    Prob>F
          -----------+----------------------------------------------------
               Model |    281.825        16   17.614063       1.61   0.0915
                     |
                drug |      46.45         3   15.483333       1.42   0.2460
                conc |     45.075         4    11.26875       1.03   0.3980
            drugconc |      190.3         9   21.144444       1.94   0.0627
                     |
            Residual |    688.125        63   10.922619
          -----------+----------------------------------------------------
               Total |     969.95        79   12.277848
```

Conclusion

The effect of drugs is insignificant at the 5% level because 0.2460 > 0.05. Thus, there is no significant difference between the 4 types of drugs used.

The effect of concentration levels is insignificant at the 5% level because 0.3980 > 0.05. Thus, there is no significant difference between the 5 levels of concentration.

There is no significant interaction effect between drugs and concentration levels at the 5% level because 0.0627 > 0.05.

The generalised linear modeling procedure of STATA

The **glm** procedure of STATA is an ideal choice for testing interaction effects of all possible orders for significance. In the example above, each of the 2 main effects (*drugs* and *concentration levels*) as well as the interaction effect between drugs and concentration levels can be tested for significance at the 5% level. Note that the variable drugconc *is the product of the variables drug and conc.*

Open up the STATA data set c:\bos\anova2.dta

Click on Statistics, Generalized Linear models, Generalized Linear Models (GLM)

Dependent variable? Select the variable *reading*

Independent variables? Select the variables *drug conc drugconc*

Click on OK

```
. use c:\bos\anova2.dta, clear

. glm reading drug conc drugconc

Iteration 0:   log likelihood = -211.27641

Generalized linear models                         Number of obs     =         80
Optimization     : ML                             Residual df       =         76
                                                  Scale parameter   =   12.12569
Deviance         =       921.5525                 (1/df) Deviance   =   12.12569
Pearson          =       921.5525                 (1/df) Pearson    =   12.12569

Variance function: V(u) = 1                       [Gaussian]
Link function    : g(u) = u                       [Identity]

                                                  AIC               =    5.38191
Log likelihood   = -211.2764072                   BIC               =   588.5185

------------------------------------------------------------------------------
             |                 OIM
     reading | Coefficient  std. err.      z    P>|z|     [95% conf. interval]
-------------+----------------------------------------------------------------
        drug |     -.3225   .8166474    -0.39   0.693      -1.9231      1.2781
        conc |     -.2625   .6743244    -0.39   0.697    -1.584152    1.059152
    drugconc |     -.0525   .2462285    -0.21   0.831    -.5350989    .4300989
       _cons |     7.0125   2.236481     3.14   0.002     2.629078    11.39592
------------------------------------------------------------------------------
```

The above result shows that none of the 3 effects is significant at the 5% level. That is, there is no significant difference among the

4 types of drugs. There is no significant difference among the 5 concentration levels. There is no significant interaction between drugs and concentration levels.

Results from SAS (Proc GLM)

proc glm data = anova2;

class drugs conc;

model reading = drugs conc drugs*conc;

run;

```
                          The SAS System

                        The GLM Procedure

                     Class Level Information

                 Class          Levels    Values

                 DRUGS               4    1 2 3 4

                 CONC                5    1 2 3 4 5

                   Number of observations    80

                        The GLM Procedure

Dependent Variable: READING   READING

                                     Sum of
Source                  DF          Squares    Mean Square    F Value    Pr > F

Model                   19      327.9500000     17.2605263       1.61    0.0823

Error                   60      642.0000000     10.7000000

Corrected Total         79      969.9500000

               R-Square     Coeff Var      Root MSE    READING Mean

               0.338110      65.09623      3.271085        5.025000

Source                  DF        Type I SS    Mean Square    F Value    Pr > F

DRUGS                    3       46.4500000     15.4833333       1.45    0.2381
CONC                     4       45.0750000     11.2687500       1.05    0.3876
DRUGS*CONC              12      236.4250000     19.7020833       1.84    0.0614

Source                  DF      Type III SS    Mean Square    F Value    Pr > F

DRUGS                    3       46.4500000     15.4833333       1.45    0.2381
CONC                     4       45.0750000     11.2687500       1.05    0.3876
DRUGS*CONC              12      236.4250000     19.7020833       1.84    0.0614
```

UNIT 10

LINEAR REGRESSION AND CORRELATION ANALYSIS

In this chapter, we will discuss applications of regression analysis. This will be done in 2 major areas: linear regression analysis and non-linear regression analysis. Linear regression analysis arises when the outcome variable of study is continuous. Non-linear regression analysis arises when the outcome variable of study is discrete. Section 1.1 of this handout deals with simple linear regression analysis. Section 1.2 deals with multiple linear regression analysis.

10.1: Simple linear regression and correlation analysis

In simple linear regression analysis, the relationship between one outcome or dependent variable (Y) and a single independent or explanatory variable (X) is investigated.

Y denotes the outcome or dependent variable of study

X denotes the independent or explanatory variable of study

Y depends on X

Example 1:

Y: score obtained in an exam

X: number of hours of study

Example 2

Y: quantity of yield obtained from a plot of land

X: quantity of fertilizer used

Relationships between Y and X

The relationship between Y and X is linear. An increase or decrease in X results in an increase or decrease.

If an increase in X results in an increase in Y, the relationship is said to be **positive**.

If an increase in X results in a decrease in Y, the relationship is said to be **negative**.

If values of Y are not affected by the values of X, the 2 variables are said to be **independent** of each other.

The line of regression of Y on X (the relationship between Y and X) is shown below:

Y $= a + bX$ *where*

a *is the Y-intercept of the line of regression*

b is the slope of the line of regression

$$b = \frac{\sum XY - n\overline{X}\overline{Y}}{\sum X^2 - n\overline{X}^2}$$

$$a = \bar{Y} - b\bar{X}$$

$$\overline{X} = \frac{\sum_{i=1}^{n} X_i}{n}$$

$$\overline{Y} = \frac{\sum_{i=1}^{n} Y_i}{n}$$

$$\sum_{i=1}^{n} X_i = X_1 + X_2 + \dots\dots.. + X_n$$

$$\sum_{i=1}^{n} X_i^2 = X_1^2 + X_2^2 + \dots\dots.. + X_n^2$$

$$\sum_{i=1}^{n} Y_i = Y_1 + Y_2 + \dots\dots.. + Y_n$$

$$\sum_{i=1}^{n} Y_i^2 = Y_1^2 + Y_2^2 + \dots\dots.. + Y_n^2$$

Possible values of the slope of the line of regression

Case 1: Positive slope (b > 0)

An increase in X results in an increase in Y.

Example:

Y: distance travelled by a car in km

X: quantity of petrol available in petrol tank

Case 2: Negative slope (b < 0)

An increase in X results in a decrease in Y.

Example:

Y: price of oil per barrel

X: supply of oil in market

Case 3: Zero slope (b = 0)

X and Y are independent of each other.

Example:

Y: prevalence of bloody diarrhoea in Kwa Zulu Natal

X: cost of textile products in Taiwan

The correlation coefficient (r)

r is a measure of the strength of interdependence existing between Y and X.

Properties of the correlation coefficient r

Values of r lie between –1 and +1 always. That is, $-1 \le r \le +1$ always.

If r = 0, Y and X are **independent** of each other. No relationship exists between Y and X.

If r = 1, Y and X are said to be **perfectly and positively correlated**. An increase (decrease) in X by one unit results in an increase (decrease) in Y by one unit.

If r = –1, Y and X are said to be **perfectly and negatively correlated**. An increase (decrease) in X by one unit results in a decrease (increase) by one unit in Y.

The correlation coefficient, r, is obtained as follows:

$$r = \frac{\sum XY - n\overline{X}\overline{Y}}{\sqrt{\left(\sum X^2 - n\overline{X}^2\right)\left(\sum Y^2 - n\overline{Y}^2\right)}}$$

The explained variation r^2

The explained variation is a measure of adequacy of the estimated line of regression.

A high value of r^2 *(at least 75%) indicates that the estimated line of regression fits the data well.*

A low value of r^2 (less than 75%) indicates that the estimated line of regression does not fit the data well.

Example:

X	1	2	3	4	5	6	7	8	9	10
Y	35	35	40	45	50	55	55	60	60	70
XY	35	70	120	180	250	350	385	480	540	700

X: Number of hours of study

Y: Percentage score obtained in exam

The above table shows data for X (number of hours of study) and Y (percentage score obtained in exam) for a class of 10 students who took a short course. Assuming that the relationship between Y and X is linear, regress Y on X.

Find the slope of the line of regression.

a) Find the Y-intercept.
b) Write down the equation of the estimated line of regression.
c) Find the correlation coefficient.
d) How large is the explained variation?
e) How large is the unexplained variation?
f) What is the score obtained by a student who studied for 4.5 hours?
g) How many hours does one have to study in order to score 65?

Solution:

n = 10

$$\sum_{i=1}^{n} X_i = X_1 + X_2 + \dots\dots + X_n = 1 + 2 + \dots + 10 = 55$$

$$\sum_{i=1}^{n} X_i^2 = X_1^2 + X_2^2 + \dots\dots + X_n^2 = 1^2 + 2^2 + \dots + 10^2 = 385$$

$$\sum_{i=1}^{n} Y_i = Y_1 + Y_2 + \dots\dots + Y_n = 35 + 35 + \dots + 70 = 505$$

$$\sum_{i=1}^{n} Y_i^2 = Y_1^2 + Y_2^2 + \dots\dots + Y_n^2 = (35)^2 + (35)^2 + \dots + (70)_2 = 26725$$

$$\bar{X} = \frac{\sum_{i=1}^{n} X_i}{n} = \frac{55}{10} = 5.5$$

$$\bar{Y} = \frac{\sum_{i=1}^{n} Y_i}{n} = \frac{505}{10} = 50.5$$

$n\bar{X}^2 = 10(5.5)2 = 302.5$

$n\bar{Y}^2 = 10(50.5)^2 = 25502.5$

$n\bar{X}\bar{Y} = 10(5.5)(50.5) = 2777.5$

$$\sum XY = 1(35) + 2(35) + \dots\dots + 10(70) = 3090$$

a) $$b = \frac{\sum XY - n\overline{XY}}{\sum X^2 - n\bar{X}^2} = \frac{3090 - 2777.5}{385 - 302.5} = \frac{312.5}{82.5} = 3.79$$

b) $a = \bar{Y} - b\bar{X} = 50.5 - 3.79(5.5) = 29.67$

c) $Y = a + bX = 29.67 + 3.79X$

d) $r = \dfrac{\sum XY - n\overline{X}\overline{Y}}{\sqrt{\left(\sum X^2 - n\overline{X}^2\right)\left(\sum Y^2 - n\overline{Y}^2\right)}}$

$$= \frac{3090-2777.5}{\sqrt{(3090-2777.5)(26725-25502.5)}} = \frac{312.5}{317.58} = 0.98$$

e) $r^2 = (0.98)^2 = 097 = 97\%$

f) $1 - r^2 = 1 - 0.97 = 0.03 = 3\%$

g) f(x) = 29.67 + 3.79X

f(4.5) = 29.67 + 3.79(4.5) = 46.7%

h) 65 = 29.67 + 3.79X

$$X = \frac{65-29.67}{3.79} = \frac{35.33}{3.79} = 9.32 \text{ hours}$$

The statistical package STATA could be used for performing the following simple linear regression analysis procedure:

Open up STATA

Open the STATA data set c:\bos\slr.dta

Click on Statistics

Click on Linear models and related

Click on Linear regression

Dependent variable? Select the variable *score* from the list of variables

Independent variable? Select the variable *hours* from the list of variables

Click on Reporting

Select 95% confidence level

Click on OK

```
. use c:\bos\slr.dta, clear

. regress  score  hours

      Source |       SS       df       MS              Number of obs =      10
-------------+------------------------------           F(  1,      8) =  244.14
       Model |  1183.71212     1  1183.71212           Prob > F      =  0.0000
    Residual |  38.7878788     8  4.84848485           R-squared     =  0.9683
-------------+------------------------------           Adj R-squared =  0.9643
       Total |      1222.5     9  135.833333           Root MSE      =  2.2019

------------------------------------------------------------------------------
       score |      Coef.   Std. Err.      t    P>|t|     [95% Conf. Interval]
-------------+----------------------------------------------------------------
       hours |   3.787879   .2424242    15.63   0.000     3.228847     4.34691
       _cons |   29.66667   1.504203    19.72   0.000     26.19797    33.13536
------------------------------------------------------------------------------
```

In the above command, *score* is the dependent or outcome variable. The variable *hours* denotes the independent, explanatory or predictor variable.

```
. corr   score    hours
(obs=10)

             |    score    hours
-------------+------------------
       score |   1.0000
       hours |   0.9840   1.0000
```

The magnitude of the correlation coefficient is very high (0.9840 = 98.4%). This shows that the variables *score* and *hours* are significantly and positively associated with each other.

Solution from SPSS

Open up the SPSS data set c:\bos\slr.sav

Click on Analyze

Click on Regression

Click on Linear

Dependent variable? Select the variable *score* by using the selection bar

Independent variable? Select the variable *hours* by clicking on the selection bar

Click on OK

A computer printout obtained from SPSS is shown below:

The following table shows the model summary table. The table shows that the Adjusted R-Square value is equal to 0.964 = 96.4%. This result shows that the fitted line of regression has accounted for or explained 96.4% of the total variation in the dependent variable of study. That is, the fitted line of regression is highly reliable. The percentage of explained variation is also known as the coefficient of determination.

Model Summary				
Model	R	R Square	Adjusted R Square	Std. Error of the Estimate
1	0.984[a]	0.968	0.964	2.202

a. Predictors: (Constant), hours

The following table shows the Analysis of Variance (ANOVA) table. The table has a probability value of less than 0.001. This indicates that the regression of variable score on variable hours is highly significant. That is, the score obtained in the exam is explained as a function of the number of hours of study satisfactorily.

ANOVAa						
Model		Sum of Squares	df	Mean Square	F	P-value
1	Regression	1183.712	1	1183.712	244.141	<.001[b]
	Residual	38.788	8	4.848		
	Total	1222.500	9			

a. Dependent Variable: score
b. Predictors: (Constant), hours

The following table shows estimated regression coefficients under column B. The P-value corresponding to variable hours is less than 0.001. The estimated regression coefficient of variable *hours* is equal to 3.788. This indicates that variable *hours* is a highly valuable predictor of variable *score*.

The table shows that the Y-intercept or constant term is equal to 29.667.

Coefficients[a]						
		Unstandardized Coefficients		Standardized Coefficients		
Model		B	Std. Error	Beta	t	P-value
1	(Constant)	29.667	1.504		19.723	<.001
	hours	3.788	0.242	0.984	15.625	<.001

a. Dependent Variable: *score*

10.2: Multiple linear regression and correlation analysis

In multiple linear regression analysis, the relationship between a **continuous** outcome (dependent) variable and several independent (explanatory) variables is studied.

The mathematical model for multiple linear regression analysis is given by:

$$Y_i = \beta_0 + \beta_1 X_1 + \beta_2 X_2 + \dots\dots\dots + \beta_k X_k + \varepsilon_i \quad for \quad i = 1, 2, \dots\dots, n$$

where

ε is a random error. The usual tests produced by most statistical packages assume that the errors are independent, and follow a normal distribution with mean 0 and constant variance σ^2. That is, $\varepsilon \sim N(0, \sigma^2 I_n)$. The variance σ^2 is estimated by the sample variance S^2.

E(Y) denotes the expected value of the dependent variable Y. The notation

E(Y|X) denotes the population mean value of Y when values of the independent variable X are known.

E(Y|X=x) denotes the population mean value of Y when X=x where X (capital X) is a random variable and x (small x) is a specific value that could be assumed by the random variable X.

The goal of multiple linear regression analysis is to estimate values of the k+1 regression coefficients $\beta_0, \beta_1, \beta_2, \ldots\ldots\ldots, \beta_k$ using methods of ordinary least square estimation in which the error sum of squares is minimized.

The fitted or estimated line of regression is expressed as:

$$\hat{Y} = \hat{\beta}_0 + \hat{\beta}_1 X_1 + \ldots\ldots\ldots + \hat{\beta}_k X_k = E(Y \mid X = x)$$

Statistical packages such as Epi-Info, SPSS, STATA and SAS provide estimates for the k+1 regression coefficients $\beta_0, \beta_1, \beta_2, \ldots\ldots \beta_k$. The fitted line of regression can be used to predict values of Y given values of the X variables.

Testing the significance of predictor variables used for regression analysis

The statistical significance of each of the regression coefficients can be tested using t-test. The null hypothesis states that the predictor variable associated with the regression coefficient does not have the capacity to account for variability in the dependent variable Y. The alternative hypothesis states that the predictor variable does have the capacity to account for variability in Y. At the α level of significance, the null hypothesis is rejected if the P-value is less than α.

Criteria for influential predictor variables in multiple linear regression analysis

In multiple linear regression analysis, the epidemiological or econometric measure of effect is the estimated regression coefficient. At the α level of significance, influential predictor variables are characterized by the following 3 criteria:

Estimated regression coefficients that differ from zero significantly 95% confidence intervals of regression coefficients that do not contain zero P-values that are smaller than the level of significance α.

The Analysis of Variance (ANOVA) table

The Analysis of Variance table in multiple linear regression analysis is used for assessing the significance of the regression of Y on the K predictor variables X1, X2, …, Xk. Whenever one attempts to predict values of Y, uncertainty or variability arises. This variability arises from lack of information on the independent variables of study. In cases where no information is available, the best one could do is to predict each observation to be equal to the sample mean.

The amount of uncertainty or variability can be measured by the Total Sum of Squares, which is the numerator of the sample variance. The ANOVA table partitions this variability into two parts. One of the two portions is accounted for by the estimated model. It's the reduction in uncertainty that occurs when the regression model is used to predict the responses. The remaining portion is the uncertainty that remains even after the model is used. The model is considered to be statistically significant if it can account for a large amount of variability in the response.

$$\text{SST} = \text{Total Sum of Squares} = \sum_{i=1}^{n}\left(Y_i - \overline{Y}\right)^2$$

$$\text{SSE} = \text{Error Sum of Squares} = \sum_{i=1}^{n}\left(Y_i - \hat{Y}\right)^2$$

$$\text{SSR} = \text{Regression Sum of Squares} = \text{SST} - \text{SSE} = \sum\left(\hat{Y} - \overline{Y}\right)^2$$

ANOVA table for multiple linear regression

Source of variation	df	Sums of squares	Means of squares	F-ratio
SSR	k – 1	$\sum(\hat{Y}-\bar{Y})^2$	$\sum(\hat{Y}-\bar{Y})^2/(k-1)$	$\frac{MSR}{MSE}$
SSE	n – k	$\sum_{i=1}^{n}(Y_i-\hat{Y})^2$	$\sum_{i=1}^{n}(Y_i-\hat{Y})^2/(n-k)$	
SST	n – 1	$\sum_{i=1}^{n}(Y_i-\bar{Y})^2$		

The Mean Squares are the Sums of Squares divided by the corresponding degrees of freedom (*df*).

The F-ratio is the test statistic used to decide whether the model as a whole has statistically significant predictive capability, that is, whether the regression SS is big enough, considering the number of variables needed to achieve it. At the α level of significance, the regression of Y on X1, X2, …., Xk is said to be significant if the F-ratio in the above ANOVA table is greater than the tabulated F-statistic, $F_{1-\alpha}\ (k-1, n-k)$.

The Root Mean Square Error (also known as the standard error of the estimate) is the square root of the Residual Mean Square. It is the standard deviation of the data about the regression line, rather than about the sample mean.

Proportion of explained variation (R^2)

$$R^2 = \frac{SSR}{SST}$$

R^2 is a measure of the variation in Y explained by the fitted line of regression. For a perfect model, $R^2 = 1$ or 100%. If a model has no predictive capability, $R^2 = 0$. In cases where $R^2 \geq 75\%$, the fitted line of regression is said to be fairly adequate.

Scatter plots

Multiple regression models have three primary characteristics: linearity, homogeneity of variance, and normally distributed residuals. Serious departures can be detected by scatter plots of the response against each predictor, residual plots (residuals against predicted values) and normal plots of the residuals.

Detecting outliers

It is common practice to distinguish between two types of outliers. Outliers in the response variable represent model failure. Such observations are called outliers. Outliers with respect to the predictors are called leverage points. They can affect the regression model, too. Their response variables need not be outliers. However, they may almost uniquely determine regression coefficients. They may also cause the standard errors of regression coefficients to be much smaller than they would be if the observation were excluded.

The ordinary or simple residuals (observed - predicted values) are the most commonly used measures for detecting outliers. The ordinary residuals sum to zero but do not have the same standard deviation. Many other measures have been offered to improve on or complement simple residuals. Standardized Residuals are the residuals divided by the estimates of their standard errors. They have mean 0 and standard deviation 1.

There are two common ways to calculate the standardized residual for the ith observation. One uses the residual mean square error from the model fitted to the full model (internally studentized residuals). The other uses the residual mean square error from the model fitted to the all of the data except the i^{th}observation (externally studentized residuals). The externally standardized residuals follow a t-distribution with $n - p$ - 2 degrees of freedom. They can be thought of as testing the hypothesis that the corresponding observation does not follow the regression model that describes the other observations.

Detecting influential observations by using Cook's Distance and DFBETA statistics

Cook's Distance for the ith observation is a measure of the effect arising from deleting an individual observation from the data set used for performing regression analysis. It is a measure of the difference between predicted responses from the model constructed from all of the data and predicted responses from the model constructed by setting the ith observation aside. For each observation, the sum of squared residuals is divided by (p + 1) times the Residual Mean Square obtained from the full regression model. In cases where Cook's distance is greater than 1 in magnitude, it is helpful to use dot plots to identify extreme observations and outliers.

Just like Cook's Distance statistics, **DFBETA statistics** are also used for measuring the effect that deleting each observation has on the estimates for the regression coefficients. $DFBETA_i$ is a measure of the scaled difference between the predicted responses from the model constructed from all of the data and the predicted responses from the model constructed by setting the ith observation aside. DBFETA statistics are similar to Cook's Distance statistics. Unlike Cook's distance, DFBETA does not look at all of the predicted values with the ith observation set aside. It looks only at predicted values for the ith observation. Also, the scaling factor uses the standard error of the estimate with the ith observation set aside. To see the effect of this, consider a dataset with one predictor in which all observations lie exactly on a straight line. The Residual Mean Square using all of the data will be positive. The standard errors of the estimate obtained by setting one observation aside in turn will be positive except for the observation that does not lie on the line. The DFFITS statistic is a scaled measure of the change in the predicted value for the ith observation and is calculated by deleting the i^{th}observation. A large value of the DFFITS statistic indicates that the observation is highly influential.

Robust regression

Robust regression is a term used to describe model fitting procedures that are insensitive to the effects of maverick observations. A least squares model can be distorted by a single observation. The fitted line or surface might be tipped so that it no longer passes through the bulk of the data. For example, if a large error is reduced from 200 to 50, its square is reduced from 40, 000 to 2, 500. Increasing an error from 5 to 15 increases its square from 25 to 225. Thus, a least squares fit might introduce many small errors in order to reduce a large one.

The Durbin-Watson test for serial autocorrelation of residuals

The Durbin-Watson statistic tests the null hypothesis that the residuals from an ordinary least-squares regression are not auto-correlated against the alternative that the residuals follow an AR1 process (autoregressive process of order 1).

- The **Durbin-Watson statistic** ranges in value from 0 to 4.
- A value **close to 2** indicates that there is **no autocorrelation**.
- A value **close to 0** indicates **positive autocorrelation**.
- A value **close to 4** indicates **negative autocorrelation**.

The likelihood ratio test for collective efficiency of predictor variables

H0: The predictor variables are collectively inefficient in accounting for variability in the outcome variable of study

H1: The predictor variables are collectively efficient in accounting for variability in the outcome variable of study

Decision rule

At the α level of significance,

Reject H0 if $P < \alpha$

Do not reject H0 if $P \geq \alpha$

Example:

The STATA data set **c:bos\mlr.dta** contains data gathered from a random sample of **n=289** participants who took part in a community survey conducted at Orange Farm on the variables weight, age, income, degree of malnutrition and gender. The variable number denotes frequency weights.

Weight: Weight of respondent in kg

Age: Age of respondent in years

Income: Standardized income indicator of respondent

Malnutrition: Degree of malnutrition (1 if none, 2 if minor, 3 if moderate, 4 if high, 5 if severe)

Gender: Gender of respondent (1 if male, 2 if female)

Number: Frequency weights

A review of the literature shows that women are more vulnerable to malnutrition. The literature also shows that the elderly are more vulnerable to malnutrition.

a) Perform the regression of the variable **weight** on **age**, **income,** **malnutrition** and **gender** without using frequency weights. Identify influential predictor variables at the 5% level of significance.
b) Repeat (a) by using frequency weights. Write down the equation of the fitted line of regression.

c) At the 5% level of significance, which of the 4 predictor variables is most useful in explaining variability in weight when frequency weights are used?
d) At the 5% level of significance, is the regression of weight on the 4 predictor variables significant when frequency weights are used?
e) How large is the proportion of explained variation when frequency weights are used?
f) Obtain normal probability plot of the residuals. Is the distribution normal?
g) Obtain the correlation coefficient between weight and age. Obtain a scatter plot of weight versus age. What does the plot show about the relationship between weight and age?

Solution:

a) Results from unweighted regression analysis (less reliable result)

Open up STATA

Open the STATA data set mlr.dta

Click on Statistics

Click on Linear models and related

Click on Linear regression

Dependent variable? Select the variable *weight* from the list of variables

Independent variables? Select the variables *age*, *income*, *malnutrition* and *gender* from the list of variables

Click on Reporting

Select 95% confidence level

Click on OK

```
. use c:\bos\mlr.dta, clear

. regress  weight age income malnutrition gender

      Source |       SS       df       MS              Number of obs =     289
-------------+------------------------------           F(  4,   284) =  232.19
       Model |  110240.032     4  27560.008           Prob > F      =  0.0000
    Residual |  33710.2932   284  118.698216           R-squared     =  0.7658
-------------+------------------------------           Adj R-squared =  0.7625
       Total |  143950.325   288  499.827518           Root MSE      =  10.895

------------------------------------------------------------------------------
      weight |      Coef.   Std. Err.      t    P>|t|     [95% Conf. Interval]
-------------+----------------------------------------------------------------
         age |   .9909198   .0358534    27.64   0.000     .9203476    1.061492
      income |   3.088182   .7160192     4.31   0.000     1.678805     4.49756
malnutrition |  -1.374205   .5532881    -2.48   0.014     -2.46327   -.2851389
      gender |   2.488247   1.337169     1.86   0.064    -.1437738    5.120267
       _cons |   8.359115   3.376079     2.48   0.014     1.713803    15.00443
------------------------------------------------------------------------------
```

At the 5% level of significance, the variables age, income and malnutrition are influential predictors of weight. The equation of the fitted line of regression is given by:

WEIGHT = 8.36 + 0.99 (AGE) + 3.09 (INCOME) – 1.37 (MALNUTRITION) + 2.49 (GENDER)

The most influential predictor variable is income, followed by gender, followed by age.

b) Results from weighted regression analysis (more reliable result)

Go to STATA

Open the STATA data set **c:\bos\mlr.dta**

Click on Statistics

Click on Linear models and related

Click on Linear regression

Dependent variable? Select the variable weight from the list of variables

Independent variables? Select the variables age, income, malnutrition and gender from the list of variables

Click on Weights

Click on Frequency weights

Frequency weight? Select the variable number from the list of variables

Click on Reporting

Select 95% confidence level

Click on OK

```
. regress  weight age income malnutrition gender  [fweight=number]

      Source |       SS       df       MS              Number of obs =  161097
-------------+------------------------------           F(  4,161092) =       .
       Model |  45927946.4     4  11481986.6           Prob > F      =  0.0000
    Residual |  13811679.3161092  85.7378349           R-squared     =  0.7688
-------------+------------------------------           Adj R-squared =  0.7688
       Total |  59739625.7161096  370.832458           Root MSE      =  9.2595

------------------------------------------------------------------------------
      weight |      Coef.   Std. Err.      t    P>|t|     [95% Conf. Interval]
-------------+----------------------------------------------------------------
         age |    .843528   .0013115   643.17   0.000     .8409574    .8460985
      income |   5.275137   .0250841   210.30   0.000     5.225972    5.324301
malnutrition |  -1.816807   .0213488   -85.10   0.000    -1.858651   -1.774964
      gender |   6.959603    .052639   132.21   0.000     6.856431    7.062774
       _cons |   2.654007   .1432801    18.52   0.000     2.373181    2.934833
------------------------------------------------------------------------------
```

When weights are used, the equation of the fitted line of regression is given by:

WEIGHT = 2.65 + 0.84 (AGE) + 5.28 (INCOME) – 1.82 (MALNUTRITION) + 6.96 (GENDER)

c) The variable gender is most useful. Its estimated regression coefficient is equal to $6.96 \neq 0$. The 95% confidence interval for the true regression coefficient of the variable gender is given by (6.86, 7.06), and does not contain 0. Its P-value is $0.000 < 0.05$.

d) The P-value for the likelihood ratio test (shown in the ANOVA table) is equal to $0.0000 < 0.05$. Hence, the regression of weight on the 4 predictor variables is highly significant at the

5% level. That is, the 4 predictor variables are **collectively efficient** in accounting for variability in weight.

e) The value of the adjusted R^2 is 0.7688 = 76.88%. This shows that the fitted line of regression explains 76.88% of the variability in weight in terms of age, income and malnutrition. That is, the relevance of the 4 predictor variables to weight is quite significant.

f) A normal probability plot is obtained as follows:

```
. predict e if e(sample), resid

. pnorm e, grid
```

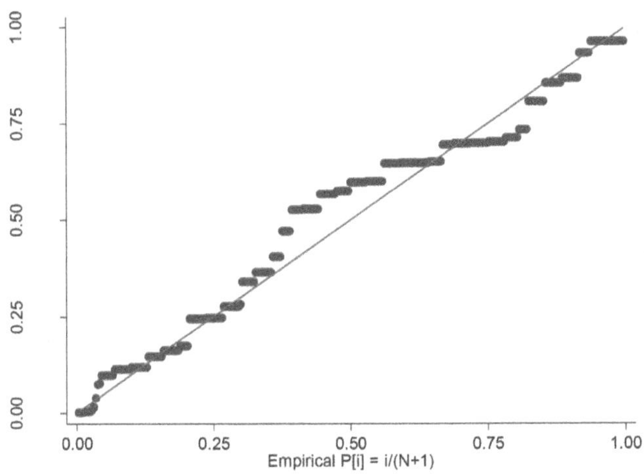

The residuals in the above normal probability plot are distributed along the diagonal axis. This shows that the distribution is normal.

Click on Graphics

Click on Distributional graphs

Click on Normal probability plot

Variable? Select the variable e

Click on OK

g) The correlation matrix is obtained as follows:

```
. corr                     (Without using frequency weights)

(obs=289)

             |   weight      age   income malnut~n   gender   number
-------------+------------------------------------------------------
      weight |   1.0000
         age |   0.8658   1.0000
      income |   0.3450   0.2943   1.0000
malnutrition |   0.0353   0.0630   0.4300   1.0000
      gender |  -0.0696  -0.1057  -0.2665  -0.0298   1.0000
      number |   0.3345   0.2572  -0.1603  -0.2850   0.1974   1.0000

. corr  [fweight=number]               (Using frequency weights)

(obs=161097)

             |   weight      age   income malnut~n   gender   number
-------------+------------------------------------------------------
      weight |   1.0000
         age |   0.8359   1.0000
      income |   0.2028   0.0262   1.0000
malnutrition |  -0.1382  -0.1076   0.3073   1.0000
      gender |   0.2028   0.1568  -0.4115  -0.1909   1.0000
      number |   0.4499   0.4216  -0.2269  -0.4885   0.3039   1.0000
```

A scatter plot of weight versus age

The scatter plot of weight versus age shown below shows that the 2 variables (weight and age) have a positive and linear relationship.

Click on Graphics

Click on Two-way graph (scatter, line, etc)

Click on Create

Click on Scatter

Y-variable? Select variable *weight* from the list

X-variable? Select variable *age* from the list

Click on Accept

Click on titles

Title? Scatter plot of weight by age

Click on OK

```
. twoway (scatter weight age), title(Scatter plot of weight by age)
```

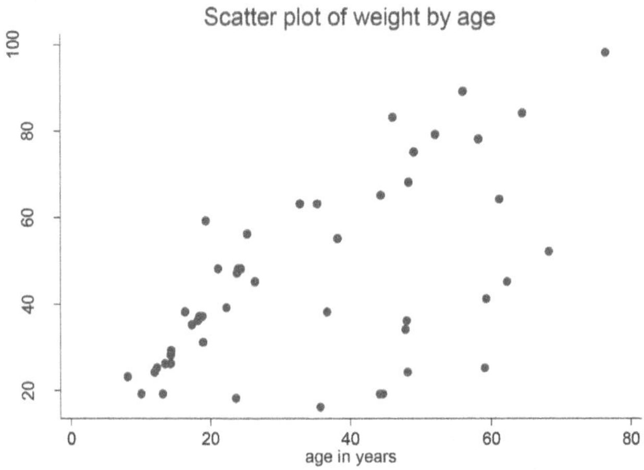

Solution from SPSS for unweighted regression analysis (without using frequency weights for performing regression analysis)

Open up the SPSS data set c:\bos\mlr.sav

Click on Analyze

Click on Regression

Click on Linear

Dependent variable? Select the variable *weight* by using the selection bar

Independent variables? Select the variables *age*, *income*, *malnutrition*, and *gender* by clicking on the selection bar

Method? Click on Stepwise

Click on Statistics

Click on Estimates

Click on Confidence Intervals

Click on Continue

Click on OK

The computer printout shown below displays estimates obtained when frequency weights are not used.

Analysis of Variance (ANOVA) table without using frequency weights

ANOVA[a]						
Model		Sum of Squares	df	Mean Square	F	P-value
1	Regression	107911.307	1	107911.307	859.362	<0.001[b]
	Residual	36039.018	287	125.571		
	Total	143950.325	288			
2	Regression	109192.038	2	54596.019	449.230	<0.001[c]
	Residual	34758.288	286	121.532		
	Total	143950.325	288			
3	Regression	109829.017	3	36609.672	305.784	<0.001[d]
	Residual	34121.309	285	119.724		
	Total	143950.325	288			

a. Dependent Variable: weight in kg
b. Predictors: (Constant), age in years
c. Predictors: (Constant), age in years, standardized income indicator
d. Predictors: (Constant), age in years, standardized income indicator, degree of malnutrition

Estimated regression coefficients without using frequency weights

Model		Unstandardized Coefficients		t	P-value	95.0% Confidence Interval for B	
		B	Std. Error			Lower Bound	Upper Bound
1	(Constant)	17.510	1.292	13.555	<0.001	14.967	20.052
	age in years	1.030	0.035	29.315	<0.001	0.961	1.099
2	(Constant)	11.773	2.177	5.409	<0.001	7.489	16.058
	age in years	0.996	0.036	27.523	<0.001	0.924	1.067
	standardized income indicator	2.047	0.631	3.246	0.001	0.806	3.288
3	(Constant)	13.085	2.234	5.857	<.001	8.688	17.482
	age in years	0.989	0.036	27.485	<.001	0.919	1.060
	standardized income indicator	2.737	0.694	3.946	<.001	1.372	4.103
	degree of malnutrition	-1.276	0.553	-2.307	0.022	-2.365	-0.187

Weighted regression analysis

Solution from SPSS for weighted regression analysis (by using frequency weights for performing regression analysis)

Open up the SPSS data set c:\bos\mlr.sav

Click on Analyze

Click on Regression

Click on Linear

Dependent variable? Select the variable *weight* by using the selection bar

Independent variables? Select the variables *age*, *income*, *malnutrition*, and *gender* by clicking on the selection bar

Method? Click on Stepwise

Click on WLS weight

Select Frequency weights by using the selection bar

Click on Statistics

Click on Estimates

Click on Confidence Intervals

Click on Continue

Click on OK

The computer printout shown below displays estimates obtained when frequency weights are used.

Analysis of Variance (ANOVA) table by using frequency weights

ANOVA[a,b]						
Model		Sum of Squares	df	Mean Square	F	P-value
1	Regression	41742556	1	41742556	665	<.001[c]
	Residual	17997069	287	62707		
	Total	59739625	288			
2	Regression	43699125	2	21849562	389	<.001[d]
	Residual	16040500	286	56085		
	Total	59739625	288			
3	Regression	45307015	3	15102338	298	<.001[e]
	Residual	14432610	285	50640		
	Total	59739625	288			
4	Regression	45927946	4	11481986	236	<.001[f]
	Residual	13811679	284	48632		
	Total	59739625	288			

a. Dependent Variable: weight in kg
b. Weighted Least Squares Regression - Weighted by frequency weights
c. Predictors: (Constant), age in years
d. Predictors: (Constant), age in years, standardized income indicator
e. Predictors: (Constant), age in years, standardized income indicator, gender of respondent
f. Predictors: (Constant), age in years, standardized income indicator, gender of respondent, degree of malnutrition

Estimated regression coefficients by using frequency weights

Model		Unstandardized Coefficients B	Unstandardized Coefficients Std. Error	t	P-value	95.0% Confidence Interval for B Lower Bound	95.0% Confidence Interval for B Upper Bound
1	(Constant)	24.516	1.386	17.683	<.001	21.787	27.245
	age in years	0.894	0.035	25.801	<.001	0.826	0.962
2	(Constant)	14.132	2.193	6.444	<.001	9.815	18.449
	age in years	0.889	0.033	27.117	<.001	0.824	0.953
	standardized income indicator	3.313	0.561	5.906	<.001	2.209	4.418
3	(Constant)	–0.657	3.351	–0.196	0.845	–7.253	5.940
	age in years	0.856	0.032	27.014	<.001	0.793	0.918
	standardized income indicator	4.707	0.588	8.010	<.001	3.551	5.864
	gender of respondent	7.198	1.277	5.635	<.001	4.684	9.713
4	(Constant)	2.654	3.412	0.778	0.437	–4.063	9.371
	age in years	0.844	0.031	27.005	<.001	0.782	0.905
	standardized income indicator	5.275	0.597	8.830	<.001	4.099	6.451
	gender of respondent	6.960	1.254	5.551	<.001	4.492	9.427
	degree of malnutrition	-1.817	0.508	-3.573	<.001	-2.818	-0.816

UNIT 11

BINARY LOGISTIC REGRESSION ANALYSIS

Binary logistic regression analysis enables researchers to perform the regression of a dichotomous dependent variable of study (Y) on a set of predictor variables that affect variable Y. The measure of effect is the odds ratio. In binary logistic regression analysis, variable Y has only 2 possible values. Example: (Yes, No), (Adequate, Inadequate), (Satisfied, Not satisfied), etc. In multiple logistic regression analysis, variable Y has 3 or more possible values (Hosmer Jr, Lemeshow & Sturdivant, 2013).

In cases where the outcome variable Y is not continuous or discrete, the relationship between Y and the predictor variables that affect Y is explored by using a non-linear regression procedure. An example of a discrete or non-continuous variable of study is the following:

Y: Degree of satisfaction in the quality of services provided

$$Y = \begin{cases} 1 & \textit{if very low} \\ 2 & \textit{if low} \\ 3 & \textit{if } \text{mod}\textit{erate} \\ 4 & \textit{if good} \\ 5 & \textit{if very good} \end{cases}$$

Binary logistic regression analysis for Y (1, 0)

The simplest form of a discrete variable is a dichotomous variable. A typical dichotomous variable has only 2 possible values (either yes or no). The relationship between a **dichotomous** outcome variable Y and a set of k explanatory variables associated with Y can be studied using binary logistic regression analysis. This method of analysis is commonly used in health-related and biomedical studies where interest is focused in outcome variables such as **sickness (yes, no)** and **exposure to hazard (yes, no)**.

Example:

Cholera sickness depends on factors such as exposure to contaminated water, literacy status, residential status, level of income, knowledge of preparing oral rehydration solutions (ORS) solutions at home, the practice of boiling drinking water, etc.

The measure of effect in logistic regression analysis is the odds ratio (OR).

The outcome variable Y is dichotomous, and has only 2 categories. That is,

$$Y = \begin{cases} 1 & if \ \ event\ occurs \\ 0 & otherwise \end{cases}$$

$X_1, X_2, \ldots\ldots, X_k$ are a combination of k discrete and continuous explanatory variables that affect the outcome variable Y.

An estimated regression coefficient is denoted by $\hat{\beta}$. In logistic regression analysis, a regression coefficient is estimated for each explanatory variable included in the model.

In general, the binary logistic regression of a dichotomous outcome variable Y on a combination of k discrete and continuous independent variables $X_1, X_2, \ldots, X_k$ is defined by the following logit function:

$$\text{logit}(p_i) = \ln\left(\frac{p_i}{1-p_i}\right) = \hat{\beta}_0 + \hat{\beta}_1 X_1 + \ldots\ldots\ldots + \hat{\beta}_k X_k$$

Interpretation of odds ratios

The odds ratio corresponding to the ith explanatory variable X_i is equal to $\exp(\hat{\beta}_i)$ where $\hat{\beta}_i$ denotes the estimated regression coefficient corresponding to X_i.

Case 1:

If $\hat{\beta} > 0$, then $\exp(\hat{\beta}) > 1$. In this case, the odds of $Y = 1$ are increased by a factor of $\exp(\hat{\beta})$.

Case 2:

If $\hat{\beta} < 0$, then $\exp(\hat{\beta}) < 1$. In this case, the odds of $Y = 1$ are decreased by a factor of $\exp(\hat{\beta})$.

Case 3:

If $\hat{\beta} = 0$, then $\exp(\hat{\beta}) = 1$. In this case, the odds of $Y = 1$ remain unchanged.

Identification of influential predictor variables

Significant predictor variables are characterised by the following 3 criteria:

1) The magnitude of the estimated odds ratio differs significantly from 1
2) The 95% confidence interval for the odds ratio does not contain 1
3) The P-value is smaller than the level of significance of test (Example: smaller than 0.05 at the 5% level of significance)

Example 1:

How to perform binary logistic regression analysis

The STATA data set **c:\bos\logistic.dta** contains data gathered from a random sample of **n = 474 mineworkers** on the following 7 variables of study:

- **Lung**: Lung disease (1 if lung function is impaired, 0 otherwise)
- **Ptb**: Pulmonary tuberculosis (1 if major, 0 otherwise)
- **Hearing**: Hearing impairment (1 if major, 0 otherwise)
- **Silica**: Exposure to silica dust (1 if major, 0 otherwise)
- **COAD**: Chronic obstructive airways disease (1 if present, 0 otherwise)
- **Jobgrade**: Job grade of mineworker (1 if machine operator, 2 if digger, 3 if driller)
- **Minetype**: Type of mine (1 if iron, 2 if copper, 3 if coal, 4 if gold)

The variable ***lung*** (1, 0) is a dichotomous outcome variable of study. The remaining 6 variables are known risk actors for chronic lung disease in the South African mining industry. The explanatory variables ***ptb*** (1, 0), ***hearing*** (1, 0), ***silica*** (1, 0) and ***COAD*** (1, 0) are each dichotomous, while the variables ***job-grade*** (1, 2, 3) and ***minetype*** (1, 2, 3, 4) are discrete variables.

The following STATA commands are suitable for performing the binary logistic regression of the dichotomous outcome variable ***lung*** (1, 0) on the 6 predictor variables shown above:

To perform a simple binary logistic regression analysis of the dichotomous outcome variable *lung* (1, 0) on all 6 predictor variables (treating all 6 predictor variables as discrete variables), use the following STATA command:

Open up the STATA data set c:\bos\logistic.dta

Click on Statistics

Click on Binary outcomes

Click on Logistic regression (reporting odds ratios)

Dependent variable? Select the variable *lung* from the list of variables

Independent variables? Select the variables *ptb*, *hearing*, *silica*, *coad*, *jobgrade* and *minetype* from the list of variables

Click on Reporting, Select 95% confidence level

Click on OK

```
. use c:\bos\logistic.dta, clear

. logistic  lung   ptb   hearing   silica   coad   jobgrade  minetype

Logistic regression                               Number of obs    =       474
                                                  LR chi2(6)       =     50.95
                                                  Prob > chi2      =    0.0000
Log likelihood = -274.82783                       Pseudo R2        =    0.0848

------------------------------------------------------------------------------
        lung | Odds Ratio   Std. Err.      z    P>|z|     [95% Conf. Interval]
-------------+----------------------------------------------------------------
         ptb |   2.802683   1.109853     2.60   0.009     1.289736    6.090417
     hearing |   1.516925   .8304918     0.76   0.447     .5187346    4.435914
      silica |   2.817107   .6884813     4.24   0.000      1.74492    4.548111
        coad |   1.334115   .3116154     1.23   0.217     .8440613    2.108688
    jobgrade |   2.041428   .5181445     2.81   0.005     1.241328    3.357234
    minetype |   1.446574   .1875004     2.85   0.004     1.122046    1.864966
------------------------------------------------------------------------------
```

Note that the categorical nature of the variables ***jobgrade*** (1, 2, 3) and ***minetype*** (1, 2, 3, 4) has been disregarded in the above STATA procedure.

To perform a stepwise binary logistic regression procedure with a probability cutoff point of 20%, use the following STATA command:

```
. sw logistic  lung  ptb  hearing  silica  coad  jobgrade  minetype, pr(0.20)

                      begin with full model
p = 0.4466 >= 0.2000  removing hearing
p = 0.2305 >= 0.2000  removing coad

Logistic regression                               Number of obs    =       474
                                                  LR chi2(4)       =     48.93
                                                  Prob > chi2      =    0.0000
Log likelihood = -275.83666                       Pseudo R2        =    0.0815

------------------------------------------------------------------------------
        lung | Odds Ratio   Std. Err.      z    P>|z|     [95% Conf. Interval]
-------------+----------------------------------------------------------------
         ptb |   2.870318   1.102859     2.74   0.006     1.351679    6.095176
    minetype |   1.382831   .1591628     2.82   0.005     1.103561    1.732773
      silica |   2.968989   .7132505     4.53   0.000     1.854051      4.7544
    jobgrade |   1.941753   .4129336     3.12   0.002     1.279903     2.94585
------------------------------------------------------------------------------
```

To treat the explanatory variables *jobgrade* (1, 2, 3) and *minetype* (1, 2, 3, 4, 5) as categorical variables in an ordinary binary logistic regression procedure, use the following STATA command:

```
. xi: logistic lung  ptb  hearing  silica  coad  i.jobgrade  i.minetype

i.jobgrade          _Ijobgrade_1-3      (naturally coded; _Ijobgrade_1 omitted)
i.minetype          _Iminetype_1-4      (naturally coded; _Iminetype_1 omitted)

note: _Ijobgrade_2 != 0 predicts success perfectly
      _Ijobgrade_2 dropped and 27 obs not used


Logistic regression                               Number of obs   =        447
                                                  LR chi2(8)      =      34.10
                                                  Prob > chi2     =     0.0000
Log likelihood = -251.54685                       Pseudo R2       =     0.0635

------------------------------------------------------------------------------
        lung | Odds Ratio   Std. Err.      z    P>|z|     [95% Conf. Interval]
-------------+----------------------------------------------------------------
         ptb |   2.000227   .8374963     1.66   0.098     .8804015    4.544414
     hearing |   .1668335   .1222766    -2.44   0.015     .0396657    .7016992
      silica |   2.587009   .6710464     3.66   0.000      1.55598    4.301222
        coad |   1.038861   .2731098     0.15   0.885     .6205574    1.739133
_Ijobgrade_3 |   .3537611   .2549721    -1.44   0.149     .0861409    1.452816
_Iminetype_2 |   .4113909   .1948321    -1.88   0.061      .162604    1.040826
_Iminetype_3 |   .6974326   .3142636    -0.80   0.424     .2883701    1.686764
_Iminetype_4 |   .9177798   .4085746    -0.19   0.847     .3835333    2.196211
------------------------------------------------------------------------------
```

To treat the discrete variables ***jobgrade*** (1, 2, 3) and ***minetype*** (1, 2, 3, 4, 5) as categorical variables in a stepwise binary logistic regression procedure with a probability cutoff point of 20%, use the following STATA command:

```
. xi: sw logistic lung ptb hearing silica coad  i.jobgrade i.minetype, pr(0.20)


i.jobgrade          _Ijobgrade_1-3      (naturally coded; _Ijobgrade_1 omitted)
i.minetype          _Iminetype_1-4      (naturally coded; _Iminetype_1 omitted)
(_Ijobgrade_2 dropped due to estimability)
(27 obs. dropped due to estimability)
                      begin with full model
p = 0.8847 >= 0.2000  removing coad
p = 0.8555 >= 0.2000  removing _Iminetype_4
p = 0.3231 >= 0.2000  removing _Iminetype_3

Logistic regression                               Number of obs   =        447
                                                  LR chi2(5)      =      33.07
                                                  Prob > chi2     =     0.0000
Log likelihood = -252.05955                       Pseudo R2       =     0.0616

------------------------------------------------------------------------------
        lung | Odds Ratio   Std. Err.      z    P>|z|     [95% Conf. Interval]
-------------+----------------------------------------------------------------
         ptb |    1.75519   .6558426     1.51   0.132     .8438494     3.65076
     hearing |   .1704557   .1156914    -2.61   0.009     .0450697    .6446705
      silica |   2.592367   .6584104     3.75   0.000     1.575825    4.264666
_Iminetype_2 |   .5373918   .1473776    -2.26   0.024     .3139442    .9198769
_Ijobgrade_3 |   .3992499   .2809074    -1.30   0.192     .1005425    1.585404
------------------------------------------------------------------------------
```

. lstat (To obtain the classification table)

```
Logistic model for lung

              -------- True --------
Classified |          D            ~D  |      Total
-----------+--------------------------+-----------
     +     |         32            32  |         64
     -     |         97           286  |        383
-----------+--------------------------+-----------
   Total   |        129           318  |        447

Classified + if predicted Pr(D) >= .5
True D defined as lung != 0
--------------------------------------------------
Sensitivity                     Pr( +| D)   24.81%
Specificity                     Pr( -|~D)   89.94%
Positive predictive value       Pr( D| +)   50.00%
Negative predictive value       Pr(~D| -)   74.67%
--------------------------------------------------
False + rate for true ~D        Pr( +|~D)   10.06%
False - rate for true D         Pr( -| D)   75.19%
False + rate for classified +   Pr(~D| +)   50.00%
False - rate for classified -   Pr( D| -)   25.33%
--------------------------------------------------
Correctly classified                        71.14%
--------------------------------------------------
```

Sensitivity is a measure of the ability of the fitted model to accurately detect mineworkers with lung disease (**lung = 1**). In highly sensitive models, percentage sensitivity is 75% or higher.

Specificity is a measure of the ability of the fitted model to accurately detect mineworkers with no lung disease (**lung = 0**). In highly specific models, percentage sensitivity is 75% or higher.

In this example, the fitted model is **poorly sensitive and highly specific**.

. lfit (To perform the Hosmer-Lemeshow goodness-of-fit test)

```
Logistic model for lung, goodness-of-fit test
       number of observations =       447
 number of covariate patterns =        14
             Pearson chi2(8) =        27.67
                 Prob > chi2 =        0.0005
```

Null hypothesis: There is no reason to doubt the reliability of the fitted model

Alternative hypothesis: There is enough reason to doubt the reliability of the fitted model

Decision rule:

Reject the null hypothesis if $P < \alpha$

Do not reject the null hypothesis if $P \geq \alpha$

Solution from SPSS

Open up the SPSS data set c:\bos\logistic.sav

Click on Analyze

Click on Regression

Click on Binary logistic

Dependent variable? Select the variable *lung* by using the selection bar

Covariates? Select the variables *ptb*, *hearing*, silica, coad, jobgrade and minetype by clicking on the selection bar

Method? Click on Backward LR

Click on Categorical variables

Select the variables *jobgrade* and *minetype* as categorical variables

Reference category? Click on first

Click on Continue

Click on Options

Click on Classification plots, Hosmer and Lemeshow goodness-of-fit test, Confidence Interval for exp(B)

Click on Continue

Click on OK

The computer printout shown below displays estimates obtained from SPSS:

Regression estimates obtained from SPSS from binary logistic regression analysis with a stepwise backward elimination procedure

		B	P-value	Exp(B)	95% C.I. for Exp(B)	
					Lower	Upper
Step 1[a]	ptb	0.693	0.098	2.000	0.880	4.544
	hearing	–1.791	0.015	0.167	0.040	0.702
	silica	0.951	<0.001	2.587	1.556	4.301
	coad	0.038	0.885	1.039	0.621	1.739
	jobgrade		0.354			
	jobgrade(1)	21.759	0.998	2815980614	0.000	.
	jobgrade(2)	–1.039	0.149	0.354	0.086	1.453
	minetype		0.116			
	minetype(1)	–0.888	0.061	0.411	0.163	1.041
	minetype(2)	–0.360	0.424	0.697	0.288	1.687
	minetype(3)	–0.086	0.847	0.918	0.384	2.196
	Constant	0.460	0.613	1.583		
Step 2[a]	ptb	0.681	0.097	1.976	0.885	4.413
	hearing	–1.801	0.014	0.165	0.040	0.691
	silica	0.958	<.001	2.606	1.582	4.293
	jobgrade		0.356			
	jobgrade(1)	21.782	0.998	2882545772	0.000	.
	jobgrade(2)	–1.036	0.151	0.355	0.087	1.457
	minetype		0.105			
	minetype(1)	–0.874	0.059	0.417	0.168	1.034
	minetype(2)	–0.360	0.425	0.698	0.289	1.687
	minetype(3)	–0.081	0.855	0.922	0.387	2.201
	Constant	0.489	0.581	1.631		

The classification table shown below indicates that the fitted binary logistic regression model classifies 73% of all cases accurately.

Classification Table[a]					
			Predicted		
			lung		
	Observed		0	1	Percentage Correct
Step 1	lung	0	309	9	97.2
		1	119	37	23.7
	Overall Percentage				73.0
Step 2	lung	0	309	9	97.2
		1	119	37	23.7
	Overall Percentage				73.0

a. The cut value is .500

At the end of Step 2 of analysis, the P-value obtained from the Hosmer-Lemeshow goodness-of-fit test is equal to 0.498. Since this figure is above 0.05, we cannot reject the null hypothesis. We conclude that we have no reason to doubt the adequacy of the fitted binary logistic regression analysis model at the 5% level.

The Hosmer and Lemeshow Goodness-of-fit test			
Step	**Chi-square**	**df**	**P-value**
1	20.844	8	0.008
2	6.360	7	0.498

UNIT 12

TIME SERIES ANALYSIS

Introduction to time series analysis

In cross-sectional data sets, data is gathered only once in time.

In time series data, data is gathered repeatedly at regular intervals (hours, days, weeks, months, quarters, years, etc).

Examples of time series data sets

Hourly price of Brent crude oil per barrel quoted at the New York Stock Exchange

The number of international flights arriving at OR Tambo airport **daily**

Monthly export of gold from South Africa

Quarterly data on the number of new cars sold by Toyota in all South African dealerships

The number of tourists who have visited Robben Island **annually** since 1994

- Time series analysis is used for quantifying factors that affect time series data.
- Time series analysis enables researchers to identify recurrent patterns in a time series so that the patterns could be quantified.
- A statistical model can be constructed once recurrent patterns are quantified.
- Forecasting is done by using the statistical models constructed.

Example 1: Number of pairs of shoes sold

Quarter	Months	2003	2004	2005	2006
1	1 to 3	54	55	49	60
2	4 to 6	58	61	69	72
3	7 to 9	94	84	95	99
4	10 to 12	70	76	88	80

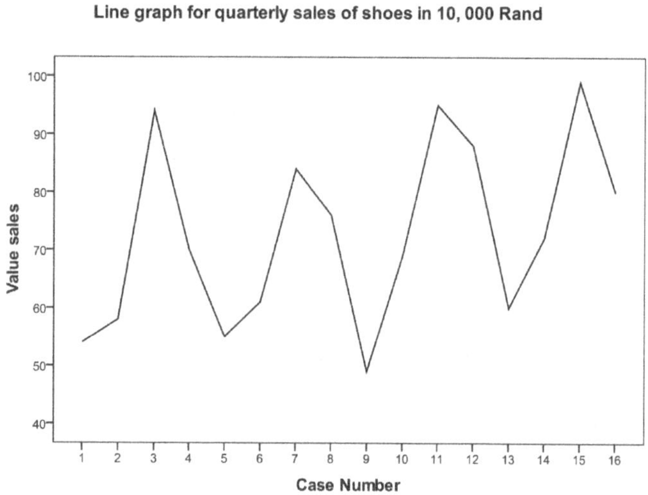

The 4 components of a time series:

1) Trend
2) Cycles
3) Seasonality
4) Irregular or random influences

T: Trends (Useful for time series analysis)

- Trend is defined as a long-term smooth underlying movement in a time series.
- Trend is explained by a smooth, continuous curve or a straight line.

- Trend analysis is used for isolating an underlying long-term movement from a time series.
- Forecast analysis (linear regression analysis) is used to quantify trend

C: Cycles

- Cycles are medium to long-term deviations from the trend.
- Cycles stimulate or depress levels of activities
- Examples of cycles are wave-like movements that describe periods of relative expansion and contraction in economic activities (Change in fiscal policy, economic sanction, etc)
- Cycles vary in terms of duration and amplitude
- A cyclical index is used for quantifying cyclical variation

S: Seasonal variations (Useful for time series analysis)

- Fluctuations in a time series that are repeated at regular intervals within a year (daily, weekly, monthly, quarterly)
- Often caused by climatic conditions, annual holidays, etc.
- A seasonal index is used for quantifying seasonal variation

I: Irregular fluctuations

- Fluctuations caused by unpredictable events in a time series
- Often caused by the outbreak of a sudden war, natural disasters, riots, strike actions, etc.

The multiplicative time series model

The multiplicative time series model is defined as follows:

$$y = T \times C \times S \times I$$

Trend analysis (2 methods)

Trend analysis can be performed based on the **moving average method** or **simple linear regression analysis**.

Example of the 3-period moving average method

A moving average removes the short-term fluctuations in a time series by taking successive averages of groups of observations. If a time series pattern repeats itself for approximately 3 consecutive time periods within a year, a 3-period moving average becomes suitable for removing short-term fluctuations.

Numerical example:

The table below shows the number of MBA students who successfully graduated from a certain Business School in the years 2003, 2004, 2005, and 2006 on a quarterly basis:

Year	Quarter	Graduates
2003	1	7
	2	3
	3	5
2004	1	9
	2	7
	3	9
2005	1	14
	2	4
	3	10
2006	1	13
	2	9
	3	10

Compute a 3-period moving average for the number of MBA graduates.

Solution:

Year	Quarter	Graduates	3-period moving total (centered)	3-period moving average
2003	1	7	-	-
	2	3	7+3+5 = 15	$\frac{15}{3} = 5$
	3	5	3+5+9 = 17	$\frac{17}{3} = 5.67$
2004	1	9	5+9+7 = 21	$\frac{21}{3} = 7$
	2	7	9+7+9 = 25	$\frac{25}{3} = 8.33$
	3	9	7+9+14 = 30	$\frac{30}{3} = 10$
2005	1	14	9+14+4 = 27	$\frac{27}{3} = 9$
	2	4	14+4+10 = 28	$\frac{28}{3} = 9.33$
	3	10	4+10+13 = 27	$\frac{27}{3} = 9$
2006	1	13	10+13+9 = 32	$\frac{32}{3} = 10.67$
	2	9	13+9+10 = 32	$\frac{32}{3} = 10.67$
	3	10	-	-

Example of simple linear regression analysis

Simple linear regression techniques are used for estimating the equation of the trend in the time series. Once that is done, future values of Y (the dependent variable of study) are predicted based on the fitted line of regression.

A simple linear regression of Y on X is performed as follows:

Y denotes values of the actual time series

The equation of the fitted line of regression is given by:

$\hat{Y} = \hat{\beta}_0 + \hat{\beta}X$

$X = 1,\ 2,\ 3,\ \ldots\ldots,\ n$ denote values of time

β_0 is the Y-intercept of the line of regression

β is the slope of the line of regression

$$\hat{\beta} = \frac{\sum XY - n\overline{X}\overline{Y}}{\sum X^2 - n\overline{X}^2}$$

$$\hat{\beta}_0 = \overline{Y} - b\overline{X}$$

$$\overline{X} = \frac{\sum_{i=1}^{n} X_i}{n}$$

$$\overline{Y} = \frac{\sum_{i=1}^{n} Y_i}{n}$$

Example:

X	1	2	3	4	5	6	7	8	9	10	11	12	13	14	15	16
Y	54	58	94	70	55	61	87	66	49	55	95	74	60	64	99	80
XY	54	116	282	280	275	366	609	528	441	550	1045	888	780	896	1485	1280

Y: Number of houses sold between Quarter 1 of 2003 and Quarter 4 of 2006

X: Indices for Quarters (1, 2, ….., 16)

a) Estimate the equation of the trend line for the number of houses sold

b) What is the expected number of houses to be sold in Quarter 1 of 2007?

Solution:

n = 16

$$\sum_{i=1}^{n} X_i = X_1 + X_2 + \dots\dots + X_n = 1 + 2 + \dots. + 16 = 136$$

$$\sum_{i=1}^{n} X_i^2 = X_1^2 + X_2^2 + \dots\dots + X_n^2 = 1496$$

$$\sum_{i=1}^{n} Y_i = Y_1 + Y_2 + \dots\dots + Y_n = 1121$$

$$\sum_{i=1}^{n} Y_i^2 = Y_1^2 + Y_2^2 + \dots\dots + Y_n^2 = 82511$$

$$\overline{X} = \frac{\sum_{i=1}^{n} X_i}{n} = \frac{136}{16} = 8.5$$

$$\overline{Y} = \frac{\sum_{i=1}^{n} Y_i}{n} = \frac{1121}{16} = 70.06$$

$$n\overline{X}^2 = 16(8.5)^2 = 1156$$

$$n\overline{Y}^2 = 16(70.06)^2 = 78534.46$$

$$n\overline{X}\overline{Y} = 16(8.5)(70.06) = 9528.16$$

$$\sum XY = 1(54) + 2(58) + \dots\dots + 16(80) = 9875$$

$$\hat{\beta} = \frac{\sum XY - n\overline{X}\overline{Y}}{\sum X^2 - n\overline{X}^2} = \frac{9875 - 9528.16}{1496 - 1156} = \frac{346.84}{340} = 1.02$$

$\hat{\beta}_0 = \overline{Y} - \hat{\beta}\overline{X} = 70.06 - 1.02(8.5) = 61.39$

a) $\hat{Y} = \hat{\beta}_0 + \hat{\beta}X = 61.39 + 1.02X = f(X)$ is the equation of the trend line.

b) $f(17) = 61.39 + 1.02(17) = 78.72 \approx$ **79 houses**

Second method:

The equation of the trend line could be obtained using STATA as shown below:

```
. use c:\bos\timeseries.dta, clear
. regress houses  x

      Source |       SS       df       MS              Number of obs =      16
-------------+------------------------------           F(  1,    14) =    1.37
       Model |  353.124265     1  353.124265           Prob > F      =  0.2619
    Residual |  3617.81324    14  258.415231           R-squared     =  0.0889
-------------+------------------------------           Adj R-squared =  0.0239
       Total |   3970.9375    15  264.729167           Root MSE      =  16.075

------------------------------------------------------------------------------
      houses |      Coef.   Std. Err.      t    P>|t|     [95% Conf. Interval]
-------------+----------------------------------------------------------------
           x |   1.019118   .8718055     1.17   0.262    -.8507191    2.888954
       _cons |       61.4   8.429958     7.28   0.000     43.31954    79.48046
------------------------------------------------------------------------------


. use c:\bos\timeseries.dta, clear
. predict yhat, xb
. list  x  houses  yhat

     +-----------------------+
     |  x   houses      yhat |
     |-----------------------|
  1. |  1       54  62.41912 |
  2. |  2       58  63.43824 |
  3. |  3       94  64.45735 |
  4. |  4       70  65.47647 |
  5. |  5       55  66.49559 |
     |-----------------------|
  6. |  6       61  67.51471 |
  7. |  7       87  68.53382 |
  8. |  8       66  69.55294 |
  9. |  9       49  70.57206 |
 10. | 10       55  71.59118 |
     |-----------------------|
 11. | 11       95  72.61029 |
 12. | 12       74  73.62941 |
 13. | 13       60  74.64853 |
 14. | 14       64  75.66765 |
 15. | 15       99  76.68677 |
     |-----------------------|
 16. | 16       80  77.70588 |
     +-----------------------+
```

```
. use c:\bos\timeseries.dta, clear

. gen future = 61.39 + 1.02*17

. list future in 1/5

     +--------+
     | future |
     |--------|
  1. |  78.73 |
  2. |  78.73 |
  3. |  78.73 |
  4. |  78.73 |
  5. |  78.73 |
     +--------+
```

UNIT 13

THE CONSUMER PRICE INDEX

The consumer price index

The consumer price index (CPI) measures changes in the price level of a weighted average market basket of consumer goods and services purchased by households. A CPI is a statistical estimate constructed using the prices of a sample of representative items whose prices are collected periodically.

Example 1:

The Consumer Price Index (CPI) and average annual wages for 4 groups of school children during their summer vacations are shown in the table below. The amounts shown in the table below are average wages in Rand per hour.

Group	A	B	C	D	CPI (1982-1984=100)
1980	7.27	9.17	5.85	4.88	82.4
1984	9.54	11.98	7.90	5.94	107.6
2001	14.84	17.65	14.61	9.82	177.1

From 1980 to 2001, the average wages went up for workers in all 4 groups. However, which wage earning groups fared best and worst in terms of their percentage change in spending power during this period?

Solution:

To determine which wage-earner groups fared best and worst in terms of their percentage change in spending power during this period, we must compute ratios of both earnings and the CPI, and then compare the ratios. Of course, one problem with these data is that we have only average hourly earnings; we do not know whether the number of hours worked per week increased, decreased, or remained fairly constant.

By 2001, the CP1 was 2.149 times its size in 1980. In 2001, the average hourly wage in group A was 2.041 times as large as its 1980 value. Corresponding multiples for groups B, C, and D were 1.925, 2.497, and 2.012, respectively. To examine changes in spending power in each employment group, we can look at the ratio of the change in wages to the change in the CPI:

For group A, the ratio is $\frac{2.041}{2.149} \times 100 = 94.97$. Therefore, workers in group A experienced a 100 – 94.97 = 5.03% decline in spending power between 1980 and 2001.

For group B, the ratio is $\frac{1.925}{2.149} \times 100 = 89.58$. Hence, workers in group B experienced a 100 – 89.58 = 10.42% decline in spending power between 1980 and 2001.

For group C, the ratio is $\frac{2.497}{2.149} \times 100 = 116.19$. Therefore, workers in group C experienced a 116.19 – 100 = 16.19% increase in spending power between 1980 and 2001.

For group D, the ratio is $\frac{2.012}{2.149} \times 100 = 93.62$. Therefore, workers in group D experienced a 100 – 93.62 = 6.38% decline in spending power between 1980 and 2001.

The wage-earners who fared best were in group C, whereas wage-earners who fared worst were in group B.

Example 2:

From 1996 to 2004, the median weekly earnings of trainee workers represented by unions went from 610 Rand to 712 Rand, while the Consumer Price Index went from 156.9 to 177.1. What was the percentage increase or decrease in real wages for the trainee workers?

Solution:

Between 1996 and 2001, the median weekly earnings of union workers grew to 1.1672 times its 1996 value. The CPI grew to 1.1287 times its 1996 value over this same period. Therefore, real earnings changed by $\frac{1.1672}{1.1287} \times 100 = 103.41$, which implies an increase of 3.41%.

Example 3:

Convert each of the following indexes so that the new base period becomes 2002:

	A	B
1999	101.3	100.0
2000	100.0	102.9
2001	103.4	104.7
2002	105.6	103.2
2003	107.9	107.5
2004	110.3	126.4
2005	116.2	122.1
2006	125.3	129.0
	2000 = 100	1999 = 100

Solution:

	A	Base 2002	B	Base 2002
1999	101.3	95.928	100.0	96.899
2000	100.0	94.697	102.9	99.709
2001	103.4	97.917	104.7	101.453
2002	105.6	**100.000**	103.2	**100.000**
2003	107.9	102.178	107.5	104.167
2004	110.3	104.451	126.4	122.481
2005	116.2	110.038	122.1	118.314
2006	125.3	118.655	129.0	125.00
	2000 = 100	**2002 = 100**	1999 = 100	**2002 = 100**

Examples of conversion calculations to be made are shown below.

Shifting the base year from 1999 to 2002 for Item A:

In 1999, the price of Item A was 103.3. If the base year is converted from 1999 to 2002, the corresponding price for Item A is obtained as follows:

$\frac{101.3}{105.6} \times 100 = 95.928$ (A decrease in price of 4.072% between 1999 and 2002)

Follow this example to calculate all other prices for Item A for the base year 2002.

Shifting the base year from 1999 to 2002 for Item B:

In 1999, the price of Item B was 100.0. If the base year is converted from 1999 to 2002, the corresponding price of Item B is obtained as follows:

$\frac{100.0}{103.2} \times 100 = 96.899$ (A decrease in price of 3.101% between 1999 and 2002)

Follow this example to calculate all other prices for Item B for the base year 2002.

The Laspeyres weighted average of price relatives

The Laspeyres Price Index is a consumer price index which is used to measure the change in the prices of a basket of goods and services relative to a specified base period weighting. Developed by German economist Etienne Laspeyres, the Laspeyres Price Index is also called the base year quantity weighted method. The Laspeyres Price Index is a composite measure.

The Laspeyres Price Index is a price index used to measure the economy's general price level and cost of living, and to calculate inflation. The index commonly uses a base year figure of 100, with periods of higher price levels shown by an index greater than 100 and periods of lower price levels by indexes lower than 100.

Laspeyres Price Index differs from the Paasche Price Index and the Fisher Price Index in that it uses weights measured in the base period.

The Laspeyres Price Index is shown below:

$$\text{Laspeyres Price Index} = \frac{\sum p_1 q_0}{\sum p_0 q_0} = \frac{725.05}{624.85} \times 100\% = 116.04\%$$

Where

p_0 is the price of the individual item at the base period

p_1 is the price of the individual item at the observation period

q_0 is the quantity of the individual item at the base period

Example:

The following table shows the price of a basket of 3 goods (a loaf of bread, a tube of tooth paste, and a bar of soap) in November 2018 and November 2019:

	Base Year (2018)		Current Year (2019)	
Items	**Unit price** (p_0)	**Quantity** (q_0)	**Unit price** (p_1)	**Quantity** (q_1)
Bread	10.15	25	10.45	23
Tooth paste	11.45	18	12.05	16
Soap	13.75	12	14.65	11

Determine Laspeyres price index, and interpret your result.

Solution:

	Base Year (2018)		Current Year (2019)		Value in period	
Items	**Unit price** (p_0)	**Quantity** (q_0)	**Unit price** (p_1)	**Quantity** (q_1)	**Base value** ($p_0 q_0$)	**Current value** ($p_1 q_0$)
Bread	10.15	25	10.45	23	253.75	261.25
Tooth paste	11.45	18	12.05	16	206.10	288.00
Soap	13.75	12	14.65	11	165.00	175.80
				Total	624.85	725.05

$$\text{Laspeyres Price Index} = \frac{\sum p_1 q_0}{\sum p_0 q_0} = \frac{725.05}{624.85} \times 100\% = 116.04\%$$

The price of the basket of 3 goods has increased by 116.04% - 100.0% = 16.04% on average between November 2018 and November 2019.

UNIT 14

AN EXAMPLE BASED ON THEMATIC ANALYSIS

A thematic analysis of determinants of nonpayment of municipal services in Soweto

By

Zeleke Worku
Tshwane School for Business and Society
159 Nana Sita Street, Pretoria 0001, South Africa
E-Mail: WorkuZ@tut.ac.za
Tel: (012) 382 3050
Cell: 082 870 2758

Abstract

The study explored factors that affect the nonpayment of municipal services in Soweto. A total of 12 one-hour-long individual in-depth interviews were conducted as part of the qualitative enquiry by using a tape recorder. Seven interview questions were used for collecting qualitative data from 12 eligible participants of research. There were 4 themes that emerged from each one of the 7 interview questions. Thus, there were a total of 28 themes in the study. Each interview was transcribed. Tallies, codes, and categories were extracted out of the transcripts. Themes were created out of tallies, codes, and categories. Open, axial and selective coding techniques were used for creating codes and categories. The study found that negative perception about leadership and accountability were key determinants of the nonpayment of municipal services. A recommendation was made to the relevant stakeholders, highlighting the need for a closer cooperation with residents and ratepayers, the provision of rewards and incentives to people who pay their municipal bills promptly, and a display of exemplary leadership.

Keywords: Soweto, Nonpayment of municipal services, Thematic analysis

Introduction and background to study

A study was carried out in Soweto, Gauteng Province, South Africa, to explore determinants of nonpayment of municipal services among residents and ratepayers. The study was carried out by conducting 12 one-hour-long individual in-depth interviews with people who live and work in Soweto. Seven interview questions were used for collecting qualitative data on socioeconomic factors that affect the payment of municipal services by residents and ratepayers. Thematic analysis (Thompson, 2022) was used for performing qualitative data analysis. This was done by creating tallies, codes and categories (Braun, Clarke and Hayfield, 2022). Multiple sources of information were used for establishing trustworthiness (Castleberry & Nolen, 2018).

Studies conducted by Aubriot (2016), Manga, Bartram, and Evans (2020) have shown that municipal water is lost in Soweto due to failure to repair and maintain broken municipal water and sewerage pipelines. The study conducted by Sinwell, Ngwane, and Maggott (2022) shows South African townships such as Soweto need to be able to use scarce resources such as water with care. An ideal method of doing so is to pay for municipal services promptly and regularly. The survey carried out in Soweto by Worku and Mboweni (2022) has shown that local municipalities such as Soweto need to develop the capacity for maintaining and expanding municipal infrastructure by way of providing economic incentives to local and international entrepreneurs. Residents and ratepayers need to be motivated enough to pay their municipal service fees in good time and on a regular basis. Failure to do this results in lack of capacity to provide satisfactory municipal services.

The survey carried out by Phillips and Petrova (2015) shows the need for building capacity for the optimal utilisation of municipal resources and infrastructure. To achieve this goal, municipalities need to be able to collect revenues that are owed to them by residents, ratepayers, and businesses that operate in their localities. Following the Covid-19 outbreak of 2020 and 2021, business enterprises, and employees working in business enterprises had lost significant revenue and, consequently, the ability to pay their municipal service fees promptly and fully.

Literature review

At the level of local municipalities, the quality of service delivery is often hampered by lack of human, financial, and logistical resources. Various surveys have shown that an appropriate remedial action is to discourage the non-payment of municipal bills by residents and ratepayers (Khale & Worku, 2015; Kambule, Yessoufou & Nwulu, 2022). The study examined the effects of nonpayment of municipal services on the delivery of services in Soweto. At the local government level (municipalities), service delivery is hampered by limited resources, yet it is a key mandate of the State that municipal and government officials are required to render essential municipal services to the people. Soweto is a major attraction to people who live in rural regions. An inflow of people into Soweto results in a higher level of demand for municipal services. People and businesses that require municipal services are required to pay for such services promptly and fully on a regular basis. In return, municipal employees are required to serve them efficiently at all times. Studies conducted by Worku (2017, 2018, and 2022) in various local municipalities within Gauteng Province have found that the capacity of local municipalities to render satisfactory municipal services is severely undermined by nonpayment of essential municipal services. The author has pointed out that key areas of nonpayment are electricity and water services.

The Municipal Finance Management Act (Act no. 32 of 2000) sets service level standards and requirements for all categories of municipal services (South African government, 2023). The Act also states that South African municipalities should render municipal services by using payments made by residents and ratepayers for municipal services. A major aspect of the duty and responsibility of municipalities is the maintenance, repair, and expansion of municipal infrastructure. The Act requires municipalities to propose and implement constructive service delivery and developmental projects, and to govern and manage municipal resources and communities in accordance with constitutional rights that are stipulated in the South African Constitution. The extent to which municipalities carry out their duties is assessed by the South African Auditor-General.

The main responsibility of ensuring satisfactory municipal level performance and the collection of service fees lies with municipalities. These municipalities are accountable to the South African Department of Cooperative Governance and Traditional Affairs (CoGTA, 2023) in terms of rendering quality and affordable municipal services to all people and business enterprises. Municipalities rely on municipal service fees, rates, and taxes to generate 92% of their income. The remaining 8% of revenue is given to them by the South African National Treasury.

The cost of repairing, maintaining and expanding municipal infrastructure in Soweto is quite high (Worku & Mboweni, 2022).

It follows that people who use municipal services need to pay their service fees promptly, fully, and regularly in order for municipalities to be able to render essential services at an affordable cost and decent service quality. Wall (2022) has shown that people and businesses that require efficient municipal services must be committed enough to pay for such services. In order to collect municipal service fees efficiently in local municipalities, services need to be rendered efficiently. All account-related queries need to be resolved promptly and accurately. Municipal employees who render such services must possess the required skills and experience to perform satisfactorily (McKay & Tantoh, 2021). An active interaction is needed between local municipalities and people and businesses that rely on municipal services on a regular basis. In this regard, effective communication and commitment to resolving account-related queries promptly and effectively are highly helpful.

Khale and Worku (2015) has pointed out the need for maintaining, repairing and expanding municipal infrastructure in South African townships. The author has shown that the demand for efficient municipal services is growing rapidly. In this regard, the main contributing factors are migration from rural to urban centres, poor municipal services in rural areas, unemployment and poverty in rural areas, and the failure of local municipalities in most rural regions (Tongwane, Ramotubei & Moeletsi, 2022). There is a considerable pressure on municipal resources to cope with a rapidly growing demand for municipal services in urban centres and townships such as Soweto. This development has resulted in a significant challenge in townships such as Soweto. In this regard, a reliable remedial action is to enhance the quality and efficiency of municipal services by providing quality services to people and businesses that pay for the services. Municipal bylaws must be enforced effectively in order to protect and preserve municipal and environmental resources and the general environment (Sucha & Duskova, 2022). Local municipalities such as Soweto need to pre-empt municipal protests by rendering efficient services to all people and businesses that deserve such services.

The study is inspired by the service excellence theory proposed by James Grunig (2006), in which the author has identified 6 pillars of service excellence (personalisation of services to clients, integrity, expectations, resolution, time and effort, and empathy).

The theory shows that it is not possible to render efficient municipal services without adhering to the basic principles of good leadership, accountability, and transparency. Adequate consultations with stakeholders are highly helpful. Studies carried out by Khale and Worku (2015), McKay and Tantoh (2021), and Worku (2022) have shown that inability to follow processes and steps stipulated in integrated development plan (IDP) documents often results in failure to render efficient and affordable municipal services in South African municipalities.

Objective of study

The objective of the research was to explore determinants of satisfactory municipal service delivery among residents and ratepayers of Soweto in Gauteng Province, South Africa.

Methods and materials of study

Individual in-depth interviews (Braun and Hayfield, 2022) were conducted with 12 eligible participants of study in Soweto. Twelve 1-hour-long individual interviews were conducted by using a digital tape-recording device. All such interviews were conducted in compliance with Covid-19 guidelines and requirements. Saturation (Thompson, 2022) was achieved after interviewing participant number 12. That is, after participant number 12 was interviewed, all subsequent interviews led to views and opinions expressed in interviews held with participants 1 to 12. Qualitative data analyses were performed by using coding, tallying, text analyses, thematic analysis, and triangulation (Castleberry & Nolen, 2018:807-815). Seven interview questions were used for gathering data from 12 participants of study. Four themes emerged from each one of the 7 interview questions. Thus, there were a total of 28 themes in the study. Each interview was transcribed. Tallies, codes, and categories were extracted out of the transcripts. Themes were created out of tallies, codes, and categories.

The manual creation of codes and categories

Codes and categories were created manually in the study and subsequently moderated by two suitably qualified, independent and well-experienced subjectmatter specialists or experts. Manual coding enables the researcher to gain an in-depth understanding of information or data gathered from respondents and the research questions that need to be answered. Manual coding enables the researcher to understand contexts of the research being carried out along with accurate interpretations of views and opinions expressed by the participants of study. Manual coding also enables the researcher to critically observe and examine sources of data. Manual coding allows the researcher to use deductive or inductive coding processes.

In deductive or concept-driven coding, the coding process begins with a set of predefined codes, which are then assigned to new qualitative data. These codes are often obtained from past experience, a review of the literature, expert opinion, and an in-depth understanding of themes that are of interest to the researcher. The process entails reading data gathered from participants, examining views expressed by participants critically, and placing similar codes into categories.

In inductive coding, codes are extracted or derived from views and opinions expressed by participants of the study. The process of inductive coding entails breaking qualitative data sets into smaller samples, examining a sample of the data critically, creating codes that cover the sample, re-examining the sample and applying the codes created, reading the newly created sample of data, and applying the codes created for the initial sample.

A combination of open, axial and selective coding processes were used for creating categories. Open coding is the first level of coding and entails breaking data into discrete parts. Axial coding is used for drawing connections between codes. Categories are created by putting like ideas, opinions and views together. Categories created by using open and axial coding should be mutually exclusive and exhaustive in order to account for all possible views expressed by participants of the study. Selective coding refers to the process of electing a core category, systematically relating it to other categories, validating those relationships, and filling in categories that need further refinement and development.

Open, axial, and selective coding are three distinct processes used in qualitative research. They are based on the basic principles of grounded theory in which views and opinions gathered from participants of the study are systematically analysed and placed in categories in order to identify patterns, themes and relationships.

In qualitative research, analysis often focuses on quotations, segments of the material that present an insight or information. A code is a simplification of the idea or insight. Open coding refers to coding the material without a pre-defined list of codes. In open coding, the researcher places similar concepts, views and opinions in distinct categories.

Assessment of trustworthiness of results

Lincoln and Guba (1985) and Adler (2022) recommend the assessment of trustworthiness by ensuring adequate transferability, credibility, dependability and confirmability. In this particular study, the level of trustworthiness was ensured by using multiple sources of empirical facts (triangulation). A pilot study (Braun, Clarke and Hayfield, 2022) was carried out by administering 1-hourlong in-dividual interviews with a purposive sample of size 12 eligible participants. The exercise was helpful for refining the 7 interview questions. Trustworthiness was ascertained by using multiple sources of credible evidence. In this study, interviews were carried out through face-to-face interactions. These interviews were transcribed and handed over to the participants of research so that they could confirm that the transcription was an accurate reflec-tion of what they said during the interviews. A pilot survey was carried out by interviewing 2 of the 12 eligible participants. This was done before carrying out the actual study. The pilot study enabled the researcher to amend and refine the list of interview questions and was quite helpful. Credibility was ascertained by sharing and corroborating valuable information with people and experts who are well informed and highly knowledgeable about the subject being researched. Three suitably qualified experts on municipal service delivery were asked to check the credibility of

information gathered from the 12 participants of study. Transferability is a measure of the ability to apply results obtained from a study to a different study with a different context and different participants of study. In this study, transferability was ascertained by having transcripts of interviews reviewed by municipal employees who were responsible for collecting revenues, generat-ing financial statements, and taking legal action against people who fail to pay their municipal service fees. Dependability was ascertained by asking the 12 participants of study to comment on how reliable and accurate the views expressed by the participants of study were. The process showed that the views expressed by the participants of study were a true reflection of the reality. Confirmability entails the corroboration of views expressed by the participants of study. In this particular study, confirmability was assessed by verifying the accuracy of views and opinions expressed by checking past records, reports, and financial statements. Authenticity was ascertained by corroborating the level of truthfulness of views and opinions expressed by participants of the study during interviews. In this study, authenticity was established by confirming that the views and opinions expressed by the 12 participants were factually correct or truthful. Each interview was validated to establish authenticity. The relevant stakeholders took part in corroborating views and opinions expressed by the 12 participants of study.

Results of study

Table A displays the distribution of gender, age, duration of residence, highest level of academic qualification, and occupation of the 12 participants of study. Studies conducted in the past by McKay and Tantoh (2021), Patji and Selepe (2022), Worku and Mboweni (2022), and Kambule, Yessoufou and Nwulu (2022) have shown that socioeconomic characteristics such as gender, age, duration of residence, highest level of academic qualification, and occupation are reliable predictors of nonpayment of municipal services in South African local municipalities.

Table A: Socioeconomic characteristics of participants (n=12)

Participant number	Gender	Age	Duration of residence in years	Highest academic qualification	Occupation of respondent
1	Male	53	24	Bachelor's degree	Civil servant
2	Female	36	11	Diploma	Hairdresser
3	Male	48	14	Diploma	Mechanic
4	Male	32	9	Diploma	Electrician
5	Male	52	13	Grade 12	Plumber

Participant number	Gender	Age	Duration of residence in years	Highest academic qualification	Occupation of respondent
6	Male	49	22	Certificate	Mini-market owner
7	Female	41	16	Bachelor's degree	Spaza shop owner
8	Male	48	19	Diploma	Truck driver
9	Male	29	8	Grade 12	Taxi driver
10	Female	26	5	Bachelor's degree	Nurse
11	Male	46	22	Honour's degree	Teacher
12	Male	44	17	Master's degree	Fast food outlet owner

Thematic analysis

A total of 12 one-hour-long individual in-depth interviews were conducted as part of the qualitative enquiry by using a tape recorder. Each interview was transcribed. Tallies, codes, and categories were created manually. Themes were created out of tallies, codes, and categories. There were 4 themes that emerged from each one of the 7 interview questions. Thus, there were a total of 28 themes in the study. Each interview was transcribed. Tallies, codes and categories were extracted out of the transcripts. Themes were created out of tallies, codes and categories. The following table shows details of themes corresponding to interview questions. All tallies, codes, categories and themes were moderated by two suitably trained and qualified moderators.

Table B: List of 7 interview questions and 28 themes

Interview questions	Theme 1	Theme 2	Theme 3	Theme 4
Q1: How satisfied are you with the quality of municipal services that are provided to you by municipal employees?	Electricity services	Water services	Waste management services	Sanitation services
Q2: What specific methods of making payment do you recommend?	Debit order	Customer care centres	Online payment	Retail outlets and vending machines
Q3: In your opinion, what are the root causes of nonpayment of municipal services?	Poor quality of services	A feeling of entitlement to free municipal services	Lack of commitment	Lack of steady income
Q4: In your opinion, what are the immediate consequences of nonpayment of municipal services?	Interruption of essential services	Closure of businesses and companies	Loss of municipal infrastructure	Loss of quality of life
Q5: Please suggest a few effective methods of communication with residents and ratepayers.	Personal door-to-door visits	Phone calls	E-Mails and text messages	Written notifications and formal letters
Q6: What are the main obstacles that you have personally experienced in the past in connection with the payment of municipal services?	Inaccurate statements	Inability of municipal employees to read meters regularly	Failure to repair or replace faulty meters	Inability to obtain prompt clarification from municipal employees about an account related query
Q7: Please suggest a few convenient methods of motivating account holders to pay their municipal bills in good time.	Educational campaigns	Enforcing credit control procedures	Litigation	Providing discounts to people who pay their bills in good time

Descriptive analysis of themes

Interview Question 1: How satisfied are you with the quality of municipal services that are provided to you by municipal employees?

Themes 1, 2, 3 and 4: Electricity, water, waste management, and sanitation services

Seven of the 12 participants of study (2, 4, 6, 7, 8, 9, and 11) stated that they were generally satisfied with the quality of electricity, water, waste management, and sanitation services. Three of the participants (1, 8, and 9) stated that service fees were fair enough. Two of the participants (3 and 5) stated that waste removal people picked up waste at variable times and that waste disposal bins were often vandalised due to late collection. Two of the participants (10 and 12) stated that the quality of electricity services was poor, as there were frequent power outages. According to participant number 10, "It is necessary to identify and disconnect illegal electricity connections". Participant number 12 had a similar view and said "People who pay for their electricity services must not be penalised due to failure to hold people who do not pay for their electricity services accountable". Participant number 11 stated that learners often failed to do their homework due to load-shedding. Participant number 12 stated that costly food items were often put to waste due to frequent load-shedding. Participant number 9 stated that "The South African Government and big businesses have a duty to pay for municipal services on behalf of those who are unable to pay for the services, as they can afford to do so easily". Participant number 12 argued that electricity, water, sanitation, and waste management services must be highly efficient, affordable, and reliable at all times in order for local businesses to remain viable. In the words of participant number 10, "Unplanned power outages cause a lot of harm to vulnerable patients and infants who require specialised neonatal health care services. Someone needs to be held accountable". In this regard, the following two suggestions were made by two participants.

Participant number 1: "The level of performance of all municipal employees must be assessed, monitored and critically evaluated against key performance indicators that are agreed upon between municipal line function managers and their subordinates. This should be done on a quarterly basis".

Participant number 7: "To avoid frequent power outages, Crime Intelligence employees, members of the SAPS and municipal employees should find out and disconnect all illegal power connections. All municipalities should criminalise the sale of power cables".

The views expressed by the 12 participants of study are in agreement with views expressed in the literature in the past by Khale and Worku (2015), and Watermeyer, Scott, Kapueja, and Ware (2022). The resounding opinion expressed by the 12 participants of study is that the performance of municipal employees must be monitored and evaluated on a regular basis to ensure the quality, efficiency, affordability, and reliability of municipal services.

Q2: What specific methods of making payment do you recommend?

Themes 1, 2, 3, and 4: Debit order, Customer care centres, Online payment, Retail outlets, and vending machines

Participants 1, 8, 10, and 11 stated that paying by debit order is a preferred choice, as doing so saves valuable time and money. In the words of participant number 8, "No time should be put to waste in queues when payment can be made by using debit orders". A similar view was expressed by participant number 10 "It saves valuable time to pay by debit order". Five of the 12 participants of study (2, 3, 4, 5, 9) indicated that customer care centres, retail outlets are convenient enough to pay municipal bills promptly. Three of the 12 participants (6, 7, 12) indicated that online payments and vending machines are convenient enough for making easy payment.

The views expressed by the 12 participants of study are in agreement with views expressed in the literature in the past by Enwereji and Uwizeyimana (2020) and Maphela and Cloete (2020). The results show that people who have steady income can afford to pay their fees by debit order, which is the most effective way of supporting and working with municipalities. People who have steady income from viable businesses can afford to pay their municipal bills by using online methods and customer care centres.

Q3: In your opinion, what are the root causes of nonpayment of municipal services?

Themes 1, 2, 3, and 4: Poor quality of services, A feeling of entitlement to free municipal services, Lack of commitment, and Lack of steady income

Participants 2, 7, 8, and 9 stated that municipal bills should be paid by the South African government or large business enterprises, as most people in Soweto did not have enough money to pay for such services. In the words of participant number 7, "It is the duty of the Government and wealthy businesses to pay for municipal services as they are the ones who have the money to do so". Five of the 12 participants of study (1, 6, 10, 11, 12) indicated that residents and ratepayers were responsible for paying municipal bills. Three of the 12 participants (3, 4, 5) indicated that lack of steady income was the root cause of nonpayment of municipal services. Participant number 4 said "If I earn enough money, I would be happy to pay my bills promptly. At times, I struggle to pay my municipal bills due to lack of money". Participants 3 and 5 indicated that paying municipal bills was not a problem at times when they earned enough money.

The views expressed by the 12 participants of study are in agreement with views expressed in the literature in the past by Kambule, Yessoufou and Nwulu (2022) and Chikwira, Vengesai and Mandude (2022). The results indicate that a sense of entitlement to free municipal services among people who do not have steady income is a major obstacle to the prompt payment of municipal services by residents and ratepayers. This finding is in agreement with findings reported in the past by Patji and Selepe (2022), and Worku and Mboweni (2022).

Q4: In your opinion, what are the immediate consequences of nonpayment of municipal services?

Themes 1, 2, 3, and 4: Interruption of essential services, Closure of businesses and companies, Loss of municipal infrastructure, Loss of quality of life

Participants 3, 4, 5, 8, and 9 indicated that the immediate consequences of nonpayment are the interruption of essential services and the closure of businesses and companies. They indicated that jobs and business opportunities would be lost as a result of nonpayment. Participants 1, 10, and 11 indicated that infrastructure would be damaged as a result of nonpayment. Participants 2, 6, 7, and 12 indicated that the quality of life would be lowered significantly as a result of nonpayment. Participant 12 said "If people stop paying service fees, the municipality would not be able to render decent services to the people". Participant number 11 said "Municipal employees and officials should make the effort to teach and motivate residents and ratepayers to pay their municipal bills promptly and honestly".

The views expressed by the 12 participants of study are in agreement with views expressed in the literature in the past by Sinwell, Ngwane, and Maggott (2022), Sucha and Duskova

(2022), and Worku (2017, 2018, 2024). The results indicate that there is a need for awareness campaigns and the provision of incentives to people who pay their municipal bills promptly.

Q5: Please suggest a few effective methods of communication with residents and ratepayers.

Themes 1, 2, 3, and 4: Personal door-to-door visits, Phone calls, E-Mails and text messages, Written notifications and formal letters

Participants 2, 3, 4, 8, and 9 indicated that door-to-door visits are most effective for having people pay their municipal bills promptly and regularly. Participants 1, 7, 10, 11, and 12 indicated that phone calls, emails and text messages are suitable and effective methods of communication with residents and ratepayers. Participants 5 and 6 indicated that written notifications and formal letters are suitable methods of communication. Participant 10 said "Door-to-door visits are not so easy. It is better to use radio talk shows, phone calls, emails and text messages". Participant number 1 said "Effective communication requires the ability to use appropriate technology for reaching out to people. Radio talk shows are suitable for doing that".

The views expressed by the 12 participants of study are in agreement with views expressed in the literature in the past by Phillips and Petrova (2021) and Worku (2022). The results indicate that there is a need for effective communication between municipal workers and residents and ratepayers who live and work in Soweto.

Q6: What are the main obstacles that you have personally experienced in the past in connection with the payment of municipal services?

Themes 1, 2, 3, and 4: Inaccurate statements, Inability of municipal employees to read meters regularly, Failure to repair or replace faulty meters, and inability to obtain prompt clarification from municipal employees about an account-related query.

Participants 2, 5, 8, and 11 indicated that municipal employees need to read water and electricity meters regularly, rather than using estimations. Participants 1, 3, 4, and 6 indicated that financial statements need to be checked and verified to establish their accuracy. They pointed out that it was not so easy to correct mistakes arising from wrong financial statements. Participants 7, 9, 10, and 12 indicated that financial statements must be prepared by employees who possess auditing and accounting skills. Participant 10 said "Auditing and accounting skills are crucially needed for generating accurate bills and statements". Participant 11 said "It takes long to make account-related queries". The views expressed by the majority of participants showed that efforts should be made to ensure the accuracy of electricity and water meter readings.

The views expressed by the 12 participants of study are in agreement with views expressed in the literature in the past by McKay and Tantoh (2021), and Ayeleru, Okonta, and Ntuli (2021).

Q7: Please suggest a few convenient methods of motivating account holders to pay their municipal bills in good time.

Themes 1, 2, 3, and 4: The use of different tariffs, Educational campaigns, Enforcing credit control procedures, Litigation, Providing discounts to people who pay their bills in good time Participants 2, 5, and 7 indicated that different tariffs should be used for people living in various regions of Soweto. Participants 3, 4, and 9 stated that discounts should be provided to people who pay their municipal bills regularly. Participants 1, 10, and 11 indicated that credit control procedures should be enforced to collect revenues effectively. Participants 8, 9, and 12 indicated that educational campaigns should be launched to highlight the importance of paying municipal service fees promptly and regularly. Said participant number 2: "Different tariffs should be used for different regions of Soweto". Participants 3, 4, and 6 indicated that litigation is appropriate in cases where people who can afford to pay their bills refuse to do so. Participant 4 said "People who pay their bills regularly and promptly need to be rewarded". Participant 11 said "Some people may not even know why the municipality cannot deliver services unless people pay their bills".

The views expressed by the 12 participants of study are in agreement with views expressed in the literature in the past by Wall (2022), Ayeleru, Okonta, and Ntuli (2021).

Discussion of results

A critical summary of the 12 individual interviews has identified the following three significant views and expressions of interest.

The first significant view expressed by the 12 participants of study is the need for capacity for rendering satisfactory services to all people and businesses who pay municipal service fees, levies, and rates. Soweto falls under the City of Johannesburg Metropolitan Municipality (CJMM). Employees of CJMM who are responsible for municipal services in Soweto need to be able to collect municipal service fees fully, promptly, and regularly from all people and businesses in their localities. It is not possible for local municipalities to render services unless they are paid their municipal service fees in good time. Municipalities in urban areas such as Soweto are exposed to an influx of migrants from rural regions of South Africa. This means they need to have the capacity to render services to an ever-growing population with a diverse range of socioeconomic characteristics.

It is not possible for municipal employees and officials working in Soweto to cope with the task of rendering municipal services and maintaining, repairing, and expanding municipal infrastructure. For this reason, it is prudent to create an enabling retail business and working environment so that vibrant retail businesses set up shop in Soweto. The private sector needs to be provided with an economic incentive so that it participates in the maintenance, repair, and expansion of municipal infrastructure.

The second significant view expressed by the 12 participants of study is the need for good leadership, accountability, good governance, and transparency among municipal employees and officials who are responsible for providing municipal services and for assessing the quality of such services. The participants of study have pointed out that there is a dire need for effective communication and accountability to residents and ratepayers. The implication is that the performance of municipal employees needs to be assessed and evaluated on a regular basis. In this regard, a view has been expressed that municipal employees and officials should be working in collaboration with community leaders and the South African Police Service (SAPS) with a view to discourage illegal electricity and water connections as well as the abuse of municipal infrastructure.

The third significant view is that municipal bylaws should be enforced effectively and that different tariffs should be used for different regions of Soweto. Municipal employees and officials should be recruited and appraised based on a clear demonstration of skills and outputs that are required for performing adequately in the line of duty. Doing so is essential for Soweto to be able to attract viable business enterprises.

Recommendations of study

The recommendations stated below are informed by results obtained from data analysis in this particular study.

The recommendations are made to employees and officials of the City of Johannesburg Metropolitan Municipality (CJMM) who are responsible for rendering municipal services to people who live and work in Soweto:

- Radio talk shows and local newspapers and television programmes are highly suitable for effective communication with residents and ratepayers of Soweto. Local newspapers are especially valuable.
- The use of different tariffs for the various regions of Soweto is very helpful for promoting the culture of payment. This recommendation has the potential for resolving problems and grievances arising from wrong valuations and inaccurate billings. This recommendation is helpful for making a distinction between residents living in low-density suburbs and those living in high-density suburbs.
- Stakeholders, especially those working in the private sector, need to be motivated and encouraged to take part in municipal infrastructural projects. Such stakeholders need to be invited to take part in municipal roadshows, workshops, ward council meetings, and surveys so that they can take part in community-based projects.
- A sense of entitlement, in which the government is expected to pay for municipal services, should be discouraged. This can be done by promoting awareness among residents of Soweto.
- Municipal bylaws need to be enforced with full commitment to discourage the culture of nonpayment.
- The CJMM should work closely with crime intelligence experts, with a view to identify and take appropriate legal action against people who abuse and harm costly municipal infrastructure.
- The CJMM should carry out an effective credit-control mechanism in which people pay for municipal services that are rendered to them promptly, fully, and regularly.

Incentives and rewards should be provided to people and businesses that pay municipal service fees promptly, fully, and regularly.

- The recruitment of municipal employees based on verifiable merits, competence, and skills is crucially helpful for collecting revenues, for resolving account-related queries, and for meeting the service-related expectations of residents and ratepayers.

List of references

Adler, R. H. (2022). Trustworthiness in qualitative research. *Journal of Human Lactation*, *38*(4), 598-602.

Aubriot, J. (2016). Water disputes in Soweto: Inequalities, social mobilizations and recourse to the law. In *Water Regimes* (pp. 183-196). New York: Routledge.

Ayeleru, O. O., Okonta, F. N., & Ntuli, F. (2021). Cost benefit analysis of a municipal solid waste recycling facility in Soweto, South Africa. *Waste Management*, *134*(1), 263-269.

Braun, V., & Clarke, V. (2022). Conceptual and design thinking for thematic analysis. *Qualitative Psychology*, *9*(1), 1-13.

Chikwira, C., Vengesai, E., & Mandude, P. (2022). The impact of microfinance institutions on poverty alleviation. *Journal of Risk and Financial Management, 15*(9), 1-13.

Castelberry, A., & Nolen, A. (2018). Thematic analysis of qualitative research data: Is it as easy as it sounds? *Currents in Pharmacy Teaching and Learning*, *10*(6), 807-815.

Enwereji, P. C., & Uwizeyimana, D. (2020). Municipal consumer debt in South African municipalities: Contexts, causes, and realities. *Research in World Economy*, *11*(3), 333-345.

Grunig, J. E., Grunig, L. A., & Dozier, D. M. (2006). The excellence theory. *Public relations theory*, *2*(21), 1-13.

Kambule, N., Yessoufou, K., & Nwulu, N. (2022). Formulating best practice recommendations for prepaid electricity meter deployment in Soweto, South Africa–Capitalising on the developed-world's experiences. *Journal of Public Affairs, 22*(4), 1-13.

Khale, S. (2015). Assessment of the quality of municipal services in the City of Tshwane, South Africa. *Journal of Corporate Ownership and Control, 13*(1), 678-695.

Khale, S., & Worku, Z. 2015. Benefits of good corporate governance principles: A study of the City of Tshwane, South Africa. *Journal of Corporate Governance and Control, 13*(1), 753-770.

Lincoln, Y. S., & Guba, E. G. (1985). *Naturalistic Inquiry.* London: SAGE Publications.

Manga, M., Bartram, J., & Evans, B. E. (2020). Economic cost analysis of low-cost sanitation technology options in informal settlement areas (case study: Soweto, Johannesburg). *International Journal of Hygiene and Environmental Health, 223*(1), 289-298.

Maphela, B., & Cloete, F. (2020). Johannesburg's implementation of the National Water Act, 1998 in Soweto, South Africa. *Development Southern Africa, 37*(4), 535-552.

McKay, T. J. M., & Tantoh, H. B. (2021). A dialogue approach to stakeholder engagement with urban communities: The case of Mofolo Park, Soweto, Johannesburg, South Africa. *Journal of Environmental Planning and Management, 64*(12), 2172-2191.

Patji, P., & Selepe, M. M. (2022). Contextualisation of non-payments of municipal rates, taxes and user charges within South African local governments. *African Renaissance, 19*(3), 1744-2532.

Saldana, J. (2021). *The coding manual for qualitative researchers*. London: SAGE Publications.

Sinwell, L., Ngwane, T., & Maggott, T. (2022). Electing to electrify: Unpacking the local crisis and state response in Sun Valley, Soweto. *Politikon, 1*(1), 1-13.

South African Department of Cooperative Governance and Traditional Affairs. (2023). *Annual report for 2020/2021.* [Online]. Available from: https://www.cogta.gov.za/index.php/category/documents/annual-reports/ [Accessed: 28 September 2023].

South African Government. (2023). *The Municipal Finance Management Act (Act no. 32 of 2000)*. [Online]. Available from: https://www.gov.za/ [Accessed: 28 September 2023].

Sucha, L., & Duskova, L. (2022). Land access mechanisms of Soweto farmers: Moving beyond legal land tenure for urban agriculture. *Land Use Policy*, *119*(1), 1-13.

Thompson, J. (2022). A guide to abductive thematic analysis. *The Qualitative Report*, *27*(5), 1410-1421.

Tongwane, M. I., Ramotubei, T. S., & Moeletsi, M. E. (2022). Influence of climate on conflicts and migrations in Southern Africa in the 19th and early 20th centuries. *Climate*, *10*(8), 1-13.

Wall, K. (2022). The 1998"'mini-constitution'for local government": A review of the assumptions of the white paper on local government. *Acta Structilia*, *29*(2), 260-292.

Watermeyer, J., Scott, M., Kapueja, L., & Ware, L. J. (2022). To trust or not to trust: An exploratory qualitative study of personal and community perceptions of vaccines amongst a group of young community healthcare workers in Soweto, South Africa. *Health Policy and Planning*, *37*(9), 1-13.

Worku, Z. (2017). Analysis of the perception of small businesses on the quality of routine municipal services in the City of Tshwane, South Africa. *Journal of Applied Business Research*, *33*(2), 247-256.

Worku, Z. (2018). Factors that affect the nonpayment of municipal services in Madibeng, Mamelodi and Soshanguve Townships of South Africa. *Journal of Applied Business Research*, *34*(1), 99-116.

Worku, Z. (2020). A critical evaluation of the quality of municipal services in Tshwane. *Journal of Critical Reviews*, *7*(3), 218-223.

Worku, Z. (2024). A qualitative enquiry of obstacles to adequate performance among municipal employees. *Specialusis Ugdymas*, *2*(43), 1321-1329.

Worku, Z., & Mboweni, M. (2022). An exploratory study of economic contributions made by migrant retail entrepreneurs in Soweto. *Journal of Northeastern University*, *25*(4), 3810-3828.

UNIT 15

AN EXAMPLE BASED ON CONFIRMATORY FACTOR ANALYSIS

A survey was conducted by gathering data from a stratified random sample of size 586 retail businesses in Johannesburg. Data was gathered on the following 9 variables of study (below). The dependent variable of study is profit (Yes, No). It is desired to use confirmatory factor analysis in order to identify the top 3 influential predictors of profitability in the retail businesses.

List of 9 variables of study and their levels

- **profit:** Profitability of retail business (Yes, No)
- **ownership:** Ownership of retail business (Yes, No)
- **duration:** Duration of business operation (5 years or less, More than 5 years)
- **wholesale:** Ability to order merchandise in bulk on credit from wholesalers (Yes, No)
- **businessplan:** Ability to draw up a business plan (Yes, No)
- **rent:** Renting business premises (Yes, No)
- **socialmedia:** Use of social media for marketing (Yes, No)
- **bankaccount:** Ownership of a bank account (Yes, No)
- **freelabour:** Use of free labour from family members (Yes, No)

Remark:

There are 9 variables of study. Dichotomise each one of these 9 variables of study (Y, X1, X2, …., X8). In this particular case, each one of the 9 variables of study is dichotomous. That is, each one of the 9 variables of study has only 2 possible values. Make sure that the possible values of these 9 variables are properly aligned. That is, category 1 (Yes) values contribute to profitability ;in retail businesses based on a review of the literature; category 2 values (No) undermine profitability.

- The dependent variable of study (Y) is profitability
- Perform two-by-two crosstab tests between Y and each of the 8 predictor variables.
- Identify 5 independent variables that are significantly associated with the dependent variable of study (Y) based on large observed values of the Pearson chi-square statistic and small P-values.

Step 1 (Obtain frequency tables for all 9 variables of study)

```
. use c:\bos\cf1.dta, clear
. tabl profit ownership wholesale duration rent businessplan socialmedia
bankaccount freelabour

-> tabulation of profit

     profit |      Freq.     Percent        Cum.
------------+-----------------------------------
         No |         84       14.33       14.33
        Yes |        502       85.67      100.00
------------+-----------------------------------
      Total |        586      100.00

-> tabulation of ownership

  ownership |      Freq.     Percent        Cum.
------------+-----------------------------------
         No |        122       20.82       20.82
        Yes |        464       79.18      100.00
------------+-----------------------------------
      Total |        586      100.00

-> tabulation of wholesale

  wholesale |      Freq.     Percent        Cum.
------------+-----------------------------------
         No |        202       34.47       34.47
        Yes |        384       65.53      100.00
------------+-----------------------------------
      Total |        586      100.00

-> tabulation of duration

           duration |      Freq.     Percent        Cum.
-------------------+-----------------------------------
  5 years or less  |        201       34.30       34.30
More than 5 years  |        385       65.70      100.00
-------------------+-----------------------------------
              Total |        586      100.00
```

```
-> tabulation of rent

       rent |      Freq.     Percent        Cum.
------------+-----------------------------------
         No |        194       33.11       33.11
        Yes |        392       66.89      100.00
------------+-----------------------------------
      Total |        586      100.00

-> tabulation of businessplan

businesspla |
          n |      Freq.     Percent        Cum.
------------+-----------------------------------
         No |         64       10.92       10.92
        Yes |        522       89.08      100.00
------------+-----------------------------------
      Total |        586      100.00

-> tabulation of socialmedia

socialmedia |      Freq.     Percent        Cum.
------------+-----------------------------------
         No |        548       93.52       93.52
        Yes |         38        6.48      100.00
------------+-----------------------------------
      Total |        586      100.00

-> tabulation of bankaccount

bankaccount |      Freq.     Percent        Cum.
------------+-----------------------------------
         No |        550       93.86       93.86
        Yes |         36        6.14      100.00
------------+-----------------------------------
      Total |        586      100.00

-> tabulation of freelabour

 freelabour |      Freq.     Percent        Cum.
------------+-----------------------------------
         No |        552       94.20       94.20
        Yes |         34        5.80      100.00
------------+-----------------------------------
      Total |        586      100.00
```

The results displayed above can also be obtained from SPSS:

- **Go to SPSS and open up the SPSS data set c:\bos\cfa1.sav**
- **Click on Analyze, Descriptive statistics, Frequencies**
- **Select the variables profit, ownership, wholesale, duration, rent, businessplan, socialmedia, bankaccount, and freelabour by clicking on the selection bar**
- **Click on OK**

profit					
		Frequency	Percent	Valid Percent	Cumulative Percent
Valid	No	84	14.3	14.3	14.3
	Yes	502	85.7	85.7	100.0
	Total	586	100.0	100.0	

ownership					
		Frequency	Percent	Valid Percent	Cumulative Percent
Valid	No	122	20.8	20.8	20.8
	Yes	464	79.2	79.2	100.0
	Total	586	100.0	100.0	

wholesale					
		Frequency	Percent	Valid Percent	Cumulative Percent
Valid	No	202	34.5	34.5	34.5
	Yes	384	65.5	65.5	100.0
	Total	586	100.0	100.0	

duration					
		Frequency	Percent	Valid Percent	Cumulative Percent
Valid	5 years or less	201	34.3	34.3	34.3
	More than 5 years	385	65.7	65.7	100.0
	Total	586	100.0	100.0	

businessplan					
		Frequency	Percent	Valid Percent	Cumulative Percent
Valid	No	194	33.1	33.1	33.1
	Yes	392	66.9	66.9	100.0
	Total	586	100.0	100.0	

rent					
		Frequency	Percent	Valid Percent	Cumulative Percent
Valid	No	64	10.9	10.9	10.9
	Yes	522	89.1	89.1	100.0
	Total	586	100.0	100.0	

socialmedia					
		Frequency	Percent	Valid Percent	Cumulative Percent
Valid	No	548	93.5	93.5	93.5
	Yes	38	6.5	6.5	100.0
	Total	586	100.0	100.0	

bankaccount					
		Frequency	Percent	Valid Percent	Cumulative Percent
Valid	No	550	93.9	93.9	93.9
	Yes	36	6.1	6.1	100.0
	Total	586	100.0	100.0	

freelabour					
		Frequency	Percent	Valid Percent	Cumulative Percent
Valid	No	552	94.2	94.2	94.2
	Yes	34	5.8	5.8	100.0
	Total	586	100.0	100.0	

Step 2 (Screening of valuable variables by using two-by-two crosstab analyses)

```
. use c:\bos\cfa1.dta, clear

. for var ownership wholesale duration rent businessplan socialmedia bankaccount
freelabour: tab2 profit X, cell exp chi2

->  tab2 profit ownership, cell exp chi2

-> tabulation of profit by ownership

+--------------------+
| Key                |
|--------------------|
|     frequency      |
| expected frequency |
|  cell percentage   |
+--------------------+

           |       ownership
    profit |        No        Yes |     Total
-----------+----------------------+----------
        No |        55         29 |        84
           |      17.5       66.5 |      84.0
           |      9.39       4.95 |     14.33
-----------+----------------------+----------
       Yes |        67        435 |       502
           |     104.5      397.5 |     502.0
           |     11.43      74.23 |     85.67
-----------+----------------------+----------
     Total |       122        464 |       586
           |     122.0      464.0 |     586.0
           |     20.82      79.18 |    100.00

          Pearson chi2(1) = 118.6236   Pr = 0.000


->  tab2 profit wholesale, cell exp chi2

-> tabulation of profit by wholesale

+--------------------+
| Key                |
|--------------------|
|     frequency      |
| expected frequency |
|  cell percentage   |
+--------------------+

           |       wholesale
    profit |        No        Yes |     Total
-----------+----------------------+----------
        No |        64         20 |        84
           |      29.0       55.0 |      84.0
           |     10.92       3.41 |     14.33
-----------+----------------------+----------
       Yes |       138        364 |       502
           |     173.0      329.0 |     502.0
           |     23.55      62.12 |     85.67
-----------+----------------------+----------
     Total |       202        384 |       586
           |     202.0      384.0 |     586.0
           |     34.47      65.53 |    100.00

          Pearson chi2(1) =  75.5551   Pr = 0.000
```

```
->  tab2 profit duration, cell exp chi2

-> tabulation of profit by duration

+--------------------+
| Key                |
|--------------------|
|     frequency      |
| expected frequency |
|  cell percentage   |
+--------------------+

           |        duration
    profit | 5 years..  More th.. |     Total
-----------+----------------------+----------
        No |        64         20 |        84
           |      28.8       55.2 |      84.0
           |     10.92       3.41 |     14.33
-----------+----------------------+----------
       Yes |       137        365 |       502
           |     172.2      329.8 |     502.0
           |     23.38      62.29 |     85.67
-----------+----------------------+----------
     Total |       201        385 |       586
           |     201.0      385.0 |     586.0
           |     34.30      65.70 |    100.00

          Pearson chi2(1) =  76.3546   Pr = 0.000


->  tab2 profit rent, cell exp chi2

-> tabulation of profit by rent

+--------------------+
| Key                |
|--------------------|
|     frequency      |
| expected frequency |
|  cell percentage   |
+--------------------+

           |          rent
    profit |        No        Yes |     Total
-----------+----------------------+----------
        No |        59         25 |        84
           |      27.8       56.2 |      84.0
           |     10.07       4.27 |     14.33
-----------+----------------------+----------
       Yes |       135        367 |       502
           |     166.2      335.8 |     502.0
           |     23.04      62.63 |     85.67
-----------+----------------------+----------
     Total |       194        392 |       586
           |     194.0      392.0 |     586.0
           |     33.11      66.89 |    100.00

          Pearson chi2(1) =  61.0498   Pr = 0.000
```

```
-> tab2 profit businessplan, cell exp chi2

-> tabulation of profit by businessplan

+--------------------+
| Key                |
|--------------------|
|     frequency      |
| expected frequency |
|  cell percentage   |
+--------------------+

           |     businessplan
    profit |        No        Yes |     Total
-----------+----------------------+----------
        No |        30         54 |        84
           |       9.2       74.8 |      84.0
           |      5.12       9.22 |     14.33
-----------+----------------------+----------
       Yes |        34        468 |       502
           |      54.8      447.2 |     502.0
           |      5.80      79.86 |     85.67
-----------+----------------------+----------
     Total |        64        522 |       586
           |      64.0      522.0 |     586.0
           |     10.92      89.08 |    100.00

          Pearson chi2(1) =  61.9539   Pr = 0.000


-> tab2 profit socialmedia, cell exp chi2

-> tabulation of profit by socialmedia

+--------------------+
| Key                |
|--------------------|
|     frequency      |
| expected frequency |
|  cell percentage   |
+--------------------+

           |      socialmedia
    profit |        No        Yes |     Total
-----------+----------------------+----------
        No |        82          2 |        84
           |      78.6        5.4 |      84.0
           |     13.99       0.34 |     14.33
-----------+----------------------+----------
       Yes |       466         36 |       502
           |     469.4       32.6 |     502.0
           |     79.52       6.14 |     85.67
-----------+----------------------+----------
     Total |       548         38 |       586
           |     548.0       38.0 |     586.0
           |     93.52       6.48 |    100.00

          Pearson chi2(1) =   2.7230   Pr = 0.099
```

```
->  tab2 profit bankaccount, cell exp chi2

-> tabulation of profit by bankaccount

+--------------------+
| Key                |
|--------------------|
|     frequency      |
| expected frequency |
|  cell percentage   |
+--------------------+

           |      bankaccount
    profit |        No        Yes |     Total
-----------+----------------------+----------
        No |        82          2 |        84
           |      78.8        5.2 |      84.0
           |     13.99       0.34 |     14.33
-----------+----------------------+----------
       Yes |       468         34 |       502
           |     471.2       30.8 |     502.0
           |     79.86       5.80 |     85.67
-----------+----------------------+----------
     Total |       550         36 |       586
           |     550.0       36.0 |     586.0
           |     93.86       6.14 |    100.00

          Pearson chi2(1) =   2.4073   Pr = 0.121
```

```
->  tab2 profit freelabour, cell exp chi2

-> tabulation of profit by freelabour

+--------------------+
| Key                |
|--------------------|
|     frequency      |
| expected frequency |
|  cell percentage   |
+--------------------+

           |      freelabour
    profit |        No        Yes |     Total
-----------+----------------------+----------
        No |        82          2 |        84
           |      79.1        4.9 |      84.0
           |     13.99       0.34 |     14.33
-----------+----------------------+----------
       Yes |       470         32 |       502
           |     472.9       29.1 |     502.0
           |     80.20       5.46 |     85.67
-----------+----------------------+----------
     Total |       552         34 |       586
           |     552.0       34.0 |     586.0
           |     94.20       5.80 |    100.00

          Pearson chi2(1) =   2.0998   Pr = 0.147
```

The following table shows a list of probability values obtained from 8 two-by-two Pearson's two-by-two tests of associations for the 8 predictor variables used for data analysis. The table ranks the 8 predictor variables in order of their strength of association with the dependent variable of study (profitability). Useful predictor variables have large observed chi-square values and small probability values.

Predictor variables ranked in order of strength (n=586)

Variable	Observed chi-square value	P-value
Ownership of business (ownership)	118.6236	0.0000
Duration of business operation (duration)	76.3546	0.0000
Ability to order merchandise from whole suppliers in bulk on credit (wholesale)	75.5551	0.0000
Ability to draw up a business plan (businessplan)	61.9539	0.0000
Having to pay rent for business premises (rent)	61.0498	0.0000
Use of social media for marketing (socialmedia)	2.7230	0.0990
Ownership of bank account (bankaccount)	2.4073	0.1210
Use of free labour from family members for conducting business (freelabour)	2.0998	0.1470

At the 5% level of significance, the first 5 variables are useful. These 5 variables are used for performing subsequent confirmatory factor analysis.

The results displayed above can also be obtained from SPSS:

Go to SPSS and open up the SPSS data set c:\bos\cfa1.sav

Click on Analyze, Descriptive statistics, Crosstabs

Select the variable profit as a row variable

Highlight and select the remaining 9 categorical variables as column variables by clicking on the selection bar

Click on Statistics, Chi-square

Click on Continue

Click on OK

Crosstabs

profit * ownership

Crosstab				
Count				
		ownership		
		No	Yes	Total
profit	No	55	29	84
	Yes	67	435	502
Total		122	464	586

Chi-Square Tests					
	Value	df	Asymptotic Significance (2-sided)	P-value (2-sided)	P-value (1-sided)
Pearson Chi-Square	118.624[a]	1	<0.001		
Continuity Correction[b]	115.482	1	<0.001		
Likelihood Ratio	96.775	1	<0.001		
Fisher's Exact Test				<0.001	<0.001
N of Valid Cases	586				

a. 0 cells (0.0%) have expected count less than 5. The minimum expected count is 17.49.

b. Computed only for a 2 × 2 table

profit * wholesale

Crosstab				
Count				
		wholesale		Total
		No	Yes	
profit	No	64	20	84
	Yes	138	364	502
Total		202	384	586

Chi-Square Tests					
	Value	df	Asymptotic Significance (2-sided)	P-value (2-sided)	P-value (1-sided)
Pearson Chi-Square	75.555[a]	1	<0.001		
Continuity Correction[b]	73.414	1	<0.001		
Likelihood Ratio	72.262	1	<0.001		
Fisher's Exact Test				<0.001	<0.001
N of Valid Cases	586				

a. 0 cells (0.0%) have expected count less than 5. The minimum expected count is 28.96.

b. Computed only for a 2 × 2 table

profit * duration

Crosstab				
Count				
		duration		Total
		5 years or less	More than 5 years	
profit	No	64	20	84
	Yes	137	365	502
Total		201	385	586

Chi-Square Tests					
	Value	df	Asymptotic Significance (2-sided)	P-value (2-sided)	P-value (1-sided)
Pearson Chi-Square	76.355[a]	1	<0.001		
Continuity Correction[b]	74.200	1	<0.001		
Likelihood Ratio	72.919	1	<0.001		
Fisher's Exact Test				<0.001	<0.001
N of Valid Cases	586				

a. 0 cells (0.0%) have expected count less than 5. The minimum expected count is 28.81.

b. Computed only for a 2 × 2 table

profit * businessplan

Crosstab				
Count				
		businessplan		
		No	Yes	Total
profit	No	59	25	84
	Yes	135	367	502
Total		194	392	586

Chi-Square Tests					
	Value	df	Asymptotic Significance (2-sided)	P-value (2-sided)	P-value (1-sided)
Pearson Chi-Square	61.050[a]	1	<0.001		
Continuity Correction[b]	59.108	1	<0.001		
Likelihood Ratio	57.334	1	<0.001		
Fisher's Exact Test				<0.001	<0.001
N of Valid Cases	586				

a. 0 cells (0.0%) have expected count less than 5. The minimum expected count is 27.81.

b. Computed only for a 2 × 2 table

profit * rent

Crosstab				
Count				
		rent		Total
		No	Yes	
profit	No	30	54	84
	Yes	34	468	502
Total		64	522	586

Chi-Square Tests					
	Value	df	Asymptotic Significance (2-sided)	P-value (2-sided)	P-value (1-sided)
Pearson Chi-Square	61.954[a]	1	<0.001		
Continuity Correction[b]	59.015	1	<0.001		
Likelihood Ratio	45.978	1	<0.001		
Fisher's Exact Test				<0.001	<0.001
N of Valid Cases	586				

a. 0 cells (0.0%) have expected count less than 5. The minimum expected count is 9.17.

b. Computed only for a 2 × 2 table

profit * socialmedia

Crosstab				
Count				
		socialmedia		
		No	Yes	Total
profit	No	82	2	84
	Yes	466	36	502
Total		548	38	586

Chi-Square Tests					
	Value	df	Asymptotic Significance (2-sided)	P-value (2-sided)	P-value (1-sided)
Pearson Chi-Square	2.723[a]	1	0.099		
Continuity Correction[b]	1.990	1	0.158		
Likelihood Ratio	3.414	1	0.065		
Fisher's Exact Test				0.147	0.069
N of Valid Cases	586				

a. 0 cells (0.0%) have expected count less than 5. The minimum expected count is 5.45.

b. Computed only for a 2 × 2 table

profit * bankaccount

Crosstab				
Count				
		bankaccount		
		No	Yes	Total
profit	No	82	2	84
	Yes	468	34	502
Total		550	36	586

Chi-Square Tests					
	Value	df	Asymptotic Significance (2-sided)	P-value (2-sided)	P-value (1-sided)
Pearson Chi-Square	2.407[a]	1	0.121		
Continuity Correction[b]	1.706	1	0.192		
Likelihood Ratio	2.989	1	0.084		
Fisher's Exact Test				0.144	0.087
N of Valid Cases	586				

a. 0 cells (0.0%) have expected count less than 5. The minimum expected count is 5.16.

b. Computed only for a 2 × 2 table

profit * freelabour

Crosstab				
Count				
		freelabour		Total
		No	Yes	
profit	No	82	2	84
	Yes	470	32	502
Total		552	34	586

Chi-Square Tests					
	Value	df	Asymptotic Significance (2-sided)	P-value (2-sided)	P-value (1-sided)
Pearson Chi-Square	2.100[a]	1	0.147		
Continuity Correction[b]	1.433	1	0.231		
Likelihood Ratio	2.580	1	0.108		
Fisher's Exact Test				0.206	0.109
N of Valid Cases	586				

a. 1 cells (25.0%) have expected count less than 5. The minimum expected count is 4.87.

b. Computed only for a 2 × 2 table

Cronbach Alpha coefficients for 5 useful predictor variables (n=586)

Variable	Observed chi-square value	P-value	Cronbach Alpha coefficients
Ownership of business (ownership)	118.6236	0.0000	0.6160
Duration of business operation (duration)	76.3546	0.0000	0.5130
Ability to order merchandise from whole suppliers in bulk on credit (wholesale)	75.5551	0.0000	0.5108

Variable	Observed chi-square value	P-value	Cronbach Alpha coefficients
Ability to draw up a business plan (businessplan)	61.9539	0.0000	0.4724
Having to pay rent for business premises (rent)	61.0498	0.0000	0.4882
Use of social media for marketing (socialmedia)	2.7230	0.0990	0.1205
Ownership of bank account (bankaccount)	2.4073	0.1210	0.1128
Use of free labour from family members for conducting business (freelabour)	2.0998	0.1470	0.1048

At the 5% level of significance, the first 5 variables are useful. These 5 variables are used for performing subsequent confirmatory factor analysis.

Estimation of Cronbach Alpha coefficients

The Cronbach Alpha coefficient is a measure of internal consistency. The statistic is used for measuring the degree to which a set of items are as a group. The Cronbach Alpha coefficient is a measure of scale reliability. Cronbach Alpha coefficients are obtained as shown below. Large magnitudes of the Cronbach Alpha coefficient indicate that the variable is valuable enough to be used for performing confirmatory factor analysis. By using a cutoff point of 0.45, the first 5 variables in the table are chosen for performing confirmatory factor analysis.

```
. use c:\bos\cfa2.dta, clear
. alpha profit ownership

Test scale = mean(unstandardized items)

Average interitem covariance:      .064123
Number of items in the scale:            2
Scale reliability coefficient:    0.6160
```

```
. alpha profit duration

Test scale = mean(unstandardized items)

Average interitem covariance:     .0601499
Number of items in the scale:            2
Scale reliability coefficient:      0.5130


. alpha profit wholesale

Test scale = mean(unstandardized items)

Average interitem covariance:     .0599049
Number of items in the scale:            2
Scale reliability coefficient:      0.5108


. alpha profit businessplan

Test scale = mean(unstandardized items)

Average interitem covariance:     .0533182
Number of items in the scale:            2
Scale reliability coefficient:      0.4724


. alpha profit rent

Test scale = mean(unstandardized items)

Average interitem covariance:     .0355999
Number of items in the scale:            2
Scale reliability coefficient:      0.4882


. alpha profit socialmedia

Test scale = mean(unstandardized items)

Average interitem covariance:     .0058925
Number of items in the scale:            2
Scale reliability coefficient:      0.1205


. alpha profit bankaccount

Test scale = mean(unstandardized items)

Average interitem covariance:     .0054024
Number of items in the scale:            2
Scale reliability coefficient:      0.1128


. alpha profit freelabour

Test scale = mean(unstandardized items)

Average interitem covariance:     .0049123
Number of items in the scale:            2
Scale reliability coefficient:      0.1048
```

The above Cronbach Alpha coefficients can be obtained from SPSS as follows:

Go to SPSS and open up the data set c:\bos\cfa2.sav

Click on Analyze, Scale, Reliability analysis

Select the variables profit and ownership as items by using the selection bar

Click on OK

Reliability Statistics	
Cronbach's Alpha	N of Items
0.616	2

Follow the above procedure for the remaining pairs of variables:

profit and duration

profit and wholesale

profit and businessplan

profit and rent

profit and socialmedia

profit and bankaccount

profit and freelabour

The results from SPSS are in the following table:

Items	Cronbach Alpha coefficients
profit and ownership	0.6160
profit and duration	0.5130
profit and wholesale	0.5108
profit and businessplan	0.4724
profit and rent	0.4882
profit and socialmedia	0.1205
profit and bankaccount	0.1128
profit and freelabour	0.1048

Steps for performing confirmatory factor analysis in SPSS:

The SPSS data set **c:\bos\cfa2.sav** contains 6 variables or columns (Y, X1, X2, X3, X4, X5)

Go to SPSS and open up the data set **c:\bos\cfa2.sav**

The variable view of SPSS shows the dependent variable of study (profit) and 9 independent variables of study:

Y: Profitability of retail business (profit)

X1: Ownership of business (ownership)

X2: Duration of business operation (duration)

X3: Ability to order merchandise from whole suppliers in bulk on credit (wholesale)

X4: Ability to draw up a business plan (businessplan)

X5: Having to pay rent for business premises (rent)

X7: Use of social media for marketing (socialmedia)

X8: Ownership of bank account (bankaccount)

X9: Use of freelabour from family members (freelabour)

Go to SPSS and open up the data set c:\bos\cfa2.sav

Click on Analyze, Dimension reduction, Factor analysis

Select the first 5 independent variables of study as factor variables

Select the dependent variable of study as a selection variable

What is the value of your selection variable? 1

Click on Continue

Click on Descriptive statistics and select the following options

Univariate descriptive

Initial solution

Coefficients

KMO (Kaiser-Meyer-Olkin Measure) and Bartlett's test of sphericity

Click on continue

Click on Extraction method and select the following options

Principal axis factoring

Correlation matrix

Scree plot

Extract based on Eigen values > 1

Click on continue

Click on Rotation

Select the following options

Varimax

Rotated solution

Click on continue

Click on scores

Select the following options

Save as variables

Regression

Display factor score coefficient matrix

Click on continue

Click on Options, missing values

Select the following options

Exclude cases listwise

Sorted by size

Click on continue

Click on OK

Computer printout from SPSS

The following table shows averages and standard deviations for 5 predictors of profitability.

Table of descriptive statistics for 5 predictors of profitability (n = 586)

Variable of study	Average	Standard deviation
Ownership of business (ownership)	0.65	0.478
Duration of business operation (duration)	0.76	0.428
Ability to order merchandise from whole suppliers in bulk on credit (wholesale)	0.76	0.428
Ability to draw up a business plan (businessplan)	0.70	0.460
Having to pay rent for business premises (rent)	0.36	0.482

The following table shows a correlation matrix for the 5 predictors of profitability. It can be seen that the correlation coefficients differ from zero significantly, indicating that the use of factor analysis is appropriate.

Table of correlation matrix for 5 predictors of profitability (n = 586)

	ownership	wholesale	duration	businessplan	rent
ownership	1.000	0.182	0.182	-0.199	0.280
wholesale	0.182	1.000	0.344	0.247	-0.167
duration	0.182	0.344	1.000	0.247	0.125
businessplan	-0.199	0.247	0.247	1.000	-0.058
rent	0.280	-0.167	0.125	-0.058	1.000

The following table shows goodness-of-fit measures for KMO and Bartlett's test (Mueller & Hancock, 2018). The observed values of these goodness-of-fit statistics indicate that the use of factor analysis is appropriate for the data set.

Table of goodness-of-fit measures for KMO and Bartlett's test (n=586)

Name of goodness-of-fit statistic	Observed value of statistic
Kaiser-Meyer-Olkin Measure (KMO) of Sampling Adequacy	0.474
Observed value of Bartlett's test of Sphericity statistic	42.052
Degrees of freedom of Bartlett's test of Sphericity statistic	10
P-value for Bartlett's test of Sphericity	0.0000

The following table shows statistics for communalities that are extracted by using principal axis factoring (Mueller & Hancock, 2018). Taking 0.2 as a cut-off point, the observed values of 2 of the 5 communalities differ from zero significantly. This indicates that 2 of the 5 factors used for factor analysis could be extracted by using principal axis factoring. These 2 factors are ownership and wholesale.

Table of communalities extracted by using principal axis factoring (n=586)

Predictor variable associated with communality	Magnitudes of extracted communalities
ownership	0.206
wholesale	0.236
duration	0.195
businessplan	0.166
rent	0.152

The following table shows components that are extracted by using the principal axis factoring method. Two factors are extracted by using the principal axis factoring method. The criterion for extraction is having Eigen values that are greater than 1. Based on this criterion, the variables *ownership* and *wholesale* are extracted by using the principal axis factoring method.

Table of rotated factor matrix by using principal axis factoring (n = 568)

Predictor variable	Component 1	Component 2
ownership	0.859	0.189
wholesale	0.017	0.627
duration	0.122	0.562
businessplan	-0.296	0.438
rent	0.328	-0.047

The following table shows Eigen values estimated for 2 influential predictors of profitability identified by performing factor analysis. These 2 influential predictor variables of profitability have Eigen values with magnitudes of 1 or more. These 2 predictor variables are *ownership* and *wholesale*. The 2 extracted factors jointly account for 59.653% of the total variation in the dependent variable of study (profitability).

Table of Eigen values from factor analysis (n = 586)

Predictor variable	Magnitude of Eigen value	Magnitudes of percentage variances explained by predictor variables	Cumulative percentages of variances explained by predictor variables
ownership	1.589	31.787	31.787
wholesale	1.393	27.865	59.653
duration	0.944	18.882	78.534
businessplan	0.602	12.042	90.577
rent	0.471	9.423	100.000

The following figure shows a scree plot obtained from factor analysis. The plot shows that the first 2 most influential predictor variables (*ownership* and *wholesale*) account for most of the variability in the dependent variable of study (profitability in retail businesses). The scree plot has 4 segments. Segments 1 and 2 have Eigen values that are greater than 1. Segments 3 and 4 have Eigen values that are less than 1. This finding shows that 2 viable factors are extracted by using the principal axis factoring method. These 2 viable factors are *ownership* and *wholesale*.

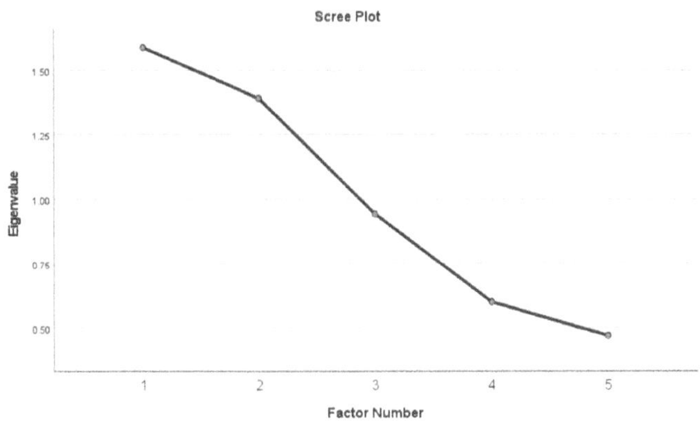

A scree plot obtained from factor analysis

UNIT 16

AN EXAMPLE BASED ON STRUCTURAL EQUATIONS MODELLING

Postgraduate level students and researchers often use STATA software (Stata Corporation, 2023) for performing economic data analysis. One appealing feature of STATA software is the use of Structural equations modelling for postgraduate level research. The lecture notes in this unit (Unit 16) are available to students who use STATA software as part of the User's Guide manual (**Documentation**). They can also be downloaded freely from the STATA website address: https://www.stata.com/features/structural-equation-modeling/

The author and publisher wish to express their sincere appreciation to Stata Corporation for their valuable contribution to this study guide.

Structural equations modeling (SEM) allows researchers to assess complex relationships that exist among 1 or more dependent variables of study and 1 or more independent variables of study. That is, it is possible to have 1 or more dependent variables of study and 1 or more independent variables of study in an SEM data analysis procedure.

In SEM analysis, it is possible to have any type of dependent and independent variables of study. That is, the dependent and independent variables of study can be continuous, ordinal, nominal, etc.

In structural equations modelling, the dependent variables of study are those variables that have one-way arrows pointing to them. The independent variables of study are those variables that do not have one-way arrows pointing to them.

Dependent variables have residuals (are not perfectly related to the other variables in the model) indicated by *e*'s (*errors*) pointing to measured variables and *d*'s pointing to latent variables.

The basic assumptions in structural equations modeling are the assumption of multivariate normality, no systematic missing data, sufficiently large sample size, and correct model specification. Structural equations modelling provides theoretically reliable estimates when the sample size of study is large (400 or above) and there are no missing values.

Individual structural equations models are illustrated by using path diagrams.

Boxes represent variables that are directly observed in the raw data set and are collected by using a questionnaire of study or are measured directly.

Circles represent variables that are not directly observed or measured in the data set. They are referred to as latent variables.

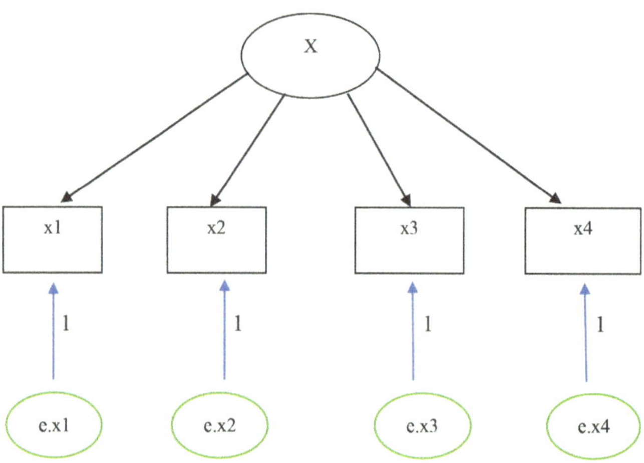

Suppose that a path points from Variable A to Variable B, it means that Variable A affects variable B.

Let $s \rightarrow d$

This means that there is a path coefficient β_k

We need to add values of β_k to the linear function of d

The diagram shown above corresponds to the equations shown below:

$$x_1 = \alpha_1 + \beta_1 X + ex_1$$

$$x_2 = \alpha_2 + \beta_2 X + ex_2$$

$$x_3 = \alpha_3 + \beta_3 X + ex_3$$

$$x_4 = \alpha_4 + \beta_4 X + ex_4$$

In the above set of equations,

X, x_1, x_2, x_3, x_4, ex_1, ex_2, ex_3, ex_4 are distributed independently and identically with mean vector and covariance matrix Σ

In the above figure, it is assumed that the *error* terms are not correlated with each other.

Variable X is a latent exogeneous variable. Thus, it needs a normalising constraint. The variable X is anchored to the first observed variable x1. As such, the path coefficient is constrained to be 1.

Go to STATA and open up the STATA data set c:\bos\marks.dta

Click on Statistics

Click on Structural Equations Modelling (SEM)

Click on Other

Click on Estimation sample summary statistics for estimation sample

Click on Display summary by equation

Click on OK

STATA will provide the following computer printout:

```
. use c:\bos\marks.dta, clear

. estat summarize, equation

after sem, option equation ignored

  Estimation sample sem                        Number of obs =        500

  -------------------------------------------------------------------
      Variable |         Mean      Std. dev.         Min          Max
  -------------+-----------------------------------------------------
            x1 |       99.518      14.35402           60          137
            x2 |       99.954       14.1939           52          140
            x3 |       99.052      14.26395           59          150
            x4 |       94.474      70.11603         -113          295
  -------------------------------------------------------------------
```

Go to STATA and open up the STATA data set **c:\bos\marks.dta**

Click on Statistics

Click on Structural Equations Modelling (SEM)

Click on Other

Click on Variance-covariance matrix of estimators (vce)

Click on Display as covariance matrix

Click on OK

STATA will provide the following computer printout:

```
. use c:\bos\marks.dta, clear
. estat vce

Covariance matrix of coefficients of sem model

             | x1                        | x2                        | x3
        e(V) |          X        _cons   |          X        _cons   |           X
-------------+---------------------------+---------------------------+------------
x1           |                           |                           |
           X |          0                |                           |
       _cons |          0    .4120755    |                           |
-------------+---------------------------+---------------------------+------------
x2           |                           |                           |
           X |          0   .00096327    |  .00589223                |
       _cons |          0   .18486939    | -.00343034   .40293364    |
-------------+---------------------------+---------------------------+------------
x3           |                           |                           |
           X |          0  -.00003457    |  .00345516  -.00268369    |  .00564043
       _cons |          0   .18392197    | -.00154673   .20612904    | -.00088264
-------------+---------------------------+---------------------------+------------
x4           |                           |                           |
           X |          0   .00426711    |   .0218024  -.03211975    |  .02175832
```

```
       _cons |          0   1.3134478 | -.01699136   1.3537311 |  -.0167814
-------------+------------------------+------------------------+-----------
/            |                        |                        |
   var(e.x1) |          0  -.21037245 |  .05289592  -.44652515 |  .04795919
   var(e.x2) |          0   .16786776 | -.00844992  -.37438071 |  -.0097117
   var(e.x3) |          0    .1783588 |  .01626385   .22884687 | -.00495673
   var(e.x4) |          0  -3.3766155 | -.05806676   4.8237325 |  .68389183
      var(X) |          0   .15046619 | -.53953563   .68954482 | -.56164925

             | x3         | x4                     | /
        e(V) |      _cons |          X       _cons | var(e.x1)   var(e.x2)
-------------+------------+------------------------+-----------------------
x3           |            |                        |
       _cons |  .40692043 |                        |
-------------+------------+------------------------+-----------------------
x4           |            |                        |
           X | -.02395708 |  .19242186             |
       _cons |  1.3951129 | -.15211112   9.8325157 |
-------------+------------+------------------------+-----------------------
/            |            |                        |
   var(e.x1) | -.36746608 |  .99703521  -1.8276463 |  59.972218
   var(e.x2) |  .03214354 |  .36660133  -.43415671 |  5.2230261   42.239426
   var(e.x3) |  .24618426 |   .4934075   .46803675 |   4.379404   1.5434496
   var(e.x4) |   4.581066 | -30.105476   28.785085 | -398.04174  -219.56735
      var(X) |  .50305364 | -4.1381284   3.2751897 | -15.591354  -2.2245074

             | /
        e(V) |  var(e.x3)   var(e.x4)      var(X)
-------------+------------------------------------
/            |
   var(e.x3) |  49.006579
   var(e.x4) |  -382.1259   21217.038
      var(X) | -6.2555545   317.61681   127.15504
```

A simple STATA command for SEM analysis:

Go to STATA and open up the STATA data set **c:\bos\marks.dta**

```
. use c:\bos\marks.dta, clear
. sem (x1 x2 x3 x4 <- X)


Endogenous variables
  Measurement: x1 x2 x3 x4

Exogenous variables
  Latent: X

Fitting target model:
Iteration 0:   log likelihood = -8487.5905
Iteration 1:   log likelihood = -8487.2358
Iteration 2:   log likelihood = -8487.2337
Iteration 3:   log likelihood = -8487.2337

Structural equations model                         Number of obs = 500
Estimation method: ml

Log likelihood = -8487.2337
```

```
 ( 1)  [x1]X = 1
------------------------------------------------------------------------------
             |                 OIM
             | Coefficient  std. err.      z    P>|z|     [95% conf. interval]
-------------+----------------------------------------------------------------
Measurement  |
  x1         |
           X |          1  (constrained)
       _cons |     99.518   .6412888   155.18   0.000      98.2611    100.7749
  -----------+----------------------------------------------------------------
  x2         |
           X |   1.033249   .0723898    14.27   0.000     .8913676     1.17513
       _cons |     99.954   .6341354   157.62   0.000     98.71112    101.1969
  -----------+----------------------------------------------------------------
  x3         |
           X |   1.063876   .0729725    14.58   0.000     .9208526      1.2069
       _cons |     99.052   .6372649   155.43   0.000     97.80298     100.301
  -----------+----------------------------------------------------------------
  x4         |
           X |   7.276754   .4277638    17.01   0.000     6.438353    8.115156
       _cons |     94.474   3.132547    30.16   0.000     88.33432    100.6137
-------------+----------------------------------------------------------------
   var(e.x1)|   115.6865   7.790423                      101.3823    132.0089
   var(e.x2)|   105.0445    7.38755                      91.51873    120.5692
   var(e.x3)|   101.2572    7.17635                      88.12499    116.3463
   var(e.x4)|   144.0406   145.2887                      19.94838    1040.069
      var(X)|   89.93921   11.07933                      70.64676    114.5001
------------------------------------------------------------------------------
LR test of model vs. saturated: chi2(2) = 1.46            Prob > chi2 = 0.4827
```

The following table shows the path coefficients for

$X \to x1, \quad X \to x2, \quad X \to x3, \quad X \to x4$

The path coefficient for $X \to x1$ is equal to 1 (constrained estimate)

The path coefficient for $X \to x2$ is equal to 1.03

The path coefficient for $X \to x3$ is equal to 1.06

The path coefficient for $X \to x4$ is equal to 7.28

The true path coefficients for

$X \to x1, \quad X \to x2, \quad X \to x3, \quad X \to x4$

are equal to 1, 1, 1 and 7 respectively.

```
. estat su

 Estimation sample sem                         Number of obs =        500

 -------------------------------------------------------------------------
     Variable |        Mean      Std. dev.          Min             Max
 -------------+-----------------------------------------------------------
           x1 |      99.518      14.35402            60             137
           x2 |      99.954       14.1939            52             140
           x3 |      99.052      14.26395            59             150
           x4 |      94.474      70.11603          -113             295
 -------------------------------------------------------------------------


. estat gof

----------------------------------------------------------------------------
Fit statistic        |      Value   Description
---------------------+------------------------------------------------------
Likelihood ratio     |
          chi2_ms(2) |      1.457   model vs. saturated
            p > chi2 |      0.483
          chi2_bs(6) |    923.468   baseline vs. saturated
            p > chi2 |      0.000
```

The Adjusted Goodness-of-fit Indicator (AGFI) statistic has a magnitude of 923.468. The likelihood ratio statistic follows the chi-squared distribution with 2 degrees of freedom. At the 5% level of significance, the calculated value of the likelihood ratio statistic is equal to 1.457. The probability value is equal to 0.483.

Null hypothesis: The estimated model fits the data well.

Alternative hypothesis: The estimated model does not fit the data well.

Decision rule:

At the 5% level, the null hypothesis is rejected if the probability value is less than 0.05.

At the 5% level, the null hypothesis cannot be rejected if the probability value is greater than or equal to 0.05.

Now, since P = 0.483 > 0.07, the null hypothesis cannot be rejected at the 5% level. We conclude that the fitted model fits the data well.

```
. estat ic
Akaike's information criterion and Bayesian information criterion

-----------------------------------------------------------------------------
       Model |          N   ll(null)  ll(model)      df         AIC        BIC
-------------+---------------------------------------------------------------
           . |        500          .  -8487.234      12    16998.47   17049.04
-----------------------------------------------------------------------------
Note: BIC uses N = number of observations. See [R] BIC note.


. estat vce
Covariance matrix of coefficients of sem model

             | x1                      | x2                      | x3
        e(V) |          X        _cons |          X        _cons |          X
-------------+-------------------------+-------------------------+------------
x1           |                         |                         |
           X |          0              |                         |
       _cons |          0    .41125135 |                         |
-------------+-------------------------+-------------------------+------------
x2           |                         |                         |
           X |          0            0 |  .00524029              |
       _cons |          0    .18585921 |          0    .40212777 |
-------------+-------------------------+-------------------------+------------
x3           |                         |                         |
           X |          0            0 |  .00292225            0 |  .00532499
       _cons |          0    .19136836 |          0    .19773118 |          0
-------------+-------------------------+-------------------------+------------
x4           |                         |                         |
           X |          0            0 |  .01935664            0 |   .0201272
       _cons |          0    1.3089311 |          0    1.3524518 |          0
-------------+-------------------------+-------------------------+------------
/            |                         |                         |
   var(e.x1) |          0            0 |  .00799912            0 |  .01061742
   var(e.x2) |          0            0 | -.02081191            0 | -.00620689
   var(e.x3) |          0            0 |  -.0090084            0 | -.01891051
   var(e.x4) |          0            0 |   .4046865            0 |  .28516024
      var(X) |          0            0 | -.48613085            0 | -.50292169

             | x3         | x4                      | /
        e(V) |      _cons |          X        _cons |  var(e.x1)  var(e.x2)
-------------+------------+-------------------------+-----------------------
x3           |            |                         |
       _cons |  .40610659 |                         |
-------------+------------+-------------------------+-----------------------
x4           |            |                         |
           X |          0 |  .18298187              |
       _cons |  1.3925405 |          0    9.8128506 |
-------------+------------+-------------------------+-----------------------
/            |            |                         |
   var(e.x1) |          0 |  .53147372            0 |  60.690683
   var(e.x2) |          0 |  .56472301            0 |  6.1543968  54.575893
   var(e.x3) |          0 |   .5610347            0 |  6.0689691  8.1535484
   var(e.x4) |          0 | -28.874143            0 | -316.67781 -413.30109
      var(X) |          0 | -3.8987616            0 | -7.1572505 -6.1543967

             | /
        e(V) |  var(e.x3)  var(e.x4)     var(X)
-------------+---------------------------------
/            |
   var(e.x3) |  51.499999
   var(e.x4) | -412.99684  21108.799
      var(X) | -6.0689691   316.6778  122.75149
```

The Satorra-Bentler (1994) goodness-of-fit test

```
. sem (x1 x2 x3 x4 <- X), vce(sbentler)


Endogenous variables
  Measurement: x1 x2 x3 x4

Exogenous variables
  Latent: X

Fitting target model:
Iteration 0:   log pseudolikelihood = -8487.5905
Iteration 1:   log pseudolikelihood = -8487.2358
Iteration 2:   log pseudolikelihood = -8487.2337
Iteration 3:   log pseudolikelihood = -8487.2337

Structural equations model                          Number of obs = 500
Estimation method: ml

Log pseudolikelihood = -8487.2337

 ( 1)  [x1]X = 1
-------------------------------------------------------------------------------
             |             Satorra-Bentler
             | Coefficient  std. err.      z    P>|z|     [95% conf. interval]
-------------+-----------------------------------------------------------------
Measurement  |
  x1         |
           X |          1  (constrained)
       _cons |     99.518   .6419311   155.03   0.000     98.25984    100.7762
-------------+-----------------------------------------------------------------
  x2         |
           X |   1.033249   .0767608    13.46   0.000     .8828006    1.183698
       _cons |     99.954   .6347705   157.46   0.000     98.70987    101.1981
-------------+-----------------------------------------------------------------
  x3         |
           X |   1.063876   .0751028    14.17   0.000     .9166773    1.211075
       _cons |     99.052   .6379032   155.28   0.000     97.80173    100.3023
-------------+-----------------------------------------------------------------
  x4         |
           X |   7.276754   .4386592    16.59   0.000     6.416998     8.13651
       _cons |     94.474   3.135684    30.13   0.000     88.32817    100.6198
-------------+-----------------------------------------------------------------
   var(e.x1)|   115.6865   7.744173                      101.4617    131.9055
   var(e.x2)|   105.0445   6.499187                      93.04833    118.5872
   var(e.x3)|   101.2572    7.00047                      88.42551    115.9509
   var(e.x4)|   144.0406   145.6607                      19.84766    1045.347
      var(X)|   89.93921    11.2763                      70.34416    114.9927
-------------------------------------------------------------------------------
LR test of model vs. saturated: chi2(2) = 1.46             Prob > chi2 = 0.4827
Satorra-Bentler scaled test:    chi2(2) = 1.59             Prob > chi2 = 0.4526
```

Comparison of fitted model with saturated model

A saturated model is a model that fits the data perfectly. The likelihood ratio test statistic follows the chi-squared distribution with 2 degrees of freedom and has an observed magnitude of 1.46 and a P-value of 0.4827, which is greater than 0.05.

Null hypothesis: The estimated model fits the data perfectly well.

Alternative hypothesis: The estimated model does not fit the data perfectly well.

Decision rule:

At the 5% level, the null hypothesis is rejected if the probability value is less than 0.05.

At the 5% level, the null hypothesis cannot be rejected if the probability value is greater than or equal to 0.05.

Now, since P = 0.4827 > 0.07, the null hypothesis cannot be rejected at the 5% level. We conclude that the fitted model fits the data perfectly well.

The Satorra–Bentler scaled goodness-of-fit test

The Satorra–Bentler scaled test statistic (Satorra and Bentler, 2010) follows the chi-squared distribution with 2 degrees of freedom and has an observed magnitude of 1.59 and a P-value of 0.4526, which is greater than 0.05. The Satorra-Bentler scaled (mean-adjusted) chi-square statistic is used to test the adequacy of the fitted structural equations model.

Satorra–Bentler scaled test: chi2(2) = 1.59 Prob > chi2 = 0.4526

Null hypothesis: The estimated model fits the data well.

Alternative hypothesis: The estimated model does not fit the data well.

Decision rule:

At the 5% level, the null hypothesis is rejected if the probability value is less than 0.05.

At the 5% level, the null hypothesis cannot be rejected if the probability value is greater than or equal to 0.05.

Now, since P = 0.4526 > 0.07, the null hypothesis cannot be rejected at the 5% level. We conclude that the fitted model fits the data well.

Goodness-of-fit tests for SEM analysis

The saturated model assumes that all variables are correlated.

The baseline model assumes that no variables are correlated (except for exogenous variables in cases when endogenous variables are present in the model).

The specified model is the model that is fitted or estimated by performing SEM analysis.

The following **likelihood ratio chi-square statistic** is used for comparing the baseline model (b) with the saturated model (s).

$$\chi^2_{bs} = 2\left(LogL_s - LogL_b\right)$$

The following likelihood ratio chi-square statistic is used for comparing the specified model (m) with the saturated model (s).

$$\chi^2_{ms} = 2\left(LogL_s - LogL_m\right)$$

L_b is the loglikelihood function for the baseline model.

L_s is the loglikelihood function for the saturated model.

L_m is the loglikelihood function for the specified model.

The degrees of freedom are given as follows:

$$df_{bs} = df_s - df_b$$

$$df_{ms} = df_s - df_m$$

Commonly used goodness-of-fit tests are shown below:

The likelihood ratio chi-square test $\chi^2_{ms} = 2\left(LogL_s - LogL_m\right)$

The Akaike Information Criterion (AIC) statistic

The Swartz Bayesian Information Criterion (BIC) statistic

The Coefficient of Determination (CD) statistic

The Coefficient of Determination (CD) statistic

The Coefficient of Determination (CD) statistic, which is equal to R^2

$$R^2 = 1 - \frac{\det\left(\hat{\psi}\right)}{\det\left(\hat{\Sigma}\right)}$$

Values of R^2 that are closer to 1 or 100% indicate that the fitted SEM model is adequate.

The Root Mean Square Error of Approximation (RMSEA) statistic

$$RMSEA = \sqrt{\frac{\left(\chi^2_{ms} - df_{ms}\right)}{(n-1)df_{ms}}}$$

At the 5% level of significance, a P-value which is larger than 0.05 indicates that the fitted SEM model is adequate.

Values of RMSEA which are smaller than 0.05 indicate that the fitted SEM is adequate.

The Comparative Fit Index (CFI) statistic is used for comparing the estimated SEM model with the baseline model.

$$CFI = 1 - \frac{\chi^2_{ms} - df_{ms}}{\chi^2_{bs} - df_{bs}}$$

At the 5% level of significance, values of CFI that are 0.95 or larger indicate that the fitted SEM model is adequate.

The Tucker-Lewis Index (TLI)

The TLI statistic compares estimated SEM model with the baseline model.

$$TLI = 1 - \frac{\left(\frac{\chi^2_{ms}}{df_{ms}}\right) - \left(\frac{\chi^2_{bs}}{df_{bs}}\right)}{\left(\frac{\chi^2_{bs}}{df_{bs}}\right) - 1}$$

At the 5% level of significance, values of TLI that are 0.95 or larger indicate that the fitted SEM model is adequate.

The Standardised Root Mean Square Residual (SRMR) statistic

The SRMR statistic is given by the following expression:

$$SRMR = \chi^2_{bs} = 2\left(LogL_s - LogL_b\right)$$

At the 5% level of significance, values of SRMR that are 0.05 or smaller indicate that the fitted SEM model is adequate.

At the 5% level, a P-value which is smaller than 0.05 indicates that the fitted model is adequate.

Akaike Information Criterion (AIC) statistic

The AIC statistic is given by

$$AIC = -2LogL_m + 2df_m$$

The Swartz Bayesian Information Criterion (BIC) statistic

The BIC statistic is given by

$$BIC = -2LogL_m + Ndf_m$$

Small values of AIC and BIC indicate that the fitted SEM model is adequate.

UNIT 17

EXAMPLES OF HOW TO USE THE AMERICAN PSYCHOLOGICAL ASSOCIATION (APA) CITATION AND REFERENCING STYLE

This unit provides various examples on how to use the American Psychological Association (APA) referencing style based on journal articles, books, and Internet-based reports. The examples show learners how to cite material in proposals and dissertations. They also show learners how to list cited materials in the list of references at the end of their proposals, dissertations, and research reports and papers. Detailed guidelines and more examples are available at the APA official website:

https://apastyle.apa.org/blog/sentence-case-titles-references

Journal article with 1 author

Moore, R. K. (2022). The Evolution of Promotional

Marketing. *Journal of Management*, *4*(2), 14-26.

To use the above in the body of the proposal,

Moore (2022) has found that ....
Moore (2022: 15) has found that ....
Moore (2022: 15-16) has found that ....

According to Miller (2022: 175), early assessment is beneficial.

According to Miller (2022: 175-176), early assessment is beneficial.

Miller (2022) has stated that early assessment is beneficial.

Miller (2022: 13) has stated that early assessment is beneficial.

Miller (2022: 13-14) has stated that early assessment is beneficial.

Poor planning leads to the loss of valuable resources (Moore, 2022).

Poor planning leads to the loss of valuable resources (Moore, 2022: 15).

Poor planning leads to the loss of valuable resources (Moore, 2022: 15-16).

Journal article with 2 authors

Ashley, K. D., & Harrison, L. B. (2022). Conducting surveys: Methods and applications. *Journal of Management, 4*(2), 41-53.

To use the above in the body of the proposal:

Ashley and Harrison (2022) have stated that .....

A similar assessment has been made by Ashley and Harrison (2022).

This method is less cumbersome and more efficient (Ashley & Harrison, 2022).

This method is less cumbersome and more efficient (Ashley & Harrison, 2022: 34).

This method is less cumbersome and more efficient (Ashley & Harrison, 2022: 34-35).

Early assessment is beneficial (Miller & Smith, 2022).

Early assessment is beneficial (Miller & Smith, 2022: 9).

Early assessment is beneficial (Miller & Smith, 2022: 9-11).

Miller and Smith (2022) have proposed a framework that could be used for risk assessment.

Miller and Smith (2022: 8) have proposed a framework that could be used for risk assessment.

Miller and Smith (2022: 8-9) have proposed a framework that could be used for risk assessment.

Journal article with 3 authors

Peter, A.P., Kent, M., & Kelvin, T. (2022). Project management: Technical processes. *Journal of Process Control, 5*(3), 32-41.

To use the above in the body of the proposal:

Peter, Kent and Kelvin (2022) have stated that .....

Peter, Kent and Kelvin (2022: 9) have stated that .....

Peter, Kent and Kelvin (2022: 9-11) have stated that .....

Peter et al. (2022) have stated that ....

Peter et al. (2022: 34) have stated that ....

Peter et al. (2022: 34-35) have stated that ....

A similar assessment has been made by Peter, Kent and Kelvin (2022).

A similar assessment has been made by Peter, Kent and Kelvin (2022: 11).

A similar assessment has been made by Peter, Kent and Kelvin (2022: 11-12).

A similar assessment has been made by Peter et al. (2022).

A similar assessment has been made by Peter et al. (2022: 11).

A similar assessment has been made by Peter et al. (2022: 11-12).

This method is less cumbersome and more efficient (Peter, Kent & Kelvin, 2022).

This method is less cumbersome and more efficient (Peter, Kent & Kelvin, 2022: 13).

This method is less cumbersome and more efficient (Peter, Kent & Kelvin, 2022: 13-14).

This method is less cumbersome and more efficient (Peter et al., 2022).

This method is less cumbersome and more efficient (Peter et al., 2022: 8).

This method is less cumbersome and more efficient (Peter et al., 2022: 8-10).

Early assessment is beneficial (Miller, Smith & Kent, 2022).

Early assessment is beneficial (Miller, Smith & Kent, 2022: 8).

Early assessment is beneficial (Miller, Smith & Kent, 2022: 8-9).

Miller, Smith and Kent (2022) have stated that early assessment is beneficial.

Miller, Smith and Kent (2022: 8) have stated that early assessment is beneficial.

Miller, Smith and Kent (2022: 8-9) have stated that early assessment is beneficial.

Book with 1 author

Maxwell, K. T. (2022). *Principles of management.* New York: John Wiley & Sons.

To use the above in the body of the proposal:

Maxwell (2022) has found that ....

Maxwell (2022: 28) has found that ....

Maxwell (2022: 28-29) has found that ....

Poor planning leads to the loss of valuable resources (Maxwell, 2022).

Poor planning leads to the loss of valuable resources (Maxwell, 2022: 34).

Poor planning leads to the loss of valuable resources (Maxwell, 2022: 34-35).

Book with 2 authors

Ashley, K. D., & Harrison, L. B. (2022). *Conducting surveys: Methods and applications.* New York: John Wiley & Sons.

To use the above in the body of the proposal,

Ashley and Harrison (2022) have stated that .....

Ashley and Harrison (2022: 8) have stated that .....

Ashley and Harrison (2022: 8-9) have stated that .....

A similar assessment has been made by Ashley and Harrison (2022).

This method is less cumbersome and more efficient (Ashley & Harrison, 2022).

This method is less cumbersome and more efficient (Ashley & Harrison, 2022: 12).

This method is less cumbersome and more efficient (Ashley & Harrison, 2022: 12-14).

Book with 3 authors

Peter, A.P., Kent, M., & Kelvin, T. (2022). *Project Management: Technical Processes.* New York: John Wiley & Sons.

To use the above in the body of the proposal:

Peter, Kent and Kelvin (2022) have stated that .....

Peter, Kent and Kelvin (2022: 8) have stated that .....

Peter, Kent and Kelvin (2022: 8-9) have stated that .....

Peter et al. (2022) have stated that ....

Peter et al. (2022: 8) have stated that ....

Peter et al. (2022: 8-9) have stated that ....

A similar assessment has been made by Peter, Kent and Kelvin (2022).

A similar assessment has been made by Peter, Kent and Kelvin (2022: 8).

A similar assessment has been made by Peter, Kent and Kelvin (2022: 8-9).

A similar assessment has been made by Peter et al. (2022).

A similar assessment has been made by Peter et al. (2022: 8).

A similar assessment has been made by Peter et al. (2022: 8-9).

This method is less cumbersome and more efficient (Peter, Kent & Kelvin, 2022).

This method is less cumbersome and more efficient (Peter, Kent & Kelvin, 2022: 8).

This method is less cumbersome and more efficient (Peter, Kent & Kelvin, 2022: 8-9).

This method is less cumbersome and more efficient (Peter et al., 2022).

This method is less cumbersome and more efficient (Peter et al., 2022: 8).

This method is less cumbersome and more efficient (Peter et al., 2022: 8-9).

Hardcopy of report published in print by the World Bank Group in Washington DC

World Bank Group. (2022). ***The World Bank Annual Report 2022.*** **Washington DC: World Bank Group.**

Internet-based report published online by the World Bank Group

World Bank Group. (2022). ***Poverty and Shared Prosperity.*** **[Online]. Available from:** https://www.worldbank.org/en/publication/poverty-and-shared-prosperity **[Accessed: 28 September 2023].**

A sample list of references based on the APA referencing style

Beh, E. J., & Lombardo, R. (2021). *An introduction to correspondence analysis*. New York: John Wiley & Sons.

Bell, E., Bryman, A., & Harley, B. (2022). *Business research methods*. Oxford: Oxford University Press.

Braun, V., & Clarke, V. (2019). Reflecting on reflexive thematic analysis. *Qualitative Research in Sport, Exercise and Health, 11*(4), 589-597.

Chatfield, C., & Collins, A. (2018). *Introduction to multivariate analysis*. New York: Routledge.

Levy, P. S., & Lemeshow, S. (2013). *Sampling of populations: Methods and applications*. New York: John Wiley & Sons.

Raosoft. (2023). *Online sample size calculator*. [Online]. Available from: http://www.raosoft.com/samplesize.html [Accessed: 28 September 2023].

South African Small Enterprise Development Agency. (2016). *Accelerating SMME growth in South Africa*. [Online]. Available from: http://www.seda.org.za/ [Accessed: 28 September 2023].

South African National Department of Trade, Industry and Competition. (2023). *Annual report for the financial year 2021/2022*. [Online]. Available from: http://www.thedtic.gov.za/ [Accessed: 28 September 2023].

Westnet. (2023). *Annual report for 2021/2022*. [Online]. Available from: https://gowestnet.co.za/ [Accessed: 28 September 2023].

Worku, Z. (2024). A guide for the measurement of entrepreneurial skills. *Tec Empresarial, 19*(1), 244-251.

Worku, Z. (2022). Determinants of satisfactory entrepreneurial skills in retail businesses. *Journal of Positive School Psychology, 6*(4), 2300-2313.

How to indent references in the APA format

An indentation is a blank space between a margin and the beginning of a line of text. In a list of references drawn up based on the APA style, each referenced item should be indented by a certain number of spaces. For example, in the following references, lines 2 and 3 are indented by a few spaces each.

Mark, T. W., & Sweeney, K. (2023). Factors that affect the effective utilisation of business loans. *Journal of Entrepreneurship, 2*(3), 11-23.

Allan, B., Peter, T., & Jarman, R. (2023). *How to Manage Municipal Projects*. New York: John Wiley & Sons.

World Bank. (2023). *Annual report* 2022. [Online]. Available from: https://www.worldbank.org/ [Accessed: 28 September 2023].

UNIT 18

A SAMPLE MBA RESEARCH PROPOSAL AND QUESTIONNAIRE

A FRAMEWORK FOR ENHANCING SOUND FINANCIAL RECORD KEEPING IN SMALL, MICRO AND MEDIUM-SIZED ENTERPRISES OPERATING AT SALDANHA BAY

A Research Proposal

By

Mark Nathaniel Williams

Submitted in partial fulfilment of the requirements for the degree

MASTER'S DEGREE IN BUSINESS ADMINISTRATION (MBA)

In the Tshwane School of Business & Society
Faculty of Management Sciences

TSHWANE UNIVERSITY OF TECHNOLOGY

Supervisor: Prof Z Worku

January 2023

TABLE OF CONTENTS

1. INTRODUCTION AND BACKGOUND TO STUDY

The study aims to determine the benefits of sound financial record keeping for ensuring sustained profitability and viability in small, micro, and medium-sized enterprises (SMMEs) that conduct retail business operations in the Saldanha Bay region of the Western Cape. SMMEs are valuable for creating livelihood and alleviating poverty among poorly skilled people worldwide. The retail industry relies on SMMEs for creating jobs, promoting economic wealth, and reducing poverty levels among the general population (Bushe, 2019: 1). A survey conducted by Wentzel, Fapohunda and Haldenwang (2022: 1-22) has found that SMMEs generate more employment opportunities and livelihood for poorly skilled and poorly resourced people than do well-established or large business enterprises. As such, they deserve tangible policy-related, administrative, and financial assistance from local municipalities and national governments. In developing nations, SMMEs alleviate poverty, generate wealth, and reduce unemployment rates among the poor (Elijah & Usaini, 2021: 3; Badenhorst-Weiss & Cilliers, 2014:2; Nkosi, Bounds & Goldman, 2013: 1). SMMEs vary with regard to size, capital, and economic sector. SMMEs play a valuable role in economic sectors such as retail, services, and manufacturing. SMMEs perform an essential function in national economies, as they are often the source of economic development, invention, and employment creation (South African Small Enterprise Development Agency, 2023: 1).

Despite the considerable and undeniable role that small businesses play in societies, the literature on small business survival reveals that, on average, 40 percent of SMMEs fail annually (Wentzel, Fapohunda & Haldenwang, 2022: 1-22). The Organisation for Economic Cooperation and Development (OECD) has reported that 20 to 40 percent of SMMEs have closed across all regions (OECD, 2021: 1-2). The reasons leading to the closure of SMMEs are often different. The South African Department of Trade, Industry and Competition (2022: 2) has listed several factors that contribute to failure among SMMEs. Examples of such factors are lack of entrepreneurial, management and marketing skills, difficulty in obtaining business loans, and intense competition from well-established businesses. Inability to use appropriate technology often leads to lack of efficiency and profitability in SMMEs. Owners and operators of emerging SMMEs in South African townships often fail to benefit from training programmes that are offered by the Small Enterprise Development Agency (SEDA) and the Department of Trade, Industry and Competition (DTIC) (Worku, 2022). Such training programmes are valuable for acquiring and improving skills in drawing up business plans, completing business loan application forms, keeping business-related records, the use of computers, taking inventory of stock, auditing, completing tax-return forms, networking, and making oral presentations (Fatoki, 2018: 3; Balagobei, 2019: 439).

Skills in the fields of auditing, accounting, and financial record–keeping are generally low among emerging SMME owners and managers (Seja & Hromuakova, 2019). Owners and operators of SMMEs are reluctant to audit daily activities thoroughly for fear of having to pay significant tax. The need for auditing and keeping sound financial records is high among emerging SMMEs in all economic sectors. Owners and operators of emerging SMMEs often fail to recognise the benefits of proper record keeping, bookkeeping, auditing, and accounting. They often fail to produce accurate financial statements and tax returns. These shortcomings hamper their chances of securing business loans from commercial banks (Babakura, 2019). Studies conducted in Gauteng Province by Marivate (2014: 53-72), Fatoki (2018: 1-10), and Worku (2022: 2301) have identified difficulty in securing business loans, lack of auditing and accounting skills, and inadequate entrepreneurial skills as major causes of failure and bankruptcy in emerging retail businesses in Gauteng Province.

Herrington and Coduras (2019: 1-24) have found that the lack of entrepreneurial skills is a key cause of failure in emerging SMMEs in all Sub-Saharan African countries, including South Africa. The authors have shown that emerging businesses do not benefit from programmes of assistance that are offered to them by SEDA and DTIC due to lack of awareness, poor motivation, and poor leadership. Emerging SMMEs often fail to comprehend the significance of sound financial record keeping, even though the problem often leads to failure in SMMEs (Bushe, 2019: 1-2). Anderson, Chandy and Zia (2018: 5559-5583) have found that most SMME owners who lack auditing and accounting skills stand to benefit from training programmes that are offered by SEDA and DTIC.

2. LITERATURE REVIEW

There is a need for skills-related training programmes among poorly resourced SMMEs in all South African regions. Due to lack of accounting and auditing skills, SMMEs often struggle to acquire equity from financial institutions. Even in cases where financial institutions permit offering equity, the requirements are always stringent and prohibitive. The lack of accounting and record-keeping practices has resulted in many SMMEs losing funding or financial opportunities, partly because the financial information required by the financial institution is unavailable. The 5-year-long study conducted by Marivate (2014: 53-72) found that programmes of assistance that are offered by SEDA and DTIC often fail to transform poorly resourced emerging retail businesses due to lack of awareness, poor political commitment, poor motivation, and poor leadership. Fatoki (2018) has constructed a practical framework that is suitable for enhancing the level of technical, financial, and managerial capacity in emerging SMMEs. The author has shown that it is essential to monitor and evaluate factors that undermine profitability in SMMEs by way of taking valuable lessons from the developed nations. The author has shown the dire need for skills in auditing, accounting, stock-taking, bookkeeping, and presentation skills. Surveys conducted in the past by Herrington and Coduras (2019: 3) and Worku (2022: 2301) show that emerging SMMEs often fail due to inadequate entrepreneurial, networking, and marketing skills. Herrington and Coduras (2019) found that the failure rate in the first year of operation among newly established South African SMMEs is more than 50%. According to the authors, about 60% of all newly established SMMEs fail before operating for three consecutive years.

Although SMMEs promote or enhance the country's economic growth, they are not growing adequately to meet the National Development Plan (NDP) targets (Diabate, Sibiri, Wang & Yu, 2019: 1-5). The NDP envisioned that the segment of SMMEs would contribute 80 percent of Gross Domestic Product (GDP) growth, generate 90 percent of the jobs, and contribute significantly to an estimated 11 million new jobs by 2030. This plan has failed to materialise. Although the Saldanha Bay Municipality GDP contributed 31 percent to the GDP of its District in 2018, the economy has not grown as fast as expected due to a slow economic growth and inability to provide meaningful support to SMMEs, which was slightly higher than in 2015; the GDP percentage growth was an average of 2.4 percent, which is still below the district average of 3 percent shared by the economic sector of the actual cost of products produced and services rendered in the municipal area for a year and have stayed the same since 2011. The primary sector (agriculture and mining) has contributed 20 percent, while the secondary sector shares the percentage below. The tertiary sector (government services, finance, insurance, real estate, and trade) has the highest, above 55 percent, even though having declined slightly. These figures prove that the tertiary sector still drives the Saldanha Bay economy (Saldanha Bay Municipality, 2021:15). The report highlights that the unemployment rate has grown exponentially on the West Coast. The report also shows that SMMEs play a crucial role in growing the local economy of Saldanha Bay. However, there are difficulties, such as poor financial management, the high cost of doing business, difficulty in securing business loans, inability to provide training opportunities to emerging SMMEs, stiff competition from well-established businesses, a high influx of migrant communities, and inability to render satisfactory municipal services to a rapidly growing population. The study aims to show the benefits of sound record keeping, auditing, bookkeeping, and financial accounting to SMMEs operating in Saldanha Bay.

Sound financial record keeping is essential for making informed business decisions and for minimising wasteful expenditure in emerging SMMEs. Economic activities are evaluated and described by monetary measures. Proper financial recordkeeping is essential for producing accurate information, financial statements, and plans for investment in all business enterprises (Qubbaja & Talahmeh, 2019: 310-317). Barnard, Amaeshi and Vaaler (2023) have found that emerging SMMEs fail due to poor record keeping and inability to make informed business decisions. It is not possible to pro-duce sound business plans in the absence of credible informa-tion. Proper record keeping is a critical success factor in emerg-ing SMMEs in all economic sectors. Inappropriate and capital structure financial problems were some of the issues identified and recognised under capacity business operations in the lack of financial management in unsuccessful businesses, among other matters (Msomi & Olarewaju, 2021: 104; Nassiuma, 2018: 34; Gidado & Babakura, 2019: 353; Aladejebi & Oladi-meji, 2019: 29; Simatele, Mishi, Kapingura & Copestake, 2022: 277). The Global Entrepreneurship Monitoring (GEM) Report for the year 2019 has shown that South African emerging SMMEs are less competitive than SMMEs in Ghana, Zambia, Kenya, and Nigeria due to lack of entrepreneurial skills (Herrington & Coduras, 2019: 3).

3. THEORETICAL FRAMEWORK OF STUDY

The study aims to test the potential benefits, relevance, and veracity of the dynamic theory of profit propounded by Clark (1908). Makadok (2011) has provided theories that are based on the dynamic theory of profit and are helpful for SMMEs operating in the Saldanha Bay region. These are the frictional theory of profits, the monopoly theory of profits, the innovations theory of profits, the risk and uncertainty bearing theory of profits, and the managerial efficiency theory of profits. The theories explain the requirements for ensuring sustained profitability in SMMEs in all economic sectors. Examples of crucial requirements for ensuring sustained profitability in SMMEs are the acquisition of adequate entrepreneurial, marketing and networking skills.

4. PROBLEM STATEMENT

The Saldanha Bay GDP for 2020 has decreased by 3.4 percent. The unemployment rate has increased rapidly and becomes the highest on the West Coast, with 17.6 percent in September (Saldanha Bay Municipality, 2022). The economic status of the district continues to be on a downward spiral, and the performance of SMMEs remains unexplored, which warrants further scrutiny. Hence, it is imperative to determine the value of financial record keeping on the performance of SMMEs in Saldanha.

For the reasons mentioned above, the study is profoundly important, as it may highlight or demystify the challenges SMMEs face. The study will propose a contextually relevant framework that is vital for promoting sound recordkeeping, auditing, and accounting processes in emerging SMMEs in Saldanha Bay Municipality. Such a contribution to emerging SMMEs will be vital in reducing bankruptcy in poorly skilled and poorly resourced owners and operators of businesses at the site of study. Findings obtained from the study will be vital for promoting sound record keeping, bookkeeping, auditing, and accounting in emerging SMMEs, thereby promoting sustained profitability and viability. The same findings will also help policymakers in reviewing the current policy in financial record-keeping in emerging SMMEs. Findings of the study will also assist Saldanha Bay Municipality by identifying feasible ways and means in which effective assistance can be provided to emerging SMMEs. Such an outcome is helpful for growing the local economy and reducing the current rate of unemployment among the youth. There is a shortage of such studies on Saldanha Bay. The study aims to fill the gap by gathering fresh empirical data from emerging SMMEs that operate in Saldanha Bay Municipality.

5. OBJECTIVES OF STUDY

Although there is a collaboration between the Saldanha Bay Municipality (WC014) and the Saldanha Bay Industrial Development Zone (IDZ), which aims to eradicate poverty and grow the economy, the unemployment rate in Saldanha has increased by 17.5 percent, becoming the highest within the West Coast. The Western Cape business survey report (2020) highlighted that 76 percent have anticipated that there would be no generated revenue or a decline of 80 percent due to the COVID-19 pandemic. The consequential impact on the working capital affects the business's operation, leading to the company's closing due to inefficiency brought on by a failure to keep and maintain finan-cial records in an appropriate accounting format and inadequately. Gidado and Babakura (2019: 350-361) have pointed out that difficulty in securing business loans is a major obstacle to profitability in poorly resourced and emerging SMMEs in South African townships. There is also a lack of skills and competencies or capability to perform allocated activities at a certain level of effectiveness and efficiency. Although Economic Development, Environmental Affairs, and Tourism have policies in place, the high unemployment in Saldanha has become a critical issue facing the municipality. Ensuring sound record-keeping and entrepreneurial competence in poorly resourced and emerging SMMEs has the potential for leading to economic development and prosperity in the West Coast. Against this background, the study aims to assess and evaluate the extent to which SMMEs operating in Saldanha Bay practice sound financial record keeping on a day-to-day basis. The study aims to assess and evaluate the potential benefits of sound financial record keeping to profitability and growth in SMMEs operating in Saldanha Bay.

The study has the following specific objectives:

- To determine the value of financial record keeping on the performance of SMMEs in Saldanha;
- To determine the typebl of financial records keeping that is utilised by the SMME owners and managers in Saldanha;
- To explore the attitude of SMME owners towards financial record keeping;
- To identify the challenges the SMME owners and managers experience regarding financial record keeping; and
- To make recommendations to ensure consistent adherence to the financial records and accounting practices.

6. METHODS AND MATERIALS OF STUDY

The study will be conducted using a cross-sectional survey method. The survey seeks to define the characteristics of subjects or phenomena, beliefs, attitudes, tastes, and perceptions of people in which the researcher is interested (Bell, Harley & Bryman, 2022). Quantitative methods will be used to collect and analyse data. Deductive reasoning (application of well-known theoretical principles) will be used for constructing research hypotheses. The questionnaire of study will be adapted from an existing questionnaire of study constructed by Fatoki (2018) for assessing skills related to record keeping, auditing, accounting, and writing business plans. The level of entrepreneurial skills of operators of SMMEs will be measured by using a composite index constructed by Worku (2024: 252-268) for assessing entrepreneurial skills in emerging SMMEs.

Sample size of study and sampling technique

The online sample size calculator, Raosoft (2023), was used for calculating the sample size of study. The level of significance of test was set at 3%. The population size was equal to 900, as the total number of SMMEs listed on the West Net (2022) database is equal to 900. The percentage of SMMEs that keep proper financial records at all times is not known. Thus, the percentage was set at 50%. By using these figures, the sample size of study became 489. Thus, data will be gathered from 489 SMMEs as part of the study. Stratified random sampling (Levy and Lemeshow, 2013) will be used for selecting eligible SMMEs into the sample. The type or economic sector of retail business carried out by SMMEs will be used for stratification.

7. STATISTICAL METHODS OF DATA ANALYSIS

Data will be gathered on socioeconomic factors that affect the ability of SMMEs to keep financial records accurately and suitably. Quantitative methods of data collection and analyses will be used for conducting the study. Examples of such methods are frequency tables, crosstab analysis (Beh and Lombardo, 2021), one and two-sample tests on proportions (Denis, 2021), confirmatory factor analysis, and structural equations modelling (Chatfield & Collins, 2018).

Measurement of variables

Validity and reliability tests will be used for ensuring accuracy in the measurement of variables. A pilot study will be used for ensuring content validity. The Cronbach Alpha test will be used for ensuring reliability and internal consistency (Beh & Lombardo, 2021).

Data collection procedures

Primary data will be collected from 489 eligible participants of study by using a structured questionnaire of study. The questionnaire of study is an adaptation of a questionnaire developed by Fatoki (2018) for assessing skills related to record keeping, auditing, accounting, and writing business plans. The reference for the questionnaire is shown in the list of references.

A pilot study will be conducted in Saldanha Bay by administering the questionnaire of study to a simple random sample of size 50 SMMEs operating in the various sectors of the retail industry. A pilot study is valuable for ensuring content validity in the questionnaire of study. The pilot study will be conducted by administering the questionnaire of study to 10 participants each from the 5 geographical zones of Saldanha Bay. This process is commonly referred to as face validity.

Sampling frame, population, sample size and sampling method

The sampling frame will be obtained from Westnet (2023). This is the list of all 900 SMMEs operating in the Saldanha Bay area. From the list, a stratified random sample of size, 489 eligible retail SMMEs, will be chosen by economic sector. Thus, economic sector will be used as a criterion for stratification. The sampling frame shows the geographical zones of SMMEs that are on the list of SMMEs belonging to Westnet (2023). These 489 SMMEs will be contacted and asked to take part in the study. The researcher has been granted a letter of permission for data collection for the planned study. A copy of the information leaflet (IL) and informed consent form (ICF) will be sent out to all 489 eligible participants of study by using their contact details (email addresses, telephone numbers, and street addresses of businesses). Data will be collected from respondents who are willing to take part in the study voluntarily.

Questionnaires will be distributed to eligible participants of study in person by the researcher. Participation in the study is voluntary. Thus, data will be collected from people who are willing to take part in the study. Eligible respondents will be provided with the questionnaire of study and politely asked to complete the questionnaire. They will be allowed to complete the questionnaire of study at their time of convenience. Completed questionnaires will be collected in person from eligible respondents of study. Distributing and collecting questionnaires is expected to be completed in the last quarter of 2023. In the course of data collection, all aspects of the South African Personal Information Protection Act will be complied with and observed.

Population: The target population is retail SMMEs that operate in the Saldanha Bay region. The sampling frame will be obtained from Westnet (2023). This is the list of all 900 SMMEs operating in the Saldanha Bay area. In order to take part in the study, eligible participants must be active owners and operators of SMMEs in the Saldanha Bay region. Business operators who are at least 18 years old (of all genders) will be allowed to take part in the study.

Sampling technique: Stratified random sampling will be used for selecting eligible participants into the study. The sampling frame will be obtained from Westnet (2023). This is the list of all 900 SMMEs operating in the Saldanha Bay area. From the list, a stratified random sample of size 489 eligible retail SMMEs will be chosen by economic sector. Thus, economic sector will be used as a criterion for stratification. A copy of the information leaflet (IL) and informed consent form (ICF) will be sent out to all 489 eligible participants of study by using their contact details (email addresses and street addresses at their places of residence or work). According to Levy and Lemeshow (2013), the sample size of study as well as the use of stratification by geographical zone is appropriate for the study.

Statistical methods of data analyses

The following methods of statistical data analyses will be used in the study:

- Frequency tables, pie charts, and bar charts for categorical variables of the study (Denis, 2021)
- Crosstab analyses for pairs of categorical variables (Beh and Lombardo, 2021)
- Confirmatory factor analysis and Structural equations modelling (Chatfield and Collins, 2018)

8. TIME TABLE OF ACTIVITIES

Research activity	**Duration**
Approval of proposal	March 2025
Ethics approval	April 2025
Data collection	May 2025
Data capturing and analysis	June 2025
Write-up of draft project report	August 2025
Review of draft research report	October 2025
Submission of final research report	November 2025

9. ETHICAL CONSIDERATIONS

The researcher will request ethical approval from the Research Ethics Committee of the Faculty of Management Sciences of Tshwane University of Technology. The researcher will administer an online questionnaire. Furthermore, the participants will be notified about the research and their rights. Participation will be done voluntarily without any form of pressure or influence. The participants will have the right to withdraw from the study when they feel like it. The researcher will observe informed consent, which includes informing the participants about the aim of the research and their rights. The researcher will ensure the respondents' anonymity and confidentiality. No identities will be revealed. Only the researcher will manage the data, which will be stored securely and backed up on different platforms, such as the vetted cloud and Microsoft drive. The participants in the study will not suffer any harm, discomfort, or injury or be forced to participate. They will be advised that they may withdraw from the study anytime the need arises.

10. LIST OF REFERENCES

Aladejebi, O., & Oladimeji, J. A. (2019). The Impact of Record-Keeping on the Performance of Selected Small and Medium Enterprises in Lagos Metropolis. *Journal of Small Business and Entrepreneurship Development*, 7(1), 28-40.

Allah, T., August, P., Bhaza, S., Chigovanyika, T., Dyan, U., Muteweye, T., Ngcoza, M., Tsiwula, N., Qambela, V., Vooi, Y., & Bruwer, J. P. (2013). Accounting information systems in the fast-food industry: *African Journal of Business Management*, 7(4), 260-264.

Anderson, S. J., Chandy, R., & Zia, B. (2018). Pathways to profits: The impact of marketing vs. finance skills on business performance. *Management Science*, *64*(12), 5559-5583.

Badenhorst-Weiss, J. A., & Cilliers, J. O. (2014). Competitive advantage of independent small businesses in Soweto. *Southern African Business Review, 18*(3), *1-21.*

Balagobei, S. (2019). Impact of record keeping practices on business performance of small and medium scale enterprises in Sri Lanka. *International Journal of Accounting and Financial Reporting, 9*(4), 439-451.

Beh, E. J., & Lombardo, R. (2021). *An Introduction to Correspondence Analysis*. New York: John Wiley & Sons.

Bell, E., Harley, B., & Bryman, A. (2022). *Business Research Methods*. Oxford: Oxford University Press.

Belitski, M., Guenther, C., Kritikos, A. S., & Thurik, R. (2022). Economic effects of the COVID-19 pandemic on entrepreneurship and small businesses. *Small Business Economics*, *58*(2), 593-609.

Chatfield, C., & Collins, A. (2018). *Introduction to Multivariate Analysis*. New York: Routledge.

Clark, J. B. (1908). *The distribution of wealth: A theory of wages, interest and profits*. London: Macmillan.

Denis, D. J. (2021). *Applied univariate, bivariate, and multivariate statistics: Understanding statistics for social and natural scientists*, with applications in SPSS and R. New York: John Wiley & Sons.

Bowmaker-Falconer, A., & Herrington, M. (2020). *Igniting start-ups for economic growth and social change: Global Entrepreneurship Monitor South Africa* (GEM SA) 2019/2020 report. [Online]. Available from: http://www.seda.org.za/ [Accessed: 28 September 2023].

Bushe, B. (2019). The causes and impact of business failure among small to micro and medium enterprises in South Africa. *Africa's Public Service Delivery and Performance Review*, *7*(1), 1-2.

Diabate, A., Sibiri, H., Wang, L., & Yu, L. (2019). Assessing SMMEs' sustainable growth through entrepreneurs' ability and entrepreneurial orientation: An insight into SMMEs in Côte d'Ivoire. *Sustainability*, *11*(24), 1-26.

Elijah, S., & Usaini, M. (2021). An empirical investigation of the role of small businesses in economic growth and poverty alleviation in North-western Nigeria. *Academy of Accounting and Financial Studies Journal*, *25*(3), 1-14.

Fatoki, O. (2018). The impact of entrepreneurial resilience on the success of small and medium enterprises in South Africa. *Sustainability*, *10*(7), 1-10.

Gidado, S. D., & Babakura, A. (2019). Accounting and managerial skills: Factors for success of small and medium scale enterprises (SMMEs) in North-West Nigeria. *International Journal of Academic Research Business and Social Sciences*, *9*(5), 350-361.

Herrington, M., & Coduras, A. (2019). The national entrepreneurship framework conditions in sub-Saharan Africa: A comparative study of GEM data/National Expert Surveys for South Africa, Angola, Mozambique and Madagascar. *Journal of Global Entrepreneurship Research, 9*(1)*, 1-24.*

Jayeolo, O., Sidek, S., Owoeye, I., & Kazeem, Y. K. (2020). Gender and the performance of informal sector enterprises. *European Scientific Journal*, *16*(4), 57-73.

Jonck, P., & Nwosu, L. (2022). The influence of demographic variables on financial record-keeping in small and medium-sized enterprises. *Journal of Economic and Financial Sciences*, *15*(1), 1-13.

Levy, P. S., & Lemeshow, S. (2013). *Sampling of populations: Methods and applications*. New York: John Wiley & Sons.

Makadok, R. (2011). Invited editorial: The four theories of profit and their joint effects. *Journal of Management*, *37*(5), 1316-1334.

Marivate, S. P. (2014). The relationship between growth in small businesses and cashflow: A study of small businesses in Tshwane. *European Journal of Research and Reflection in Management Sciences*, *2*(2), 53-72.

Mashimba, S. H., & Kuhl, R. (2014). Performance of micro and small-scale enterprises (MSEs) in Tanzania: Growth hazards of fruit and vegetables processing vendors. *Journal of Applied Economics and Business Research*, *4*(2), 120-133.

McKenzie, D. (2021). Small business training to improve management practices in developing countries: Re-assessing the evidence for 'training doesn't work.' *Oxford Review of Economic Policy*, *37*(2), 276-301.

Msomi, T. S., & Olarewaju, O. M. (2021). Factors affecting small and medium enterprises' financial sustainability in South Africa. *African Journal of Inter/Multidisciplinary Studies*, *3*(1), 103-117.

Muhammad, L., & Isah, A. I. (2018). Impact of financial record-keeping in the growth and survival of small and medium enterprises (SMMEs) in Zaria. *Katsina Journal of Economics and Development*, *1*(2), 293-301.

Musah, A. (2017). Benefits and challenges of bookkeeping and accounting practices of S.M.E.s and its effect on growth and performance in Ghana. *Journal of Accounting, Business and Management*, *24*(2), 16-36.

Nkosi, E., Bounds, M., & Goldman, G. (2013). Skills required for the management of Black-owned small enterprises in Soweto. *Acta Commercii*, *13*(1), 1-10.

Nassiuma, B. (2019). Relationship between record keeping practices and performance of small and medium enterprises in Uasin Gishu County. *Open Journal of Economics and Commerce*, *2*(1), 34-40.

Organisation for Economic Cooperation and Development. (2021). *SMME and entrepreneurship policy frameworks across OECD countries: An OECD strategy for SMMEs and entrepreneurship*. [Online]. Available from: https://doi.org/10.1787/9f6c41ce-en [Accessed: 28 September 2023].

Qubbaja, A. A. A., & Talahmeh, I. A. (2020). A Challenge of Accounting Practices on Small and Medium Enterprises (SMMEs): Case Study of Palestine. *International Journal of Multidisciplinary Research and Analysis*, *3*(12), 310-317.

Raosoft. (2023). *Online Sample Size Calculator*. [Online]. Raosoft online sample size calculator. Available from: http://www.raosoft.com/samplesize.html [Accessed: 23 September 2023].

Saldanha Bay Municipality. (2022). *Annual report for 2019/2021*. [Online]. Available from: https://sbm.gov.za/ [Accessed: 28 September 2023].

Simatele, M., Mishi, S., Kapingura, F., & Copestake, J. (2022). Guest editorial: Introduction to the special issue on contemporary issues in micro and small business development in Africa. *African Journal of Economic and Management Studies*, *13*(3), 321-327.

South African National Department of Trade and Industry. (2012). National strategy for the development and promotion of small business: White Paper. [Online]. Available from: https://www.gov.za/ [Accessed: 28 September 2023].

South African Small Enterprise Development Agency. (2023). Annual report 2021 – 2022. [Online]. Small Enterprise Development Agency (SEDA). Available from: http://www.seda.org.za/ [Accessed: 28 September 2023].

Warmbrod, J. R. (2014). Reporting and Interpreting Scores Derived from Likert-type scales. *Journal of Agricultural Education*, *55*(5), 30-47.

Wentzel, L., Fapohunda, J. A., & Haldenwang, R. (2022). The relationship between the integration of CSR and sustainable business performance: Perceptions of SMMEs in the South African construction industry. *Sustainability*, *14*(3), 1-22.

Westnet. (2023). *Annual report for 2021/2022.* [Online]. Westnet. [Available from: https://gowestnet.co.za/ [Accessed: 28 September 2023].

Worku, Z. (2024). A composite index for the measurement of basic entrepreneurial skills in emerging enterprises. *Tec Empresarial, 19*(1), 252-268.

Worku, Z. (2022). Determinants of satisfactory entrepreneurial skills in retail businesses. *Journal of Positive School Psychology*, *6*(4), 2300-2313.

Tshwane University of Technology

We empower people

Tshwane Univeristy of Technology
Business School

Questionnaire of DBA study in the field of Business Administration

Name of student	Mark Nathaniel Williams
Student number	500555318
Degree	DBA degree in Business Administration (DBA)
Faculty	Management Sciences
University	Tshwane University of Technology

Title of DBA study: **A framework for enhancing sound financial record keeping in Small, Micro and Medium Enterprises operating at Saldanha Bay**

This questionnaire is designed to collect data as part of the DBA study at the Tshwane University of Technology business school in Pretoria. I am collecting data per the Informed Consent Form (ICF) you signed voluntarily. The study aims to determine the value of financial record-keeping on the performance of SMMEs in Saldanha.

Thank you for agreeing to take part in the study. The questionnaire of the study has two sections (1 and 2)

Copyright issues:

The questionnaire of study is an adaptaion of existing questionnaires developed by Fatoki (2018) and Worku (2024) for assessing entrepreneurial skills in emerging SMMEs. The references are shown below:

Fatoki, O. (2018). The impact of entrepreneurial resilience on the success of small and medium enterprises in South Africa. *Sustainability, 10*(7), 1-10.

Worku, Z. (2024). A composite index for the measurement of basic entrepreneurial skills in emerging enterprises. *Tec Entrepresarial, 19*(1), 252-268.

Instruction:

This questionnaire of study consists of two parts. Part 1 of the questionnaire assesses the general characteristics of respondents. Part 2 of the questionnaire evaluates the quality of the record–keeping, auditing and entrepreneurial skill. p. In both parts of the questionnaire, please provide the answer that best reflects your response by circling the number corresponding to your reply.

Part I: General characteristics of respondents

1. What is your gender?

Male	1
Female	2
Other	3

2. What is your age in years?

18 to 20 years	1
21 to 30 years	2
31 to 40 years	3
41 to 50 years	4
51 years or more	5

3. What is your highest level of formal education?

Less than NQF Level 4 (Grade 12 or matric level)	1
NQF Level 4 (Grade 12 or matric level)	2
NQF Level 5 (N6 Level Certificate)	3
NQF Level 6 (National Diploma or Diploma)	4
NQF Level 7 (bachelor's degree, Advanced Diploma or BTech degree)	5
NQF Level 8 (Honours degree or Postgraduate diploma)	6
NQF Level 9 (master's degree)	7
NQF Level 10 (Doctoral degree)	8

4. How long have you been in this business?

3 years or less	1
4 to 7 years	2
8 to 10 years	3
11 years or more	4

5. what type of business you are in?

Trading	1
Service	2
Manufacturing	3
Other Specify	4

Part 2: Assessment Related to Record-Keeping, Auditing, Accounting and Writing Business

In this part of the questionnaire, a 5-point ordinal or Likert scale is used for assessing the views and experience of respondents of the study in areas that are related to record-keeping, auditing, accounting, and writing business plans financial. Each question has 5 possible answers that vary from 1 (lowest degree of agreement with the statement provided) to 5 (highest degree of agreement with the statement provided). For each one of the 36 statements stated below, please indicate your degree of agreement with the statement by circling the number corresponding to your choice of answer. The 5 possible answers to each statement are defined as follows:

1 = Strongly disagree (SD)

2 = Disagree (D)

3 = Not sure or neutral (NS)

4 = Agree (A)

5 = Strongly agree (SA)

For each one of the statements listed in the table below, please indicate your degree of agreement with each statement by circling the number corresponding to your choice of answer.

Record keeping system	SD	D	NS	A	SA
These businesses maintain financial records.	1	2	3	4	5
The keeping of financial records is the responsibility of the business owner and store manager	1	2	3	4	5
These businesses employ both manual and automated record-keeping methods.	1	2	3	4	5
It is generally advisable to keep records of all business transactions.	1	2	3	4	5
Some businesses, such as SMMEs, do not require record keeping.	1	2	3	4	5

Record-keeping is a tiresome task.	1	2	3	4	5
Hiring an accountant to assist with record-keeping is a waste of money	1	2	3	4	5
Even though I don't keep records, my business has been quite profitable.	1	2	3	4	5
Record-keeping is essential to a business's success.	1	2	3	4	5
If given the chance, I would like to learn more about keeping records and journals.	1	2	3	4	5
Adequacy and updated ness of records					
The business records all pertinent information about its operations.	1	2	3	4	5
The data collected is precise, comprehensible, and significant.	1	2	3	4	5
The information recorded is complete and accurate.	1	2	3	4	5
Maintaining accurate and current financial records is the most challenging task.	1	2	3	4	5
Archiving and retrieval					
The owners are satisfied with their memory recordings.	1	2	3	4	5
The SMMEs has well – established record – keeping procedures.	1	2	3	4	5
The business makes surely related transaction records are logically structured.	1	2	3	4	5
Records are safeguarded from accidental and deliberate deletion or alteration.	1	2	3	4	5
Authorised staff in the record centre to retrieve records.	1	2	3	4	5
The challenge of record keeping					
Lack of facilities	1	2	3	4	5
Lack the knowledge and expertise for record-keeping	1	2	3	4	5
Preparing business records is costly and time-consuming	1	2	3	4	5

(Contd.)

Profitability					
A common metric for evaluating the performance of SMMEs is profitability.	1	2	3	4	5
The SMMEs have performed well in terms of profits.	1	2	3	4	5
The business occasionally makes bad profits.	1	2	3	4	5
Maintaining records enables business owners to track their profitability.	1	2	3	4	5
Customer Profile					
It is acceptable that not everything is going according to plan in terms of customer volume.	1	2	3	4	5
It seems like fewer people are coming in as time goes by.	1	2	3	4	5
The business 's products and services are expertly crafted to appeal to the tastes and preferences of its customers.	1	2	3	4	5
The business has always delivered the goods on time. Services provided in response to customer demand.	1	2	3	4	5
The business has been able to keep most of its regular customers.	1	2	3	4	5
Entrepreneurial skill					
Are you capable of completing a business plan?	1	2	3	4	5
Do you believe that having a business plan is essential	1	2	3	4	5
To write a business strategy, did you receive any business training?	1	2	3	4	5
Have you created a business plan for your business	1	2	3	4	5

END OF QUESTIONS

THANK YOU FOR TAKING PART IN MY STUDY

LIST OF REFERENCES

Ali, F. H., Liaqat, F., Azhar, S., & Ali, M. (2021). Exploring the quantity and quality of occupational health and safety disclosure among listed manufacturing companies: Evidence from Pakistan, a lower-middle income country. *Safety Science*, *143*(1), 1-13.

Amoah, C., & Simpeh, F. (2021). Implementation challenges of COVID-19 safety measures at construction sites in South Africa. *Journal of Facilities Management*, *19*(1), 111-128.

Arana-Landín, G., Laskurain-Iturbe, I., Iturrate, M., & Landeta-Manzano, B. (2023). Assessing the influence of industry 4.0 technologies on occupational health and safety. *Heliyon*, *9*(3), 1-13.

Barbosa, A. D. S., Bueno da Silva, L., de Souza, V. F., & Morioka, S. N. (2022). Integrated management systems: Their organizational impacts. *Total Quality Management & Business Excellence*, *33*(7-8), 794-817.

Barnard, H., Amaeshi, K., & Vaaler, P. M. (2023). Theorizing international business in Africa. *Journal of International Business Policy*, *1*(1), 1-19.

Beh, E. J., & Lombardo, R. (2021). *An Introduction to Correspondence Analysis*. New York: John Wiley & Sons.

Bell, E., Harley, B., & Bryman, A. (2022). *Business Research Methods*. Oxford: Oxford University Press.

Chatfield, C., & Collins, A. J. (2018). *Introduction to Multivariate Analysis*. New York: Routledge.

De Lucas Ancillo, A., del Val Núñez, M. T., & Gavrila, S. G. (2021). Workplace change within the COVID-19 context: a grounded theory approach. *Economic Research-Ekonomska Istraživanja, 34*(1), 2297-2316.

Denis, D. J. (2021). Applied univariate, bivariate, and multivariate statistics: Understanding statistics for social and natural scientists, with applications in SPSS and R. New York: John Wiley & Sons.

De Oliveira Neto, G. C., Tucci, H. N. P., Godinho Filho, M., Lucato, W. C., & Correia, J. M. F. (2021). Performance evaluation of occupational health and safety in relation to the COVID-19 fighting practices. *Safety Science, 141*(1), 1-13.

Gauteng Provincial Government. (2021). Annual report for 2019/2020. [Online]. Available from: https://www.gauteng.gov.za/Publications/ [Accessed: 28 September 2023].

Herrington, M. (2018). *Global Entrepreneurship Monitor South Africa Report for 2016 to 2017*. [Online]. Available from: https://www.gemconsortium.org/report/49833 [Accessed: 28 September 2023].

Hosmer Jr, D. W., Lemeshow, S., & Sturdivant, R. X. (2013). *Applied logistic regression*. New York: John Wiley and Sons.

Hoeft, M., & Trask, C. (2022). Safety built right in exploring the occupational health and safety potential of BIM-based platforms. *Sustainability, 14*(10), 1-13.

Ispas, L., & Mironeasa, C. (2022). The identification of common models applied for the integration of management systems: A review. *Sustainability, 14*(6), 1-11.

Johnstone, R., Bluff, E., & Quinlan, M. (2023). A special focus on work health and safety law and policy and work for digital labor platforms. *Journal of World Health and Safety Regulation, 1*(1), 17-29.

Khale, S. (2015). Assessment of the quality of municipal services in the City of Tshwane, South Africa. *Corporate Ownership & Control, 13*(1), 674-691.

Malomane, R., Musonda, I., & Okoro, C. S. (2022). The opportunities and challenges associated with the implementation of fourth industrial revolution technologies to manage health and safety. International Journal of Environmental Research and Public Health, 19(2), 1-13.

Marivate, S. P. (2014). The impact of entrepreneurial skills on the viability and long-term survival of small businesses *European Journal of Business, Economics and Accountancy, 2*(2), 53-72.

Mathole, R., & Ross, E. (2022). How do you stay at home if you don't have a home? Experiences of homeless persons at homeless shelters in Tshwane, South Africa during the COVID-19 pandemic. *Journal of Social Distress and Homelessness, 1*(1), 1-10.

Montgomery, D. C., Peck, E. A., & Vining, G. G. (2021). *Introduction to Linear Regression Analysis*. New York: John Wiley & Sons.

Nguyen, N. T. (2023). How does adopting occupational health and safety management practices affect outcomes for employees? The case of Vietnamese SMEs. *International Review of Economics & Finance, 83*(1), 629-640.

Nyaruwata, S., & Mbasera, M. (2021). A critique of contribution of tourism to jobs in Southern African Development Community (SADC): Implications for post COVID19 pandemic. *International Tourism and Hospitality Journal, 4*(5), 1-18.

Pardoe, I. (2020). *Applied regression modelling*. New York: John Wiley & Sons.

Riano-Casallas, M. I., & Tompa, E. (2018). Cost-benefit analysis of investment in occupational health and safety in Colombian companies. *American Journal of Industrial Medicine, 61*(11), 893-900.

Rikhotso, O., Morodi, T. J., & Masekameni, D. M. (2023). Hearing conservation programme costs at selected South African companies. *Annals of Work Exposures and Health, 67*(4), 448-461.

Satorra, A., & Bentler, P. M. (2010). Ensuring positiveness of the scaled difference chi-square test statistic. *Psychometrika, 75*(2), 243.

Sepadi, M. M., & Nkosi, V. (2023). Personal PM2. 5 exposure monitoring of informal cooking vendors at indoor and outdoor markets in Johannesburg, South Africa. *International Journal of Environmental Research and Public Health, 20*(3), 1-13.

Stata Corporation. (2023). *Structural equation modeling.* [Online]. Available from: https://www.stata.com/features/structural-equation-modeling/ [Accessed: 28 September 2023].

Stride, M., Renukappa, S., Suresh, S., & Egbu, C. (2023). The effects of COVID-19 pandemic on the UK construction industry and the process of future-proofing business. *Construction Innovation, 23*(1), 105-128.

Talapatra, S., Uddin, K., Doiro, M., & Santos, G. (2023). The linkage between corporate social responsibility and the main benefits obtained from the integration of multiple management systems in Bangladesh. *Social Responsibility Journal, 19*(1), 79-100.

Vaske, J. J. (2019). Survey research and analysis. Chicago: Sagamore-Venture.

Worku, Z. (2024). A guide for the measurement of entrepreneurial skills. *Tec Empresarial*, *19*(1), 244-251.

Yang, Y., Jia, F., Chen, L., Wang, Y., & Xiong, Y. (2021). Adoption timing of OHSAS 18001 and firm performance: An institutional theory perspective. *International Journal of Production Economics*, *231*(1), 1-13.

Zhou, Q., Mei, Q., Liu, S., & Wang, Q. (2020). Dual-effects of core enterprise management and media attention on occupational health and safety of small and medium suppliers in China. *Technology in Society*, *63*(1), 1-13.

Zondo, R. W. (2021). Assessing the effectiveness of an occupational health and safety system in a selected automotive assembly organisation in South Africa. *South African Journal of Economic and Management Sciences*, *24*(1), 1-13.

APPENDIX A

THE F-TABLE AT THE 0.05 LEVEL OF SIGNIFICANCE

Page 1 of 4									
	d_1								
d_2	1	2	3	4	5	6	7	8	9
1	161.4	199.5	215.7	224.6	230.2	234.0	236.8	238.9	240.5
2	18.51	19.00	19.16	19.25	19.3	19.33	19.35	19.37	19.38
3	10.13	9.55	9.28	9.12	9.01	8.94	8.89	8.85	8.81
4	7.71	6.94	6.59	6.39	6.26	6.16	6.09	6.04	6.00
5	6.61	5.79	5.41	5.19	5.05	4.95	4.88	4.82	4.77
6	5.99	5.14	4.76	4.53	4.39	4.28	4.21	4.15	4.10
7	5.59	4.74	4.35	4.12	3.97	3.87	3.79	3.73	3.68
8	5.32	4.46	4.07	3.84	3.69	3.58	3.50	3.44	3.39
9	5.12	4.26	3.86	3.63	3.48	3.37	3.29	3.23	3.18
10	4.96	4.10	3.71	3.48	3.33	3.22	3.14	3.07	3.02
11	4.84	3.98	3.59	3.36	3.20	3.09	3.01	2.95	2.90
12	4.75	3.89	3.49	3.26	3.11	3.00	2.91	2.85	2.80
13	4.67	3.81	3.41	3.18	3.03	2.92	2.83	2.77	2.71
14	4.60	3.74	3.34	3.11	2.96	2.85	2.76	2.70	2.65
15	4.54	3.68	3.29	3.06	2.90	2.79	2.71	2.64	2.59
16	4.49	3.63	3.24	3.01	2.85	2.74	2.66	2.59	2.54
17	4.45	3.59	3.20	2.96	2.81	2.70	2.61	2.55	2.49
18	4.41	3.55	3.16	2.93	2.77	2.66	2.58	2.51	2.46
19	4.38	3.52	3.13	2.90	2.74	2.63	2.54	2.48	2.42
20	4.35	3.49	3.10	2.87	2.71	2.60	2.51	2.45	2.39
21	4.32	3.47	3.07	2.84	2.68	2.57	2.49	2.42	2.37
22	4.30	3.44	3.05	2.82	2.66	2.55	2.46	2.40	2.34
23	4.28	3.42	3.03	2.80	2.64	2.53	2.44	2.37	2.32
24	4.26	3.40	3.01	2.78	2.62	2.51	2.42	2.36	2.30
25	4.24	3.39	2.99	2.76	2.60	2.49	2.40	2.34	2.28

(Contd.)

Page 2 of 4									
	d_1								
d_2	1	2	3	4	5	6	7	8	9
26	4.23	3.37	2.98	2.74	2.59	2.47	2.39	2.32	2.27
27	4.21	3.35	2.96	2.73	2.57	2.46	2.37	2.31	2.25
28	4.20	3.34	2.95	2.71	2.56	2.45	2.36	2.29	2.24
29	4.18	3.33	2.93	2.70	2.55	2.43	2.35	2.28	2.22
30	4.17	3.32	2.92	2.69	2.53	2.42	2.33	2.27	2.21
40	4.08	3.23	2.84	2.61	2.45	2.34	2.25	2.18	2.12
60	4.00	3.15	2.76	2.53	2.37	2.25	2.17	2.10	2.04
120	3.92	3.07	2.68	2.45	2.29	2.17	2.09	2.02	1.96
inf	3.84	3.00	2.60	2.37	2.21	2.10	2.01	1.94	1.88

Page 3 of 4										
	d_1									
d_2	10	12	15	20	24	30	40	60	120	inf
1	241.9	243.9	245.9	248.0	249.1	250.1	251.1	252.2	253.3	254.3
2	19.4	19.41	19.43	19.45	19.45	19.46	19.47	19.48	19.49	19.5
3	8.79	8.74	8.70	8.66	8.64	8.62	8.59	8.57	8.55	8.53
4	5.96	5.91	5.86	5.80	5.77	5.75	5.72	5.69	5.66	5.63
5	4.74	4.68	4.62	4.56	4.53	4.50	4.46	4.43	4.40	4.36
6	4.06	4.00	3.94	3.87	3.84	3.81	3.77	3.74	3.70	3.67
7	3.64	3.57	3.51	3.44	3.41	3.38	3.34	3.30	3.27	3.23
8	3.35	3.28	3.22	3.15	3.12	3.08	3.04	3.01	2.97	2.93
9	3.14	3.07	3.01	2.94	2.90	2.86	2.83	2.79	2.75	2.71
10	2.98	2.91	2.85	2.77	2.74	2.70	2.66	2.62	2.58	2.54
11	2.85	2.79	2.72	2.65	2.61	2.57	2.53	2.49	2.45	2.40
12	2.75	2.69	2.62	2.54	2.51	2.47	2.43	2.38	2.34	2.30
13	2.67	2.60	2.53	2.46	2.42	2.38	2.34	2.30	2.25	2.21
14	2.60	2.53	2.46	2.39	2.35	2.31	2.27	2.22	2.18	2.13
15	2.54	2.48	2.40	2.33	2.29	2.25	2.20	2.16	2.11	2.07
16	2.49	2.42	2.35	2.28	2.24	2.19	2.15	2.11	2.06	2.01
17	2.45	2.38	2.31	2.23	2.19	2.15	2.10	2.06	2.01	1.96
18	2.41	2.34	2.27	2.19	2.15	2.11	2.06	2.02	1.97	1.92
19	2.38	2.31	2.23	2.16	2.11	2.07	2.03	1.98	1.93	1.88
20	2.35	2.28	2.20	2.12	2.08	2.04	1.99	1.95	1.90	1.84

Page 4 of 4										
d_1										
d_2	10	12	15	20	24	30	40	60	120	inf
21	2.32	2.25	2.18	2.10	2.05	2.01	1.96	1.92	1.87	1.81
22	2.30	2.23	2.15	2.07	2.03	1.98	1.94	1.89	1.84	1.78
23	2.27	2.20	2.13	2.05	2.01	1.96	1.91	1.86	1.81	1.76
24	2.25	2.18	2.11	2.03	1.98	1.94	1.89	1.84	1.79	1.73
25	2.24	2.16	2.09	2.01	1.96	1.92	1.87	1.82	1.77	1.71
26	2.22	2.15	2.07	1.99	1.95	1.90	1.85	1.80	1.75	1.69
27	2.20	2.13	2.06	1.97	1.93	1.88	1.84	1.79	1.73	1.67
28	2.19	2.12	2.04	1.96	1.91	1.87	1.82	1.77	1.71	1.65
29	2.18	2.10	2.03	1.94	1.90	1.85	1.81	1.75	1.70	1.64
30	2.16	2.09	2.01	1.93	1.89	1.84	1.79	1.74	1.68	1.62
40	2.08	2.00	1.92	1.84	1.79	1.74	1.69	1.64	1.58	1.51
60	1.99	1.92	1.84	1.75	1.70	1.65	1.59	1.53	1.47	1.39
120	1.91	1.83	1.75	1.66	1.10	1.55	1.50	1.43	1.35	1.25
inf	1.83	1.75	1.67	1.57	1.52	1.46	1.39	1.32	1.22	1.00

APPENDIX B

THE F-TABLE AT THE 0.01 LEVEL OF SIGNIFICANCE

Page 1 of 4									
				d_1					
d_2	1	2	3	4	5	6	7	8	9
1	4052	4999.5	5403	5625	5764	5859	5928	5982	6022
2	98.50	99.00	99.17	99.25	99.30	99.33	99.36	99.37	99.39
3	34.12	30.82	29.46	28.71	28.24	27.91	27.67	27.49	27.35
4	21.20	18.00	16.69	15.98	15.52	15.21	14.98	14.80	14.66
5	16.26	13.27	12.06	11.39	10.97	10.67	10.46	10.29	10.16
6	13.75	10.92	9.78	9.15	8.75	8.47	8.26	8.10	7.98
7	12.25	9.55	8.45	7.85	7.46	7.19	6.99	6.84	6.72
8	11.26	8.65	7.59	7.01	6.63	6.37	6.18	6.03	5.91
9	10.56	8.02	6.99	6.42	6.06	5.80	5.61	5.47	5.35
10	10.04	7.56	6.55	5.99	5.64	5.39	5.2	5.06	4.94
11	9.65	7.21	6.22	5.67	5.32	5.07	4.89	4.74	4.63
12	9.33	6.93	5.95	5.41	5.06	4.82	4.64	4.50	4.39
13	9.07	6.70	5.74	5.21	4.86	4.62	4.44	4.30	4.14
14	8.86	6.51	5.56	5.04	4.69	4.46	4.28	4.14	4.03
15	8.68	6.36	5.42	4.89	4.56	4.32	4.14	4.00	3.89
16	8.53	6.23	5.29	4.77	4.44	4.20	4.03	3.89	3.78
17	8.40	6.11	5.18	4.67	4.34	4.10	3.93	3.79	3.68
18	8.29	6.01	5.09	4.58	4.25	4.01	3.84	3.71	3.60
19	8.18	5.93	5.01	4.50	4.17	3.94	3.77	3.63	3.52
20	8.10	5.85	4.94	4.43	4.10	3.87	3.70	3.56	3.46
21	8.02	5.78	4.87	4.37	4.04	3.81	3.64	3.51	3.40
22	7.95	5.72	4.82	4.31	3.99	3.76	3.59	3.45	3.35

(Contd.)

Page 2 of 4									
	d_1								
d_2	1	2	3	4	5	6	7	8	9
23	7.88	5.66	4.76	4.26	3.94	3.71	3.54	3.41	3.30
24	7.82	5.61	4.72	4.22	3.90	3.67	3.50	3.36	3.26
25	7.77	5.57	4.68	4.18	3.85	3.63	3.46	3.32	3.22
26	7.72	5.53	4.64	4.14	3.82	3.59	3.42	3.29	3.18
27	7.68	5.49	4.60	4.11	3.78	3.56	3.39	3.26	3.15
28	7.64	5.45	4.57	4.07	3.75	3.53	3.36	3.23	3.12
29	7.60	5.42	4.54	4.04	3.73	3.50	3.33	3.20	3.09
30	7.56	5.39	4.51	4.02	3.70	3.47	3.30	3.17	3.07
40	7.31	5.18	4.31	3.83	3.51	3.29	3.12	2.99	2.89
60	7.08	4.98	4.13	3.65	3.34	3.12	2.95	2.82	2.72
120	6.85	4.79	3.95	3.48	3.17	2.96	2.79	2.66	2.56
inf	6.63	4.61	3.78	3.32	3.02	2.80	2.64	2.51	2.41

Page 3 of 4										
	d_1									
d_2	10	12	15	20	24	30	40	60	120	inf
1	6056	6106	6157	6209	6235	6261	6287	6313	6339	6366
2	99.40	99.42	99.43	99.45	99.46	99.47	99.47	99.48	99.49	99.50
3	27.23	27.05	26.87	26.69	26.60	26.50	26.41	26.32	26.22	26.13
4	14.55	14.37	14.20	14.02	13.93	13.84	13.75	13.65	13.56	13.46
5	10.05	9.89	9.72	9.55	9.47	9.38	9.29	9.20	9.11	9.02
6	7.87	7.72	7.56	7.40	7.31	7.23	7.14	7.06	6.97	6.88
7	6.62	6.47	6.31	6.16	6.07	5.99	5.91	5.82	5.74	5.65
8	5.81	5.67	5.52	5.36	5.28	5.20	5.12	5.03	4.95	4.86
9	5.26	5.11	4.96	4.81	4.73	4.65	4.57	4.48	4.40	4.31
10	4.85	4.71	4.56	4.41	4.33	4.25	4.17	4.08	4.00	3.91
11	4.54	4.40	4.25	4.10	4.02	3.94	3.86	3.78	3.69	3.60
12	4.30	4.16	4.01	3.86	3.78	3.70	3.62	3.54	3.45	3.36
13	4.10	3.96	3.82	3.66	3.59	3.51	3.43	3.34	3.25	3.17
14	3.94	3.80	3.66	3.51	3.43	3.35	3.27	3.18	3.09	3.00
15	3.80	3.67	3.52	3.37	3.29	3.21	3.13	3.05	2.96	2.87

Page 4 of 4										
	d_1									
d_2	10	12	15	20	24	30	40	60	120	inf
16	3.69	3.55	3.41	3.26	3.18	3.10	3.02	2.93	2.84	2.75
17	3.59	3.46	3.31	3.16	3.08	3.00	2.92	2.83	2.75	2.65
18	3.51	3.37	3.23	3.08	3.00	2.92	2.84	2.75	2.66	2.57
19	3.43	3.30	3.15	3.00	2.92	2.84	2.76	2.67	2.58	2.49
20	3.37	3.23	3.09	2.94	2.86	2.78	2.69	2.61	2.52	2.42
21	3.31	3.17	3.03	2.88	2.80	2.72	2.64	2.55	2.46	2.36
22	3.26	3.12	2.98	2.83	2.75	2.67	2.58	2.50	2.40	2.31
23	3.21	3.07	2.93	2.78	2.70	2.62	2.54	2.45	2.35	2.26
24	3.17	3.03	2.89	2.74	2.66	2.58	2.49	2.40	2.31	2.21
25	3.13	2.99	2.85	2.70	2.62	2.54	2.45	2.36	2.27	2.17
26	3.09	2.96	2.81	2.66	2.58	2.50	2.42	2.33	2.23	2.13
27	3.06	2.93	2.78	2.63	2.55	2.47	2.38	2.29	2.20	2.10
28	3.03	2.90	2.75	2.60	2.52	2.44	2.35	2.26	2.17	2.06
29	3.00	2.87	2.73	2.57	2.49	2.41	2.33	2.23	2.14	2.03
30	2.98	2.84	2.70	2.55	2.47	2.39	2.30	2.21	2.11	2.01
40	2.80	2.66	2.52	2.37	2.29	2.20	2.11	2.02	1.92	1.80
60	2.63	2.50	2.35	2.20	2.12	2.03	1.94	1.84	1.73	1.60
120	2.47	2.34	2.19	2.03	1.95	1.86	1.76	1.66	1.53	1.38
inf	2.32	2.18	2.04	1.88	1.79	1.70	1.59	1.47	1.32	1.00

INDEX